STUDIES IN PHILOSOPHY
OUTSTANDING DISSERTATIONS

Edited by

Robert Nozick
Pellegrino University Prc
at Harvard University

A ROUTLEDGE SERIES

STUDIES IN PHILOSOPHY

ROBERT NOZICK, *General Editor*

Anthropic Bias

Observation Selection Effects in Science and Philosophy

Nick Bostrom

Routledge
New York & London

Published in 2002 by
Routledge
270 Madison Ave,
New York NY 10016

Published in Great Britain by
Routledge
2 Park Square, Milton Park,
Abingdon, Oxon, OX14 4RN

Routledge is an imprint of the Taylor & Francis Group

Transferred to Digital Printing 2010

Library of Congress Cataloging-in-Publication Data

Bostrom, Nick, 1973–
    Anthropic bias : observation selection effects in science and philosophy / by
Nick Bostrom.
        p. cm. — (Studies in philosophy)
    Includes bibliographical references and index.
    ISBN 0-415-93858-9
    1. Methodology. 2. Anthropic principle. 3. Selectivity (Psychology)
4. Observation (Scientific method) I. Title. II. Studies in philosophy (New York,
N.Y.)
BD241.B657 2002
121'.6—dc21   2001058887

ISBN10: 0-415-93858-9 (hbk)
ISBN10: 0-415-88394-6 (pbk)

ISBN13: 978-0-415-93858-7 (hbk)
ISBN13: 978-0-415-88394-8 (pbk)

Publisher's Note
The publisher has gone to great lengths to ensure the quality of this
reprint but points out that some imperfections in the original may be apparent.

This book is dedicated to my father—*tack pappa!*

Contents

Acknowledgments

This work has benefited from copious feedback generated by previously published bits and pieces. Over the years, I must have corresponded with several hundreds of people about these issues. In addition, I've received comments from conference audiences, journal referees, authors, and students. For all this, I am extremely grateful!

There is a website associated with the book, www.anthropic-principle.com, containing a preprint archive of relevant writings that are available online, an updated bibliography, primers on various topics, and other resources to aid scholars and interested laypersons to get up to speed with the latest research on observation selection effects.

Although I cannot name everybody who has helped me in some way with this project, there are some who must be singled out for my special thanks: Paul Bartha, Darren Bradley, John Broome, Jeremy Butterfield, Erik Carlson, Brandon Carter, Douglas Chamberlain, Robin Collins, Pierre Cruse, Wei Dai, J-P Delahaye, Jean-Michel Delhotel, Dennis Dieks, William Eckhardt, Ellery Eells, Adam Elga, Hal Finney, Paul Franceschi, Richard Gott, Mark Greenberg, Robin Hanson, Daniel Hill, Christopher Hitchcock, Richard Jeffrey, Bill Jefferys, Vassiliki Kambourelli, Loren A. King, Kevin Korb, Eugene Kusmiak, Jacques Mallah, Neil Manson, Peter Milne, Bradley Monton, Floss Morgan, Samuel Newlands, Jonathan Oliver, Ken Olum, Don N. Page, David Pearce, Elliott Sober, Richard Swinburne, Max Tegmark, Alexander Vilenkin, Saar Wilf, and Roger White. I am so grateful to all those friends, named and unnamed, without whose input this book could not have been written. (The faults that it contains, however, I was perfectly capable of producing all by myself!)

I want to especially thank John Leslie for his exceedingly helpful guidance, Colin Howson and Craig Callender for long assistance and advice, Nancy Cartwright for stepping in and removing a seemingly insurmountable administrative obstacle, and Milan M. Ćirković for keeping up collaboration with me on a paper whilst bombs were detonating around him in Belgrade. Finally, I want to thank Robert Nozick for encouraging rapid publication.

I gratefully acknowledge a research grant from the John Templeton Foundation that has helped fund large parts of this work. I'm thankful to *Synthese, Mind, Analysis, Journal of Evolution and Technology,* and *Erkenntnis* for permitting texts to be republished.

Preface

This book explores how to reason when you suspect that your evidence is biased by observation selection effects. An explanation of what observation selection effects are has to await chapter 1. Suffice it to say here that the topic is intellectually fun, difficult, and important. We will be discussing many interesting applications. Philosophical thought experiments and paradoxes aside, we will use our results to address several juicy bits of contemporary science: cosmology (how many universes are there?), evolution theory (how improbable was the evolution of intelligent life on our planet?), the problem of time's arrow (can it be given a thermodynamic explanation?), game theoretic problems with imperfect recall (how to model them?), traffic analysis (why is the "next lane" faster?) and a lot more—the sort of stuff that intellectually active people like to think about...

One note to the reader before we start. Whether because of an intrinsic organic quality of the subject matter or because of defects in my presentation skills, I have found it difficult to organize the exposition in a completely linear sequence where each chapter can be fully comprehended without having read what comes after. Instead, some important themes are revisited many times over the course of this book, and some essential qualifications are added in a piecemeal fashion. I would plead that the reader not rush to a judgement until the last page has been reached and the idea-complex has been grasped in its entirety.

ANTHROPIC BIAS

CHAPTER 1

Introduction

OBSERVATION SELECTION EFFECTS

How big is the smallest fish in the pond? You catch one hundred fishes, all of which are greater than six inches. Does this evidence support the hypothesis that no fish in the pond is much less than six inches long? Not if your net can't catch smaller fish.

Knowledge about limitations of your data collection process affects what inferences you can draw from the data. In the case of the fish-size-estimation problem, a *selection effect*—the net's sampling only the big fish—vitiates any attempt to extrapolate from the catch to the population remaining in the water. Had your net instead sampled randomly from all the fish, then finding a hundred fishes all greater than a foot would have been good evidence that few if any of the fish remaining are much smaller.

In 1936, the *Literary Digest* conducted a poll to forecast the result of the upcoming presidential election. They predicted that Alf Landon, the Republican candidate, would win by a large margin. In the actual election, the incumbent Franklin D. Roosevelt won a landslide victory. The *Literary Digest* had harvested the addresses of the people they sent the survey to mainly from telephone books and motor vehicle registries, thereby introducing an important selection effect. The poor of the depression era, a group where support for Roosevelt was especially strong, often did not have a phone or a car. A methodologically more sophisticated forecast would either have used a more representative polling group or at least factored in known and suspected selection effects.[1]

---

[1] The *Literary Digest* suffered a major reputation loss as a result of the infamous poll and soon went out of business, being superceded by a new generation of pollsters such as George Gallup, who not only got the 1936 election right but also predicted what the *Literary Digest's* prediction would be to within 1%, using a sample size just one thousandth the size of the *Digest's* but more successfully avoiding selection effects. The infamous 1936 poll has secured a place in the annals

Or to take yet another example, suppose you're a young investor pondering whether to invest your retirement savings in bonds or equity. You are vaguely aware of some studies showing that over sufficiently lengthy periods of time, stocks have, in the past, substantially outperformed bonds (an observation which is often referred to as the "equity premium puzzle"). So you are tempted to put your money into equity. You might want to consider, though, that a selection effect might be at least partly responsible for the apparent superiority of stocks. While it is true that most of the readily available data does favor stocks, this data is mainly from the American and British stock exchanges, which both have continuous records of trading dating back over a century. But is it an accident that the best data comes from these exchanges? Both America and Britain have benefited during this period from stable political systems and steady economic growth. Other countries have not been so lucky. Wars, revolutions, and currency collapses have at times obliterated entire stock exchanges, which is precisely why continuous trading records are not available elsewhere. By looking at only the two greatest success stories, one would risk overestimating the historical performance of stocks. A careful investor would be wise to factor in this consideration when designing her portfolio. (For one recent study that attempts to estimate this survivorship bias by excavating and patching together the fragmentary records from other exchanges, see (Jorion and Goetzmann 2000); for some theory on survivorship biases, see (Brown 1995).)

In these three examples, a selection effect is introduced by the fact that the instrument you use to collect data (a fishing net, a mail survey, preserved trading records) samples only from a proper subset of the target domain. Analogously, there are selection effects that arise not from the limitations of some measuring device but from the fact that all observations require the existence of an appropriately positioned observer. Our data is filtered not only by limitations in our instrumentation but also by the precondition that somebody be there to "have" the data yielded by the instruments (and to build the instruments in the first place). The biases that occur due to that precondition—we shall call them *observation* selection effects—are the subject matter of this book.

Anthropic reasoning, which seeks to detect, diagnose, and cure such biases, is a philosophical goldmine. Few fields are so rich in empirical implications, touch on so many important scientific questions, pose such intricate paradoxes, and contain such generous quantities of conceptual and methodological confusion that need to be sorted out. Working in this area is a lot of intellectual fun.

Let's look at an example where an observation selection effect is involved: We find that intelligent life evolved on Earth. Naively, one might

---

of survey research as a paradigm example of selection bias, yet just as important was a nonresponse bias compounding the error referred to in the text (Squire 1988).—The fishing example originates from Sir Arthur Eddington (Eddington 1939).

think that this piece of evidence suggests that life is likely to evolve on most Earth-like planets. But that would be to overlook an observation selection effect. For no matter how small the proportion of all Earth-like planets that evolve intelligent life, we will find ourselves on a planet that did (or we will trace our origin to a planet where intelligent life evolved, in case we are born in a space colony). Our data point—that intelligent life arose on our planet—is predicted equally well by the hypothesis that intelligent life is very improbable even on Earth-like planets as by the hypothesis that intelligent life is highly probable on Earth-like planets. This datum therefore does not distinguish between the two hypotheses, provided that on both hypotheses intelligent life would have evolved somewhere. (On the other hand, if the "intelligent-life-is-improbable" hypothesis asserted that intelligent life was so improbable that is was unlikely to have evolved *anywhere* in the whole cosmos, then the evidence that intelligent life evolved on Earth *would* count against it. For this hypothesis would not have predicted our observation. In fact, it would have predicted that there would have been no observations at all.)

We don't have to travel long on the path of common sense before we enter a territory where observation selection effects give rise to difficult and controversial issues. Already in the preceding paragraph we passed over a point that is contested. We understood the explanandum, that intelligent life evolved on our planet, in a "non-rigid" sense. Some authors, however, argue that the explanandum should be: why did intelligent life evolve on *this* planet (where "this planet" is used as a rigid designator). They then argue that the hypothesis that intelligent life is quite probable on Earth-like planets would indeed give a higher probability to this fact (Hacking 1987; Dowe 1998; White 2000). But we shall see in the next chapter that that is not the right way to understand the problem.

The impermissibility of inferring from the fact that intelligent life evolved on Earth to the fact that intelligent life probably evolved on a large fraction of all Earth-like planets does not hinge on the evidence in this example consisting of only a single data point. Suppose we had telepathic abilities and could communicate directly with all other intelligent beings in the cosmos. Imagine we ask all the aliens, did intelligent life evolve on their planets too? Obviously, they would all say: Yes, it did. But equally obvious, this multitude of data would still not give us any reason to think that intelligent life develops easily. We only asked about the planets where life did in fact evolve (since those planets would be the only ones which would be "theirs" to some alien), and we get no information whatsoever by hearing the aliens confirming that life evolved on those planets (assuming we don't know the number of aliens who replied to our survey or, alternatively, that we don't know the total number of planets). An observation selection effect frustrates any attempt to extract useful information by this procedure. Some other method would have to be used to do that. (If all the aliens also reported that theirs was some Earth-like planet, this would suggest that intelligent life is *unlikely* to evolve on planets that are *not* Earth-like; for otherwise some aliens would likely have evolved on non-Earth like planets.)

Another example of reasoning that invokes observation selection effects is the attempt to provide a possible (not necessarily the only) explanation of why the universe appears fine-tuned for intelligent life in the sense that if any of various physical constants or initial conditions had been even very slightly different from what they are then life as we know it would not have existed. The idea behind this possible anthropic explanation is that the totality of spacetime might be very huge and may contain regions in which the values of fundamental constants and other parameters differ in many ways, perhaps according to some broad random distribution. If this is the case, then we should not be amazed to find that in our own region physical conditions appear "fine-tuned". Owing to an obvious observation selection effect, only such fine-tuned regions are observed. Observing a fine-tuned region is precisely what we should expect if this theory is true, and so it can potentially account for available data in a neat and simple way, without having to assume that conditions *just happened* to turn out "right" through some immensely lucky—and arguably a priori extremely improbable—cosmic coincidence. (Some skeptics doubt that an explanation for the apparent fine-tuning of our universe is needed or is even meaningful. We examine the skeptical arguments in chapter 2 and consider the counterarguments offered by proponents of the anthropic explanation.)

Here are some of the topics we shall be covering: cosmic fine-tuning arguments for the existence of a multiverse or alternatively a cosmic "designer"; so-called anthropic principles (and how they fall short); how to derive observational predictions from inflation theory and other contemporary cosmological models; the Self-Sampling Assumption; observation selection effects in evolutionary biology and in the philosophy of time; the Doomsday argument, the Adam & Eve, UN^{++} and Quantum Joe paradoxes; alleged observer-relative chances; the Presumptuous Philosopher gedanken; the epistemology of indexical belief; game theoretic problems with imperfect recall; and much more.

Our primary objective is to construct a theory of observation selection effects. We shall seek to develop a methodology for how to reason when we suspect that our evidence is contaminated with anthropic biases. Our secondary objective is to apply the theory to answer some interesting scientific and philosophical questions. Actually, these two objectives are largely overlapping. Only by interpolating between theoretical desiderata and the full range of philosophical and scientific applications can we arrive at a satisfactory account of observation selection effects. At least, that is the approach taken here.

We'll use a Bayesian framework, but a reader who doesn't like formalism should not be deterred. There isn't an excessive amount of mathematics; most of what there is, is elementary arithmetic and probability theory, and the results are conveyed verbally also. The topic of observation selection effects *is* extremely difficult. Yet the difficulty is not in the math, but in grasping and analyzing the underlying principles and in selecting appropriate models.

A BRIEF HISTORY OF ANTHROPIC REASONING

Even trivial selection effects can sometimes easily be overlooked:

> It was a good answer that was made by one who when they showed him hanging in a temple a picture of those who had paid their vows as having escaped shipwreck, and would have him say whether he did not now acknowledge the power of the gods,—'Aye,' asked he again, 'but where are they painted that were drowned after their vows?' And such is the way of all superstition, whether in astrology, dreams, omens, divine judgments, or the like; wherein men, having a delight in such vanities, mark the events where they are fulfilled, but where they fail, though this happens much oftener, neglect and pass them by. (Bacon 1620)

When even a plain and simple selection effect, such as the one that Francis Bacon comments on in the quoted passage, can escape a mind that is not paying attention, it is perhaps unsurprising that *observation selection effects*, which tend to be more abstruse, have only quite recently been given a name and become a subject of systematic study.[2]

The term "anthropic principle", which has been used to label a wide range of things only some of which bear a connection to observation selection effects, is less than three decades old. There are, however, precursors from much earlier dates. For example, in Hume's *Dialogues Concerning Natural Religion*, one can find early expressions of some ideas of anthropic selection effects. Some of the core elements of Kant's philosophy about how the world of our experience is conditioned on the forms of our sensory and intellectual faculties are not completely unrelated to modern ideas about observation selection effects as important methodological considerations in theory-evaluation, although there are also fundamental differences. In Ludwig Boltzmann's attempt to give a thermodynamic account of time's arrow (Boltzmann 1897), we find for perhaps the first time a scientific argument that makes clever use of observation selection effects. We shall discuss Boltzmann's argument in one of the sections of chapter 4, and show why it fails. A more successful invocation of observation selection effects was

---

[2] Why isn't the selection effect that Bacon refers to an "observational" one? After all, nobody could observe the bottom of the sea at that time.—Well, one could have observed that the sailors had gone missing. Fundamentally, the criterion we can use to determine whether something is an observation selection effect is whether a theory of observation selection effects is needed to model it. That doesn't seem necessary for the case Bacon describes.

made by R. H. Dicke (Dicke 1961), who used it to explain away some of the "large-number coincidences", rough order-of-magnitude matches between some seemingly unrelated physical constants and cosmic parameters, that had previously misled such eminent physicists as Eddington and Dirac into a futile quest for an explanation involving bold physical postulations.

The modern era of anthropic reasoning dawned quite recently, with a series of papers by Brandon Carter, another cosmologist. Carter coined the term "anthropic principle" in 1974, clearly intending it to convey some useful guidance about how to reason under observation selection effects. We shall later look at some examples of how he applied his methodological ideas to both physics and biology. While Carter himself evidently knew how to apply his principle to get interesting results, he unfortunately did not manage to explain it well enough to enable all his followers to do the same.

The term "anthropic" is a misnomer. Reasoning about observation selection effects has nothing in particular to do with homo sapiens, but rather with observers in general. Carter regrets not having chosen a better name, which would no doubt have prevented much of the confusion that has plagued the field. When John Barrow and Frank Tipler introduced anthropic reasoning to a wider audience in 1986 with the publication of *The Anthropic Cosmological Principle*, they compounded the terminological disorder by minting several new "anthropic principles", some of which have little if any connection to observation selection effects.

A total of over thirty anthropic principles have been formulated and many of them have been defined several times over—in nonequivalent ways—by different authors, and sometimes even by the same authors on different occasions. Not surprisingly, the result has been some pretty wild confusion concerning what the whole thing is about. Some reject anthropic reasoning out of hand as representing an obsolete and irrational form of anthropocentrism. Some hold that anthropic inferences rest on elementary mistakes in probability calculus. Some maintain that at least some of the anthropic principles are tautological and therefore indisputable. Tautological principles have been dismissed by some as empty and thus of no interest or ability to do explanatory work. Others have insisted that like some results in mathematics, though analytically true, anthropic principles can nonetheless be interesting and illuminating. Others still purport to derive empirical predictions from these same principles and regard them as testable hypotheses. We shall want to distance ourselves from most of these would-be codifications of the anthropic organon. Some reassurance comes from the meta-level consideration that anthropic reasoning is used and taken seriously by a range of leading physicists. One would not expect this bunch of hard-headed scientists to be just blowing so much hot air. And we shall see that once one has carefully removed extraneous principles, misconceptions, fallacies and misdescriptions, one does indeed find a precious core of methodological insights.

Brandon Carter also originated the notorious Doomsday argument, although he never published on it. First to discuss it in print was philosopher John Leslie, whose prolific writings have also elucidated a wide range of other issues related to anthropic reasoning. A version of the Doomsday argument was invented independently by Richard Gott, an astrophysicist. The Doomsday argument has generated a bulky literature of its own, which sometimes suffers from being disconnected from other areas of anthropic reasoning. One lesson from this book is, I think, that different applications of anthropic reasoning provide important separate clues to what the correct theoretical account of observation selection effects must look like. Only when we put all the pieces of the puzzle together in the right way does a meaningful picture emerge.

The field of observational selection has begun to experience rapid growth in recent years. Many of the of the most important results date back only about a decade or less. Philosophers and scientists (especially cosmologists) deserve about equal parts of the credit for the ideas that have already been developed and which this book can now use as building blocks.

SYNOPSIS OF THIS BOOK

Our journey begins in chapter 2 with a study of the significance of cosmic "fine-tuning", referring to the apparent fact that if any of various physical parameters had been very slightly different then no observers would have existed in the universe. There is a sizable literature on what to make of such "coincidences". Some have argued that they provide some evidence for the existence of an ensemble of physically real universes (a "multiverse"). Others, of a more religious bent, have used arguments from fine-tuning to attempt to make a case for some version of the design hypothesis. Still others claim that comic fine-tuning can have no special significance at all. The latter view is incorrect. The finding that we live in a fine-tuned universe (if that is indeed so) would, as we shall see, provide support for explanations that essentially involve observation selection effects. Such explanations raise interesting methodological issues which we will be exploring in chapter 2. I argue that only by working out a theory of observation selection effects can we get to the bottom of the fine-tuning controversies. Using analogies, we begin to sketch out a preliminary account of how observation selection effects operate in the cosmological context, which allows us to get a clearer understanding of the evidential import of fine-tuning. Later, in chapter 11, we will return to the fine-tuning arguments and use the theory that we'll have developed in the intervening chapters to more rigorously verify the informal conclusions of chapter 2.

Given that observation selection effects are important, we next want to know more precisely what kind of beast they are and how they affect methodology. Is it possible to sum up the essence of observation selection effects in a simple statement? A multitude of so-called "anthropic principles" attempt to do just that. Chapter 3 takes a critical look at the main contenders, and finds that they fall short. Many "anthropic principles" are simply confused. Some, especially those drawing inspiration from Brandon Carter's seminal papers, are sound, but we show that although they point in the right direction they are too weak to do any real scientific work. In particular, I argue that existing methodology does not permit any observational consequences to be derived from contemporary cosmological theories, in spite of the fact that these theories quite plainly can be and are being tested empirically by astronomers. What is needed to bridge this methodological gap is a more adequate formulation of how observation selection effects are to be taken into account. A preliminary formulation of such a principle, which we call the *Self-Sampling Assumption*, is proposed towards the end of chapter 3. The basic idea of the Self-Sampling Assumption is, very roughly put, that you should think of yourself as if you were a random observer from a suitable reference class.

Chapter 4 begins to build a "philosophical" case for our theory by conducting a series of thought experiments that show that something like the Self-Sampling Assumption describes a plausible way of reasoning about a wide range of cases.

Chapter 5 shows how the Self-Sampling Assumption enables us to link up cosmological theory with observation in a way that is both intuitively plausible and congruent with scientific practice. This chapter also applies the new methodology to illuminate problems in several areas, to wit: thermodynamics and the problem of time's arrow; evolutionary biology (especially questions related to how improbable was the evolution of intelligent life on Earth and how many "critical" steps there were in our evolutionary past); and an issue in traffic analysis. An important criterion for a theory of observation selection effects is that it should enable us to make sense of contemporary scientific reasoning and that it can do interesting work in helping to solve real empirical problems. Chapter 5 demonstrates that our theory satisfies this criterion.

The notorious Doomsday argument, which seeks to show that we have systematically underestimated the probability that humankind will go extinct relatively soon, forms the subject matter for chapter 6. We review and criticize the literature on this controversial piece of reasoning, both papers that support it and ones that claim to have refuted it. I think that the Doomsday argument is inconclusive. But the reason is complicated and must await explanation until we have developed our theory further, in chapter 10.

The Doomsday argument deserves the attention it has attracted, however. Getting to the bottom of what is wrong or inconclusive about it can give us invaluable clues about how to build a sound methodology of observation selection effects. It is therefore paramount that the Doomsday argument not be dismissed for the wrong reasons. Lots of people think that they have refuted the Doomsday argument, but not all these objections can be right— many of the "refutations" are inconsistent with one another, and many presuppose ideas that can be shown unacceptable when tried against other criteria that a theory of anthropic reasoning must satisfy. Chapter 7 examines several recent criticisms of the Doomsday argument and explains why they fail.

In chapter 8, we refute an argument purporting to show that anthropic reasoning gives rise to paradoxical observer-relative chances. We then give an independent argument showing that there are cases where anthropic reasoning does generate probabilities that are "observer-relative" in an interesting but non-paradoxical sense.

Paradoxes lie in ambush in chapter 9. We explore the thought experiments *Adam & Eve*, UN^{++}, and *Quantum Joe*. These reveal some counterintuitive aspects of the most straightforward version of the Self-Sampling Assumption.

Is there a way out? At the end of chapter 9 we find ourselves in an apparent dilemma. On the one hand, something like the Self-Sampling Assumption seems philosophically justified and scientifically indispensable on the grounds explained in chapters 4 and 5. On the other hand, we seem then to be driven towards a counterintuitive (albeit coherent) position vis-à-vis the gedanken experiments of chapter 9. What to do?

Chapter 10 goes back and reexamines the reasoning that led to the formulation of the original version of the Self-Sampling Assumption. But now we have the benefit of lessons gleaned from the preceding chapters. We understand better the various constraints that our theory has to satisfy. And we have a feel for what is the source of the problems. Combining these clues, we propose a solution that enables us to escape the paradoxes while still catering to legitimate methodological needs. The first step of the solution is to strengthen the Self-Sampling Assumption so that it applies to "observer-moments" rather than just observers. This increases our analytical firepower. A second step is to relativize the reference class. The result is a general framework for modeling anthropic reasoning, which is given a formal expression in an equation, the Observation Equation, that specifies how to take into account evidence that has an indexical component or that has been subjected to an observation selection effect.

In chapter 11, we illustrate how this theory of observation selection effects works by applying it to a wide range of philosophical and scientific problems. We show how it confirms (and makes more precise) the preliminary conclusions that were arrived at by less rigorous analogy-based arguments in earlier chapters. Chapter 11 also provides an analysis of the Sleeping Beauty problem (and a fortiori its closely related game-theoretic analogues, the Absent-Minded Driver problem and the Absent-Minded Passenger problem). It is argued that the solution is more complex than previously recognized and that this makes it possible to reconcile the two opposing views that dominate the literature. We close with a discussion of the element of subjectivity that may reside in the choice of a prior credence function for indexical propositions. We compare it with the more widely recognized aspect of subjectivity infesting the non-indexical component of one's credence function, and we suggest that the issue throws light on how to rank various applications of anthropic reasoning according to how scientifically rigorous they are. At the very end, there are some pointers to avenues for further research.

CHAPTER 2

Fine-Tuning in Cosmology

One aspect of anthropic reasoning that has attracted plenty of attention, from both philosophers and physicists, is its use in cosmology to explain the apparent fine-tuning of our universe. "Fine-tuning" refers to the supposed fact that there is a set of cosmological parameters or fundamental physical constants that are such that had they been very slightly different, the universe would have been void of intelligent life. For example, in the classical big bang model, the early expansion speed seems fine-tuned. Had it been very slightly greater, the universe would have expanded too rapidly and no galaxies would have formed. There would only have been a very low density hydrogen gas getting more and more dispersed as time went by. In such a universe, presumably, life could not evolve. Had the early expansion speed been very slightly less, then the universe would have recollapsed very soon after the big bang, and again there would have been no life. Our universe, having just the right conditions for life, appears to be balancing on a knife's edge (Leslie 1989). A number of other parameters seem fine-tuned in the same sense—e.g. the ratio of the electron mass to the proton mass, the magnitudes of force strengths, the smoothness of the early universe, the neutron-proton mass difference, perhaps even the metric signature of space-time (Tegmark 1997).

Some philosophers and physicists take fine-tuning to be an explanandum that cries out for an explanans. Two possible explanations are usually envisioned: the design hypothesis and the ensemble hypothesis. Although these explanations are compatible, they tend to be viewed as competing. If we knew that one of them were correct, there would be less reason to accept the other.

The design hypothesis states that our universe is the result of purposeful design. The "agent" doing the designing need not be a theistic God, although that is of course one archetypal version of the design hypothesis. Other universe-designers have been considered in this context. For example, John Leslie (Leslie 1972, 1979, 1989) discusses the case for a neoplatonist "causally efficacious ethical principle", which he thinks might have been responsible for creating the world and giving physical constants and cosmological parameters the numerical values they have. Derek Parfit (Parfit 1998) considers various "universe selection principles", which, although they are very different from what people have traditionally thought of as "God" or a "Designer," can nevertheless suitably be grouped under the heading of design hypotheses for present purposes. We can take "purposeful designer" in a very broad sense to refer to any being, principle or mechanism external to our universe responsible for selecting its properties, or responsible for making it in some sense probable that our universe should be fine-tuned for intelligent life. Needless to say, it is possible to doubt the meaningfulness of many of these design hypotheses. Even if one admits that a given design hypothesis represents a coherent possibility, one may still think that it should be assigned an extremely low degree of credence. For people who are already convinced that there is a God, however, the design hypothesis is likely to appear as an attractive explanation of why our universe is fine-tuned. And if one is not already convinced about the existence of a Designer, but thinks that it is a coherent possibility, one may be tempted to regard fine-tuning as a reason for increasing one's credence in that hypothesis. One prominent champion of the fine-tuning argument for God's existence is Richard Swinburne (Swinburne 1991). Several other theologians and philosophers also support this position (see e.g. (Polkinghorne 1986; Craig 1988, 1997; Manson 1989)).

The main rival explanation of fine-tuning is the ensemble hypothesis, which states that the universe we observe is only a small part of the totality of physical existence. This totality itself need not be fine-tuned. If it is sufficiently big and variegated, so that it was likely to contain as a proper part the sort of fine-tuned universe we observe, then an observation selection effect can be invoked to explain why we see a fine-tuned universe. The usual form of the ensemble hypothesis is that our universe is but one in a vast ensemble of actually existing universes, the totality of which we can call "the multiverse". What counts as a universe in such a multiverse is a somewhat vague matter, but "a large, causally fairly disconnected spacetime region" is precise enough for our aims. If the world consists of a sufficiently huge number of such universes, and the values of physical constants vary among these universes according to some suitably broad probability distribution, then it may well be the case that it was quite probable that a fine-tuned universe like ours would come into existence. The actual existence of such a multiverse—an ensemble of "possible universes" would not do—provides the basis on which the observation selection effect operates. The argument then goes like this: Even though the vast majority of the universes are not suitable for intelligent life, it is no wonder that we should observe one of the exceptional universes which are fine-tuned; for the other universes contain no observers and hence are not observed. To observers in such a multiverse, the world will look as though it were fine-tuned. But that is because they see only a small and unrepresentative part of the whole. Observers may marvel at the fact that the universe they find themselves in is so exquisitely balanced, but once they understand the bigger picture they can realize that there is really nothing to be astonished by. On the ensemble theory, there *had* to be such a universe (or at least, it was not so improbable that there would be), and since the other universes have no observers in them, a fine-tuned universe is precisely what the observers should expect to observe given the existence of the ensemble. The multiverse itself need not be fine-tuned. It can be robust in the sense that a small change in its basic parameters would not alter the fact that it contains regions where intelligent life exists.

In contrast to some versions of the design hypothesis, the meaningfulness of the ensemble hypothesis is not much in question. Only those subscribing to a very strict verificationist theory of meaning would deny that it is possible that the world might contain a large set of causally fairly disconnected spacetime regions with varying physical parameters. And even the most hardcore verificationist would be willing to consider at least those ensemble theories according to which other universes are in principle physically accessible from our own universe. (Such ensemble theories have been proposed, although they represent only a special case of the general idea.) But there are other philosophical perplexities that arise in this context. One can wonder, for example, in what sense the suggested anthropic explanation of fine-tuning—it is "anthropic" because it involves the idea of an observation selection effect—is really explanatory and how it would relate to a more directly causal account of how our universe came to be. Another important issue is whether fine-tuning provides some evidence for a multiverse. The first question that we shall consider, however, is whether fine-tuning stands in any need of explanation at all.

DOES FINE-TUNING NEED EXPLAINING?

First a few words about the supposition that our universe is in fact fine-tuned. This is an empirical assumption that is not trivial. It is certainly true that our current best physical theories, in particular the Grand Unified Theory of the strong, weak, and electromagnetic forces and the big bang theory in cosmology, have a number (twenty or so) of free parameters. There is quite strong reason to think at least some of these parameters are fine-tuned—the universe would have been inhospitable to life if their values had been slightly different.[1] While it is true that our knowledge of "exotic" life forms possible under different physical laws than the ones that hold in the actual world is very limited (Feinberg and Shapiro 1980; Smith 1985;

---

[1] A good overview of the case for fine-tuning can be found in chapter 2 of (Leslie 1989). For a recent discussion of some complications, see (Aguirre 2001).

Wilson 1991), it does seem quite reasonable to believe, for instance, that life would not have evolved if the universe had contained only a highly diluted hydrogen gas or if it had recollapsed before the temperature anywhere had dropped below 10,000 degrees (referring to the seeming fine-tuning in the early expansion speed) (Hawking 1974; Leslie 1985). What little direct evidence we have supports this suggestion. Life does not seem to evolve easily even in a universe like our own, which presumably has rather favorable conditions—complex chemistry, relatively stable environments, large entropy gradients etc. (Simpson 1964; Papagiannis 1978; Hart 1982; Carter 1983; Mayr 1985; Raup 1985; Hanson 1998). There are as yet no signs that life has evolved in the observable universe anywhere outside our own planet (Tipler 1982; Brin 1983).

One should not jump from this to the conclusion that our universe is fine-tuned. For it is possible that some future physical theory will be developed that uses fewer free parameters or uses only parameters on which life does not sensitively depends. Even if we *knew* that our universe were not fine-tuned, the issue of what fine-tuning would have implied could still be philosophically interesting. But in fact, the case for fine-tuning is quite strong. Given what we know, it is reasonable to doubt that there is a plausible physical theory on which our universe is not fine-tuned. Inflation theory, which was originally motivated largely by a desire to avoid the fine-tuning regarding the flatness and smoothness of the universe required by the ordinary big bang theory, seems to require some fine-tuning of its own to get the inflation potential right. More recent inflation theories may overcome this problem, at least partly; but they do so by introducing a multiverse and an observation selection effect—in other words by making exactly the kind of move that this chapter will scrutinize. The present best candidate for a single-universe theory that could reduce the number of free parameters may be superstring theories (e.g. (Kane 2000), but they too seem to require at least some fine-tuning (because there are many possible compactification schemes and vacuum states). The theories that currently seem most likely to be able to do away with fine-tuned free parameters all imply the existence of a multiverse. On these theories, *our* universe might still be fine-tuned, although the multiverse as a whole might not be, or might be fine-tuned only to a less degree.

However, since the empirical case for fine-tuning is separate from the philosophical problem of how to react if our universe really is fine-tuned, we can set these scruples to one side. Let's assume the most favorable case for fine-tuning enthusiasts: that the physics of our universe has several independent free parameters which are fine-tuned to an extremely high degree. If that is so, is it something that cries out for explanation or should we be happy to accept it as one of those brute facts that just happen to obtain?

The answer to this question has two parts, one of which is fairly unproblematic. This easier part is as follows: In general, simplicity is one desideratum on plausible scientific theories. Other things equal, we prefer theories which make a small number of simple assumptions to ones that involve a large number of ad hoc stipulations. This methodological principle is used successfully in all of science and it has, in particular, a strong track record in cosmology. For example, think of the replacement of the complicated Ptolomaic theory of planetary motion by the far simpler Copernican heliocentric theory. (Some people might regard Einstein's relativity theory as more complicated than Newton's theory of gravitation, although "more difficult" seems a more accurate description in this case than "more complicated". But note that the *ceteris paribus* includes the presupposition that the two theories predict known data equally well, so this would not be a counterexample. Newton's theory does not fit the evidence.) Thus, one should admit that there is something intellectually dissatisfying about a cosmological theory which tells us that the universe contains a large number of fine-tuned constants. Such a theory might be true, but we should not be keen to believe that until we have convinced ourselves that there is no simpler theory that can account for our data. So if the universe looks fine-tuned, this can be an indication that we should look harder to see if we cannot find a theory which reduces the number of independent assumptions needed. This is one reason for why a universe that looks fine-tuned (whether or not it actually *is* fine-tuned) is crying out for explanation.

We should note two things about this easy part of the answer. First, there might not be an explanation even if the universe is "crying out" for one in this sense. There is no guarantee that there is a simpler theory using fewer free parameters that can account for the data. At most, there is a prima facie case for looking for one, and for preferring the simpler theory if one can be found.

Second, the connection to fine-tuning is merely incidental. In this part of the answer, it is not fine-tuning *per se,* only fine-tuning *to the extent that it is coupled to having a wide range of free parameters,* that is instigating the hunt for a better explanation. Fine-tuning is neither necessary nor sufficient for the hunting horns to sound in this instance. It is not sufficient, because in order for a theory to be fine-tuned for intelligent life, it needs to have but a single free parameter. If a theory has a single physical constant on which the existence of intelligent life very sensitively depends, then the theory is fine-tuned. Yet a theory with only one free parameter could be eminently simple. If a universe cries out for explanation even though such a theory accounts for all available evidence, it must be on some other basis than that of a general preference for simpler theories. Also, fine-tuning is not necessary for there to be a cry for explanation. One can imagine a cosmological theory that contains a large number of free parameters but is not fine-tuned because life does not sensitively depend on the values assigned to these parameters.

The easy part of the answer is therefore: Yes, fine-tuning cries out for explanation to the extent to which it is correlated with an excess of free parameters and a resultant lack of simplicity.[2] This part of the answer has been overlooked in discussions of fine-tuning, yet it is important to separate out this aspect in order to rightly grasp the more problematic part to which we shall now turn. The problematic part is the question of whether fine-tuning *especially* cries out for explanation, beyond the general desideratum of avoiding unnecessary complications and ad hoc assumptions. In other words, is *the fact that the universe would have been lifeless* if the values of fundamental constants had been very slightly different (assuming this is a fact) relevant in assessing whether an explanation is called for of why the constants have the values they have? And does it give support to the multiverse hypothesis? Or, alternatively, to the design hypothesis? The rest of this chapter will focus on these questions (though the design hypothesis will be discussed only as it touches on the other two questions).

Let's begin by examining some answers given in the literature.

No "Inverse Gambler's Fallacy"

Can an anthropic argument based on an observation selection effect together with the assumption that an ensemble of universes exists explain the apparent fine-tuning of our universe? Ian Hacking has argued that this depends on the nature of the ensemble. If the ensemble consists of all possible big-bang universes (a position he ascribes to Brandon Carter) then, says Hacking, the anthropic explanation works:

> Why do we exist? Because we are a possible universe [sic], and all possible ones exist. Why are we in an orderly universe? Because the only universes that we could observe are orderly ones that support our form of life . . . nothing is left to chance. Everything in this reasoning is deductive. (Hacking 1987), p. 337

Hacking contrasts this with a seemingly analogous explanation that seeks to explain fine-tuning by supposing that a Wheeler-type multiverse exists. In the Wheeler cosmology, there is a never-ending sequence of universes each of which begins with a big bang and ends with a big crunch which bounces

---

[2] At the risk of redundancy, let me stress that the simplicity principle used here is not that every phenomenon must have an explanation (which would be version of the principle of sufficient reason, which I do not accept). Rather, what I mean is that we have an a priori epistemic bias in favor of hypotheses which are compatible with us living in a relatively simple world. Therefore, if our best account so far of some phenomenon involves very non-simple hypotheses (such as that a highly remarkable coincidence happened just by chance), then we may have prima facie reason for thinking that there is some better (simpler) explanation of the phenomenon that we haven't yet thought of. In that sense, the phenomenon is crying out for an explanation. Of course, there might not be a (simple) explanation. But we shouldn't be willing to believe in the complicated account until we have convinced ourselves that no simple explanation would work.

back in a new big bang, and so forth. The values of physical constants are reset in a random fashion in each bounce, so that we have a vast ensemble of universes with varying properties. The purported anthropic explanation of fine-tuning based on such a Wheeler ensemble notes that, given that the ensemble is large enough, it could be expected to contain at least one fine-tuned universe like ours. An observation selection effect can be invoked to explain why we observe a fine-tuned universe rather than one of the non-tuned ones. On the face of it, this line of reasoning looks very similar to the anthropic reasoning based on the Carter multiverse, which Hacking endorses. But according to Hacking, there is a crucial difference. He thinks that the version using the Wheeler multiverse commits a terrible mistake, which he dubs the "Inverse Gambler's Fallacy". This is the fallacy of a dim-witted gambler who thinks that the apparently improbable outcome he currently observes is made more probable if there have been many trials preceding the present one.

> [A gambler] enters the room as a roll is about to be made. The kibitzer asks, 'Is this the first role of the dice, do you think, or have we made many a one earlier tonight? . . . slyly, he says 'Can I wait until I see how this roll comes out, before I lay my bet with you on the number of past plays made tonight?' The kibitzer . . . agrees. The roll is a double six. The gambler foolishly says, 'Ha, that makes a difference—I think there have been quite a few rolls.' (Hacking 1987), p. 333

The gambler in this example is clearly in error. But so is Hacking in thinking that the situation is analogous to the one regarding fine-tuning. As pointed out by three authors (Leslie 1988; McGrath 1988; Whitaker 1988) independently replying to Hacking's paper, there is no observation selection effect in his example—an essential ingredient in the purported anthropic explanation of fine-tuning.

One way of introducing an observation selection effect in Hacking's example is by supposing that the gambler has to wait outside the room until a double six is rolled. Knowing that this is the setup, the gambler does obtain some reason upon entering the room and seeing the double six for thinking that there probably have been quite a few rolls already. This is a closer analogy to the fine-tuning case. The gambler can only observe certain outcomes—we can think of these as the "fine-tuned" ones—and upon observing a fine-tuned outcome he obtains reason to think that there have been several trials. Observing a double six would then be surprising on the hypothesis that there were only one roll, but it would be expected on the hypothesis that there were very many. Moreover, a kind of *explanation* of why the gambler is seeing a double six is provided by pointing out that there were many rolls and the gambler would be let in to observe the outcome only upon getting a double six.

When we make the kibitzer example more similar to the fine-tuning situation, we thus find that it supports, rather than refutes, the analogous reasoning based on the Wheeler cosmology.

What makes Hacking's position especially peculiar is that he thinks that the anthropic reasoning works with a Carter multiverse but not with a Wheeler multiverse. Many think the anthropic reasoning works in both cases, some think it doesn't work in either case, but Hacking is probably alone in thinking it works in one but not the other. The only pertinent difference between the two cases seems to be that in the Carter case one *deduces* the existence of a universe like ours whereas in the Wheeler case one infers it probabilistically. The Wheeler case can be made to approximate the Carter case by having the probability that a universe like ours should be generated in some cycle be close to 1 (which, incidentally, is actually the case in the Wheeler scenario if there are infinitely many cycles and there is a fixed finite probability in each cycle of a universe like ours resulting). It is hard to see the appeal of a doctrine that drives a methodological wedge between the two cases by insisting that the anthropic explanation works perfectly in one and fails completely in the other.

ROGER WHITE AND PHIL DOWE'S ANALYSIS

Recently, a more challenging attack on the anthropic explanation of fine-tuning has been made by Roger White (White 2000) and Phil Dowe (Dowe 1998). They eschew Hacking's doctrine that there is an essential difference between the Wheeler and the Carter multiverses as regards the prospects for an anthropic explanation. But they take up another idea of Hacking's, namely that what goes wrong in the Inverse Gambler's Fallacy is that the gambler fails to take into account the most specific version of the explanandum that he knows when making his inference to the best explanation. If all the gambler had known were that *a* double six had been rolled, then it need not have been a fallacy to infer that there probably were quite a few rolls, since that would have made it more probable that there would be at least one double six. But the gambler knows that *this* roll, the latest one, was a double six; and that gives him no reason to believe there were many rolls, since the probability that that specific roll would be a double six is one in thirty-six independently of how many times the dice have been rolled before. So Hacking argues that when seeking an explanation, we must use the most specific rendition of the explanandum that is in our knowledge:

> If F is known, and E is the best explanation of F, then we are supposed to infer E. However, we cannot give this rule carte blanche. If F is known, then FvG is known, but E* might be the best explanation of FvG, and yet knowledge of F gives not the slightest reason to believe E*. (John, an excellent swimmer, drowns in Lake Ontario. Therefore he drowns in either Lake Ontario or the Gulf of Mexico. At the time of his death, a hurricane is rav-

aging the Gulf. So the best explanation of why he drowned is that he was overtaken by a hurricane, which is absurd.) We must insist that F, the fact to be explained, is the most specific version of what is known and not a disjunctive consequence of what is known. (Hacking 1987), p. 335

Applying this to fine-tuning, Hacking, White, and Dowe charge that the purported anthropic explanation of fine-tuning fails to explain the most specific version of what is known. We know not only that *some* universe is fine-tuned; we know that *this* universe is fine-tuned. Now, if our explanandum is, why is *this* universe fine-tuned? (where "this universe" is understood rigidly) then it would seem that postulating many universes cannot move us any closer to explaining that; nor would it make the explanandum more probable. For how could the existence of many other universes make it more likely that this universe be fine-tuned?

At this stage it is useful to introduce some abbreviations. In order to focus on the point that White and Dowe are making, we can make some simplifying assumptions.[3] Let us suppose that there are n possible configurations of a big bang universe $\{T_1, T_2, \ldots, T_n\}$ and that they are equally "probable", $P(T_i) = 1/n$. We assume that T_1 is the only configuration that permits life to evolve. Let x be a variable that ranges over the set of actual universes. We assume that each universe instantiates a unique T_i, so that $\forall x\, \exists! i (T_i x)$. Let m be the number of actually existing universes, and let "α" rigidly denote our universe. We define

E := $T_1 \alpha$ ("α is life-permitting.")

E' := $\exists x\, (T_1 x)$ ("Some universe is life-permitting.")

M := $m \gg 0$ ("There are many universes."—the multiverse hypothesis)

White claims that, while there being many universes increases the probability that there is a life-permitting universe, $(P(E'|M) > P(E'|\neg M))$, it is not the case that there being many universes increases the probability that our universe is life-permitting. That is, $P(E|M) = P(E|\neg M) = 1/n$. The argument White gives for this is that

the probability of [E, i.e. the claim that α instantiates T1] is just $1/n$, regardless of how many other universes there are, since α's initial conditions and constants are selected randomly from a set of n equally probable alternatives, a selection which is independent of the existence of other universes. The events which give rise to universes are not causally related in such a

---

[3] I will adopt White's formalism to facilitate comparison. The simplifying assumptions are also made by White, on whose analysis we focus since it is more detailed than Dowe's.

way that the outcome of one renders the outcome of another more or less probable. They are like independent rolls of a die. (White 2000), pp. 262–3

Since we should conditionalize on the most specific information we have when evaluating the support for the multiverse hypothesis, and since E is more specific than E', White concludes that our knowledge that our universe is life-permitting gives us no reason to think there are many universes.

This argument has some initial plausibility. Nonetheless, I think it is fallacious. We get a strong hint that something has gone wrong if we pay attention to a certain symmetry. Let α, β_1, . . . , β_{m-1} be the actually existing universes, and for $i = \alpha$, β_1. . . , β_{m-1}, let E_i be the proposition that if some universe is life-permitting then i is life-permitting. Thus, E is equivalent to the conjunction of E' and E_α. According to White, if all we knew was E' then that would count as evidence for M; but if we know the more specific E then that is not evidence for M. So he is committed to the following ((White 2000), p. 264):

$$P(M \mid E') > P(M), \text{ and}$$

$$P(M \mid E) = P(M)$$

Since by definition $P(M \mid E'E_\alpha) = P(M \mid E)$, this implies:

$$P(M \mid E'E_\alpha) < P(M \mid E') \qquad (*)$$

Because of the symmetry of the β_j :s, $P(M \mid E'E_{\beta j}) = c$, for every β_j, for no ground has been given for why *some* of the universes β_j would have given more reason, had it been the fine-tuned one, for believing M, than would any other β_j similarly fine-tuned. E' implies the disjunction $E' E_\alpha \vee E' E_{\beta_1} \vee E' E_{\beta_2} \vee \ldots \vee E' E_{m-1}$. This together with (*) implies:

$$P(M \mid E'E_{\beta j}) > P(M \mid E') \text{ for every } \beta_j \qquad (**)$$

In other words, White is committed to the view that, given that some universe is life-permitting, then: conditionalizing on α being life-permitting *decreases* the probability of M, while conditionalizing on any of β_1. . . , β_{m-1}, *increases* the probability of M.

But that seems wrong. Given that some universe is life-permitting, why should the fact it is *this* universe that is life-permitting, rather than any of the others, lower the probability that there are many universes? If it had been some other universe instead of this one that had been life-permitting, why should that have made the multiverse hypothesis any more likely? Clearly, such discrimination could be justified only if there were something special that we knew about *this* universe that would make the fact that it is this universe rather than some other that is life-permitting significant. I can't see what sort of knowledge that would be. It is true that *we* are in this universe and not in any of the others—but that fact *presupposes* that this universe is life-permitting. It is not as if there is a remarkable coincidence between our universe being life-permitting and us being in it. So it's hard to see how the fact that we are in this universe could justify treating its being life-permitting as giving a lower probability to the multiverse hypothesis than any other universe's being life-permitting would have given it.

So what, precisely, is wrong in White's argument? His basic intuition for why P(M|E) = P(M) seems to be that "The events which give rise to universes are not causally related in such a way that the outcome of one renders the outcome of another more or less probable." A little reflection reveals that this assertion is highly problematic for several reasons.

First, there's no empirical warrant for it. Very little is yet known about the events which give rise to universes. There are models on which the outcomes of some such events *do* causally influence the outcome of others. To illustrate, in Lee Smolin's (admittedly highly speculative) evolutionary cosmological model (Smolin 1997), universes create "baby-universes" whenever a black hole is formed, and these baby-universes inherit, in a somewhat stochastic manner, some of the properties of their parent. The outcomes of chance events in one such conception can thus influence the outcomes of chance events in the births of other universes. Variations of the Wheeler oscillating universe model have also been suggested where some properties are inherited from one cycle to the next. And there are live speculations that it might be possible for advanced civilizations to spawn new universes and transfer some information into them by determining the values of some of their constants (as suggested by Andrei Linde, of inflation theory fame), by tunneling into them through a wormhole (Morris, Thorne et al. 1988), or otherwise (Ćirković and Bostrom 2000; Garriga, Mukhanov et al. 2000).

Even if the events which give rise to universes are not causally related in the sense that the outcome of one event causally influences the outcome of another (as in the examples just mentioned), that does not mean that one universe cannot carry information about another. For instance, two universes can have a partial cause in common. This is the case in the multiverse models associated with inflation theory (arguably the best current candidates for a multiverse cosmology). In a nutshell, the idea is that universes arise from inflating fluctuations in some background space. The existence of this background space and the parameters of the chance mechanism that lead to the creation of inflating bubbles are at least partial causes of the universes that are produced. The properties of the produced universes could thus carry information about this background space and the mechanism of bubble creation, and hence indirectly also about other universes that have been produced by the same mechanism. The majority of multiverse models that have actually been proposed, including arguably the most plausible one, directly negate White's claim.

Second, even if we consider the hypothetical case of a multiverse model where the universes bear no causal relations to one another, it is *still* not generally the case that P(M|E) = P(M). This holds even setting aside any issues related to anthropic reasoning. We need to make a distinction between objective chance and epistemic probability. If there is no causal connection (whether direct or indirect via a common cause) between the universes, then there is no correlation in the physical chances of the outcomes of the events in which these universes are created. It does not follow that the outcomes of those events are uncorrelated in one's rational epistemic probability assignment. Consider this toy example:

> Suppose you have some background knowledge K and that your prior subjective probability function P, conditionalized on K, assigns non-negligible probability to only three possible worlds and assigns an equal probability to these: $P(w_1|K) = P(w_2|K) = P(w_3|K)$. In w_1 there is one big universe, *a*, and one small universe, *d*; in w_2 there is one big, *b*, and one small, *e*; and in w_3 there is one big, *c*, and one small, *e*. Now suppose you learn that you are in universe *e*. This rules out w_1. It thus gives you information about the big universe—it is now more likely to be either *b* or *c* than it was before you learnt that the little universe is *e*. That is, P("The big universe is *b* or *c*" | K&"The little universe is *e*") > P("The big universe is *b* or *c*" | K).

No assumption whatever is made here about the universes being causally related. White presupposes that any such subjective probability function P must be irrational or unreasonable (independently of the exact nature of the various possible worlds under consideration). Yet that seems implausible. Certainly, White provides no argument for it.

Third, White's view that P(M|E') > P(M) seems to commit him to denying just this assumption. For how could E' (which says that some universe is life-permitting) be probabilistically relevant to M unless the outcome of one universe-creating event *x* (namely that event, or one of those events, that created the life-permitting universe(s)) can be probabilistically relevant to the outcome of another *y* (namely one of those events that created the universes other than *x*)? If *x* gives absolutely no information about *y*, then it is hard to see how knowledge that there is some life-permitting universe, the one created by *x*, could give us grounds for thinking that there are many other universes, such as the one created by *y*. So on this reasoning, it seems we would have P(M|E') = P(M), pace White.

This last point connects back to our initial observation regarding the symmetry and the implausibility of thinking that because it is *our* universe that is life-permitting there is less support for the multiverse hypothesis than if it had been some other universe instead that were life-permitting. All these problems are avoided if we acknowledge that not only P(M | E') > P(M) but also P(M | E) > P(M).

I conclude that White's argument against the view that fine-tuning lends some support to the multiverse hypothesis fails. And so do consequently Phil Dowe's and Ian Hacking's arguments, the latter failing on other accounts as well, as we have seen.

SURPRISING VS. UNSURPRISING IMPROBABLE EVENTS

If, then, the fact that our universe is life-permitting *does* give support to the multiverse hypothesis, i.e. P(M | E) > P(M), it follows from Bayes' theorem that P(E | M) > P(E). How can the existence of a multiverse make it more probable that *this* universe should be life-permitting? One may be tempted to say: By making it more likely that this universe should exist. The problem with this reply is that it would seem to equally validate the inference to many universes from any sort of universe whatever. For instance, let E* be the proposition that α is a universe that contains nothing but chaotic light rays. It seems wrong to think that P(M | E*) > P(M). Yet, if the only reason that P(E | M) > P(E) is that α is more likely to exist if M is true, then an exactly analogous reason would support P(E* | M) > P(E*), and hence P(M | E*) > P(M). This presents the anthropic theorizer with a puzzle. Somehow, the "life-containingness" of α must be given a role to play in the anthropic account. But how can that be done?

Several prominent supporters of the anthropic argument for the multiverse hypothesis have sought to base their case on a distinction between events (or facts) that are surprising and ones that are improbable but not surprising (see e.g. John Leslie (Leslie 1989) and Peter van Inwagen (van Inwagen 1993)).[4]

---

[4] Some authors who are skeptical about the claim that fine-tuning is evidence for a multiverse still see a potential role of an anthropic explanation using the multiverse hypothesis as a way of reducing the surprisingness or amazingness of the observed fine-tuning. A good example of this tack is John Earman's paper on the anthropic principle (Earman 1987), in which he criticizes a number of illegitimate claims made on behalf of the anthropic principle by various authors (especially concerning those misnamed "anthropic principles" that don't involve any observation selection effects and hence bear little or no relation to Brandon Carter's original ideas on the topic (Carter 1974, 1983, 1989, 1990). But in the conclusion he writes: "There remains a potentially legitimate use of anthropic reasoning to alleviate the state of puzzlement into which some people have managed to work themselves over various features of the observable portion of our universe. . . . But to be legitimate, the anthropic reasoning must be backed by substantive reasons for believing in the required [multiverse] structure." (p. 316). Similar views are espoused by Ernan McMullin (McMullin 1993), Bernulf Karnitscheider (Kanitscheider 1993), and (less explicitly) by George Gale (Gale 1996). I agree that anthropic reasoning reduces puzzlement only given the existence of a suitable multiverse, but I disagree with the claim that the potential reduction of puzzlement is no ground whatever for thinking that the multiverse hypothesis is true. My reasons for this will become clear as we proceed.

Suppose you toss a coin one hundred times and write down the results. Any particular sequence *s* is highly improbable (P(*s*) = 2^-100), yet most sequences are not surprising. If *s* contains roughly equally many heads and tails in no clear pattern then *s* is improbable and unsurprising. By contrast, if *s* consists of 100 heads, or of alternating heads and tails, or some other highly patterned outcome, then *s* is surprising. Or to take another example, if *x* wins a lottery with one billion tickets, this is said to be unsurprising ("someone had to win . . . it could just as well be *x* as anybody else . . . shrug."); whereas if there are three lotteries with a thousand tickets each, and *x* wins all three of them, this is surprising. We evidently have some intuitive concept of what it is for an outcome to be surprising in cases like these.

The idea, then, is that a fine-tuned universe is surprising in a sense in which a particular universe filled with only chaotic electromagnetic radiation would not have been. And that's why we need to look for an explanation of fine-tuning but would not have had any reason to suppose there were an explanation for a light-filled universe. The two potential explanations for fine-tuning that typically are considered are the design hypothesis and the multiple universe hypothesis. An inference is then made that at least one of these hypotheses is quite likely true in light of available data, or at least more likely true than would have been the case if this universe had been a "boring" one containing only chaotic light. This is similar to the 100 coin flips example. An unsurprising outcome does not lead us to search for an explanation, while a run of 100 heads does cry out for explanation and gives at least some support to potential explanations such as the hypothesis that the coin flipping process was biased. Likewise in the lottery example. The same person winning all three lotteries could make us suspect that the lottery had been rigged in the winner's favor.

A key assumption in this argument is that fine-tuning is indeed surprising. Is it? Some dismiss the possibility out of hand. For example, Stephen Jay Gould writes:

> Any complex historical outcome—intelligent life on earth, for example—represents a summation of improbabilities and becomes therefore absurdly unlikely. But something has to happen, even if any particular "something" must stun us by its improbability. We could look at any outcome and say, "Ain't it amazing. If the laws of nature had been set up a tad differently, we wouldn't have this kind of universe at all." (Gould 1990), p. 183

From the other side, Peter van Inwagen mocks that way of thinking:

> Some philosophers have argued that there is nothing in the fact that the universe is fine-tuned that should be the occasion for any surprise. After all (the objection runs), if a machine has dials, the dials have to be set some way, and any particular setting is as unlikely as any other. Since any setting of the dial is as unlikely as any other, there can be nothing more surprising

about the actual setting of the dials, whatever it may be, than there would be about any possible setting of the dials if that possible setting were the actual setting. . . . This reasoning is sometimes combined with the point that if "our" numbers hadn't been set into the cosmic dials, the equally improbable setting that did occur would have differed from the actual setting mainly in that there would have been no one there to wonder at its improbability. (van Inwagen 1993), pp. 134–5

Opining that this "must be one of the most annoyingly obtuse arguments in the history of philosophy", van Inwagen asks us to consider the following analogy. Suppose you have to draw a straw from a bundle of 1,048,576 straws of different lengths. It has been decreed that unless you draw the shortest straw you will be instantly killed so that you don't have time to realize that you didn't draw the shortest straw. "Reluctantly—but you have no alternative—you draw a straw and are astonished to find yourself alive and holding the shortest straw. What should you conclude?" According to van Inwagen, only one conclusion is reasonable: that you did not draw the straw at random but that instead the situation was somehow rigged to your advantage by some unknown benefactor. The following argument to the contrary is dismissed as "silly":

> Look, you had to draw some straw or other. Drawing the shortest was no more unlikely than drawing the 256,057th-shortest: the probability in either case was .000000954. But your drawing the 256,057th-shortest straw isn't an outcome that would suggest a 'set-up' or would suggest the need for any sort of explanation, and, therefore, drawing the shortest shouldn't suggest the need for an explanation either. The only real difference between the two cases is that you wouldn't have been around to remark on the unlikelihood of drawing the 256,057th-shortest straw. (van Inwagen 1993), p. 135

Given that the rigging hypothesis did not have too low a prior probability and given that there was only one straw lottery, it is hard to deny that this argument would indeed be silly. What we need to ponder though, is whether the example is analogous to our epistemic situation regarding fine-tuning.

Erik Carlson and Erik Olsson (Carlson and Olsson 1998), criticizing van Inwagen's argument, argue that there are three points of disanalogy between van Inwagen's straw lottery and fine-tuning.

First, they note that whether we would be willing to accept the "unknown benefactor" explanation after drawing the shortest straw depends on our prior probability of there being an unknown benefactor with the means to rig the lottery. If the prior probability is sufficiently tiny—given certain background beliefs it may be very hard to see how the straw lottery *could* be rigged—we would not end up believing in the unknown benefactor hypothesis. Obviously, the same applies to the fine-tuning argument: if the prior probability of a multiverse is small enough then we won't accept that hypothesis even after discovering a high degree of fine-tuning in our universe. The multiverse supporter can grant this and argue that the prior probability of a multiverse is not too small. Exactly how small it can be for us still to end up accepting the multiverse hypothesis depends on both how extreme the fine-tuning is and what alternative explanations are available. If there is plenty of fine-tuning, and the only alternative explanation on the table is the design hypothesis, and if that hypothesis is assigned a much lower prior probability than the multiverse hypothesis, then the argument for the multiverse hypothesis would be vindicated. We don't need to commit ourselves to these assumptions; and in any case, different people might have different prior probabilities. What we are primarily concerned with here is to determine whether fine-tuning is in a relevant sense a *surprising* improbable event, and whether taking fine-tuning into account should substantially *increase* our credence in the multiverse hypothesis and/or the design hypothesis, not what the absolute magnitude of our credence in those hypotheses should be. Carlson and Olsson's first point is granted but it doesn't have any bite. Van Inwagen never claimed that his straw lottery example could settle the question of what the prior probabilities should be.

Carlson and Olsson's second point would be more damaging for van Inwagen, if it weren't incorrect. They claim that there is a fundamental disanalogy in that we understand at least roughly what the causal mechanisms are by which intelligent life evolved from inorganic matter, whereas no such knowledge is assumed regarding the causal chain of events that led you to draw the shortest straw. To make the lottery more closely analogous to the fine-tuning, we should therefore add to the description of the lottery example that at least the proximate causes of your drawing the shortest straw are known. Carlson and Olsson then note that:

> In such a straw lottery, our intuitive reluctance to accept the single-drawing-plus-chance hypothesis is, we think, considerably diminished. Suppose that we can give a detailed causal explanation of why you drew the shortest straw, starting from the state of the world twenty-four hours before the drawing. A crucial link in this explanation is the fact that you had exactly two pints of Guinness on the night before the lottery. . . . Would you, in light of this explanation of your drawing the shortest straw, conclude that, unless there have been a great many straw lotteries, somebody intentionally caused you to drink two pints of Guinness in order to ensure that you draw the shortest straw? . . . To us, this conclusion does not seem very reasonable. (Carlson and Olsson 1998), pp. 271–2

The objection strikes me as unfair. Obviously, if you knew that your choosing the shortest straw depended crucially and sensitively on your precise choice of beverage the night before, you would feel disinclined to accept the rigging hypothesis. That much is right. But this disinclination is fully accounted for by the fact that it is tremendously hard to see, under such circumstances, how anybody *could* have rigged the lottery. If we knew that successful rigging required predicting in detail such a long and tenuous causal chain of events, we could well conclude that the prior probability of rigging was negligible. For *that* reason, surviving the lottery would not make us believe the rigging hypothesis.

We can see that it is this—rather than our understanding of the proximate causes per se—that defeats the argument for rigging by considering the following variant of van Inwagen's example. Suppose that the straws are scattered over a vast area. Each straw has one railway track leading up to it, and all the tracks start from the same central station. When you pick the shortest straw, we now have a causal explanation that can stretch far back in time: you picked it because it was at the destination point of a long journey along a track that did not branch. How long the track was makes no difference to how willing we are to believe in the rigging hypothesis. What matters is only whether we think there is some plausibility to the idea that an unknown benefactor could have put you on the right track to begin with. So contrary to what Carlson and Olsson imply, what is relevant is not the known backward length of the causal chain, but whether that chain would have been sufficiently predictable by the hypothetical benefactor to give a large enough prior probability to the hypothesis that she rigged the lottery. Needless to say, the designer referred to in the design hypothesis is typically assumed to have superhuman epistemic capacities. It is not at all farfetched to suppose that *if* there were a cosmic designer, she would have been able to anticipate which boundary conditions of the universe were likely to lead to the evolution of life. We should therefore reject Carlson and Olsson's second objection against van Inwagen's analogy.

The third alleged point of disanalogy is somewhat subtler. Carlson and Olsson discuss it in the context of refuting certain claims by Arnold Zuboff (Zuboff 1991) and it is not clear how much weight they place on it as an objection against van Inwagen. But it's worth mentioning. The idea, as far as I can make it out, is that the reason why your existing after the straw lottery is surprising, is related to the fact that you existed before the straw lottery. You could have antecedently contemplated your survival as one of a variety of possible outcomes. In the case of fine-tuning, by contrast, your existing (or intelligent life existing) is not an outcome which could have been contemplated prior to its obtaining.

> For conceptual reasons, it is impossible that you know in advance that your existence lottery is going to take place. Likewise, it is conceptually impossible that you make any ex ante specification of any possible outcome of this lottery. . . . The existence of a cosmos suitable for life does not seem to be a coincidence for anybody; nobody was ever able to specify this outcome of the cosmos lottery, independently of its actually being the actual outcome. (Carlson and Olsson 1998), p. 268

This might look like a token of the "annoyingly obtuse" reasoning that van Inwagen thought to refute through his straw lottery example. Nevertheless, there is a disanalogy between the two cases: nobody could have contemplated the existence of intelligent life unless intelligent life existed, whereas someone, even the person immediately involved, could have thought about drawing the shortest straw before drawing it. The question is whether this difference is relevant. Again it is useful to cook up a variant of the straw-drawing example:

> Suppose that in an otherwise lifeless universe there is a big bunch of straws and a simple (non-cognitive, non-conscious) automaton is about to randomly select one of the straws. There is also an "incubator" in which one person rests in an unconscious state; we can suppose she has been unconscious since the beginning of time. The automaton is set up in such a way that the person in the incubator will be woken if and only if the automaton picks the shortest straw. You wake up in the incubator. After examining your surroundings and learning about how the experiment was set up, you begin to wonder about whether there's anything surprising about the fact that the shortest straw was drawn.

This example shares with the fine-tuning case the feature that nobody would have been there to contemplate anything if the "special" outcome had failed to obtain. So what should we say about this case? In order for Carlson and Olsson's criticism to work, we would have to say that the person waking up in the incubator should not think that there is anything surprising at all about the shortest straw having been selected. Van Inwagen would, presumably, simply deny that that would be the correct attitude. For what it's worth, my intuition in this instance sides with van Inwagen, although the case is perhaps less obvious than the original straw lottery gedanken where the subject had a life before the lottery.

It would be nice to have an independent account of what makes an event or a fact surprising. We could then apply the general account to the straw lotteries or directly to fine-tuning and see what follows. Let us therefore briefly review what efforts have been made to develop such an account of surprisingness. (I'm indebted here to the literature-survey and discussion in (Manson 1998).) To anticipate the upshot, I will argue that these are dead ends as far as anthropic reasoning is concerned. The strategy relied on by those anthropic theorizers who base their case on an appeal to what is surprising is therefore ultimately of very limited utility: the strategy is based on intuitions that are no more obvious or secure than the thesis which they are employed to support. This may seem disappointing. In fact, it clears the path for a better understanding what is required to support anthropic reasoning.

The following remark by F. P. Ramsey is pertinent to the goal of determining what distinguishes surprising improbable events from unsurprising improbable events:

> What we mean by an event not being a coincidence, or not being due to chance, is that if we came to know it, it would make us no longer regard our system as satisfactory, although on our system the event may be no more improbable than any alternative. Thus 1,000 heads running would not be due to chance; i.e. if we observed it we should change our system of chances for that penny. (Ramsey 1990), p. 106

This looks like an auspicious beginning. It seems to fit the other example we considered near the beginning of this section: one person winning three lotteries with a thousand tickets could make us suspect foul play, whereas one person winning a billion-ticket lottery would not in general have any tendency do so. Or ponder the case of a monkey typing out the sequence "Give me a banana!". This is surprising and makes us change our belief that the monkey types randomly. We would think that maybe the monkey had been trained to type that specific sequence, or maybe that there was something funny about the typewriter. The chance hypothesis would be confirmed. By contrast, if the monkey types "r78o479024io; jl;", this is unsurprising and does not challenge our assumptions about the setup. So far so good.

What Ramsey's suggestion does not tell us is what it is about events such as the monkey's typing a meaningful sentence or the run of 1000 heads that makes us change our minds about the system of chances. And we need to know that if the suggestion is to throw light on the fine-tuning case. For the problem there is precisely that it is not immediately clear—lest the question be begged—whether we ought to change our system and find some alternative explanation or be satisfied with regarding fine-tuning as a coincidence and letting chance pay the bill. Ramsey's suggestion is thus insufficient for the present purpose.

Paul Horwich takes the analysis a little further. He proposes the following as a necessary condition for the truth of a statement E being surprising:

> [T]he truth of E is surprising only if the supposed circumstances C, which made E seem improbable, are themselves substantially diminished in probability by the truth of E . . .and if there is some initially implausible (but not widely implausible) alternative view K about the circumstances, relative to which E would be highly probable. (Horwich 1982), p. 101

If we combine this with the condition that "our beliefs C are such as to give rise to $P(E) \approx 0$", we get what Horwich thinks is a necessary and sufficient condition for the truth of a statement being surprising. We can sum this up by saying that the truth of E is surprising iff the following holds:

(i) $P(E) \approx 0$

(ii) $P(C \mid E) << P(C)$

(iii) $P(E \mid K) \approx 1$

(iv) $P(K)$ is small but not too small

Several authors who think that fine-tuning cries out for explanation endorse views that are similar to Horwich's (Manson 1989). For instance, van Inwagen writes:

> Suppose there is a certain fact that has no known explanation; suppose that one can think of a possible explanation of that fact, an explanation that (if only it were true) would be a very *good* explanation; then it is wrong to say that that event stands in no more need of an explanation than an otherwise similar event for which no such explanation is available. (van Inwagen 1993), p. 135

And John Leslie:

> A chief (or the only?) reason for thinking that something stands in [special need for explanation], i.e. for justifiable reluctance to dismiss it as how things just happen to be, is that one in fact glimpses some tidy way in which it might be explained. (Leslie 1989), p. 10

D. J. Bartholomew also appears to support a similar principle (Bartholomew 1984). Horwich's analysis provides a reasonably good explication of these ideas.

George Schlesinger (Schlesinger 1991) has criticized Horwich's analysis, arguing that the availability of a tidy explanation is not necessary for an event being surprising. Schlesinger asks us to consider the case of a tornado that touches down in three different places, destroying one house in each place. We are surprised to learn that these houses belonged to the same person and that they are the only buildings that this misfortunate capitalist owned. Yet no neat explanation suggests itself. Indeed, it seems to be *because* we can see no tidy explanation (other than the chance hypothesis) that this phenomenon would be so surprising. So if we let E to be the event that the tornado destroys the only three buildings that some person owns and destroys nothing else, and C the chance hypothesis, then (ii)–(iv) are not satisfied. According to Horwich's analysis, E is not surprising—which seems wrong.

Surprise being ultimately a psychological matter, we should perhaps not expect any simple definition to perfectly capture all the cases where we would feel surprised. But maybe Horwich has provided at least a sufficient condition for when we ought to feel surprised? Let's run with this for a second and see what happens when we apply his analysis to fine-tuning.

In order to do this we need to determine the probabilities referred to in (i)–(iv). Let's grant that the prior probability of fine-tuning (E) is very small, $P(E) \approx 0$. Further, anthropic theorizers maintain that E makes the chance hypothesis substantially less probable than it would have been without conditionalizing on E, so let's suppose that $P(C|E) << P(C)$[5]. Let K be a multiverse hypothesis. In order to have $P(C|K) \approx 1$, it might count as necessary to think of K as more specific than the proposition that there is some multiverse; we may have to define K as the proposition that there is a "suitable" multiverse (i.e. one such that $P(E|K) \approx 1$ is satisfied). But let us suppose that even such a strengthened multiverse hypothesis has a prior probability that is not "too small". If we make these assumptions then Horwich's four conditions are satisfied, and the truth of E would consequently count as surprising. This is the result that the anthropic theorizer would welcome.

Unfortunately, we can construct a parallel line of assumptions to show that any other possible universe would have been equally surprising. Let $E^{\#}$ be the proposition that α has some particular boring character. For instance, we can let $E^{\#}$ say that α is a universe which consists of nothing but such-and-such a pattern of electromagnetic radiation. We then have $P(E^{\#}) \approx 0$. Let K be the same as before. Now, if we suppose that $P(C|E^{\#}) << P(C)$ and $P(E^{\#}|K) \approx 1$ then the truth of $E^{\#}$ will be classified as surprising. This is counterintuitive. And if it were true that every possible universe would be just as surprising as any other, then fine-tuning being surprising can surely not be what legitimizes the inference from fine-tuning to the multiverse hypothesis. We must therefore deny either $P(C|E^{\#}) << P(C)$ or $P(E^{\#}|K) \approx 1$ (or both). At the same time, if the truth of E is to be surprising, we must maintain that $P(C|E) << P(C)$ and $P(E|K) \approx 1$. This means that the anthropic theorizer wishing to ground her argument in an appeal to surprise must treat $E^{\#}$ differently from E as regards these conditional probabilities. It may be indeed be correct to do so. But what is the justification? Whatever is it, it cannot be that the truth of E is surprising whereas the truth of $E^{\#}$ is not. For although that might be true, to simply assume it would be to make the argument circular.

The appeal to the surprisingness of E is therefore quite ineffective. In order to make the appeal persuasive, it must be backed up by some argument for the claim that: $P(C|E) << P(C)$, $P(E|K) \approx 1$ but not both $P(C|E^{\#})$

---

[5] This follows from Bayes' theorem if the probability that C gives to E is so tiny that $P(E|C) << P(E)$.

$<< P(C)$ and $P(E^{\#} \mid K) \approx 1$. But suppose we had such an argument. We could then sidestep considerations about surprisingness altogether! For it follows already from $P(E \mid K) \approx 1$, $P(E) \approx 0$, and P(K) being "not too small", that $P(K \mid E) \approx 1$, i.e. that fine-tuning is strong evidence for the multiverse hypothesis. (To see this, simply plug the values into Bayes' formula, $P(K \mid E) = P(E \mid K) \, P(K) / P(E)$.)

To make progress beyond this point, we need to abandon vague talk of what makes events surprising and focus explicitly on the core issue, which is to determine the conditional probability of the multiverse hypothesis/ chance hypothesis/design hypothesis given the evidence we have. If we figure out how to think about these conditional probabilities, we can hopefully use this insight to sort out the quandary about whether fine-tuning should be regarded as surprising. At any rate, that quandary becomes much less important if we have a direct route to assigning probabilities to the relevant hypotheses that skips the detour through the dark netherworld of amazement and surprise. Let's do that.

MODELING OBSERVATION SELECTION EFFECTS: THE ANGEL PARABLE

I submit that the only way to get a plausible model of how to reason from fine-tuning is by explicitly taking observation selection effects into account. This section will outline parts of a theory of how to do that. Later chapters will expand and support themes that are merely alluded to here. A theory of observation selection effects has applications in many domains. In this section we focus on cosmology.

As before, let "α" rigidly denote our universe. We know some things K about α (it's life-permitting; it contains the Eiffel tower; it's quite big etc.). Let h_M be the multiverse hypothesis; let h_D be the design hypothesis; and let h_C be the chance hypothesis. In order to determine what values to assign to the conditional probabilities $P(h_M \mid K)$, $P(h_D \mid K)$, and $P(h_C \mid K)$, we need to take account of the observation selection effects through which our evidence about the world has been filtered.

How should we model these observation selection effects? Suppose that you are an angel. So far nothing physical exists, but six days ago God told you that He was going away for a week to create a cosmos. He might create either a single universe or a multiverse; let's say your prior probabilities for these two hypotheses are about 50%. Now a messenger arrives and informs you that God's work is completed. The messenger tells you that universe α exists but does not say whether there are other universes in addition. Should you think that God created a multiverse or only α?

To answer this, we need to know something more about the situation. Consider two alternative stories of what happened:

Case 1. The messenger decided to travel to realm of physical existence and look at the universe or one of the universes that God had created. This universe was α, and this is what he reports to you.

Case 2. The messenger decided to find out whether God created α. So he travels to the realm of physical existence and looks until he finds α, and reports this back to you.

In Case 1, the messenger's tidings do not in general give you any reason to believe h_M. He was bound to bring back news about some universe, and the fact that he tells you about α rather than some other universe is not significant—*unless* α has some special feature F. (More on this proviso shortly.)

In Case 2 on the other hand, the fact that the messenger tells you that α exists is evidence for h_M. If the messenger selected α randomly from the class of all possible universes, or from some sizeable subclass thereof (for example only big bang universes with the same laws of nature as in our universe, or only universes which contain more good than evil), then the finding that God created α suggests that God created many universes.

Our actual epistemic situation is not analogous to the angel's in Case 2. It is not as if we first randomly selected α from a class containing both actual and non-actual possible universes and then discovered that—lo and behold!—α actually exists. The fact that we know whether α exists surely has everything to do with it actually existing and we being among its inhabitants. There is an observation selection effect amounting to the following: direct observation occurs only of universes that actually exist. Case 1 comes closer to modeling our epistemic situation in this respect, since it mirrors this selection effect.

However, Case 1 is still an inadequate model because it overlooks another observational effect. The messenger could have retrieved information about any of the actual universes, and the angel could have found out about some universe β that doesn't contain any observers. If there are no angels, gods or heavenly messengers, however, then universes that don't contain observers are not observed. Assuming the absence of extramundane observers, the selection effect restricts what is observed not only to the extent that non-actual universes are not observed but actual universes that lack observers are also not observed. This needs to be reflected in our model. If we want to continue to use the creation story, we must therefore modify it as follows:

Case 3. The messenger decided to travel to the realm of physical existence and look for some universe that contains observers. He found α, and reports this back to you.

Does this provide you with any evidence for h_M? It depends.

If you knew (call this *Case 3a*) that God had set out to create at least one observer-containing universe, then the news that α is actual does not give any support to h_M (unless you know that α has some special feature). For then you were guaranteed to learn about the existence of some observer-containing universe or other, and learning that it is α does not give any more evidence for h_M than if you had learnt about some other universe instead. The messenger's tidings T contain no relevant new information. The probably you assign to h_M remains unchanged. In Case 3a, therefore, $P(h_M | T) = P(h_M)$.

But there is second way of specifying Case 3. Suppose (*Case 3b*) that God did not set out especially to create at least one observer-containing universe, and that for any universe that He created there was only a fairly small chance that it would be observer-containing. In this case, when the messenger reports that God created the observer-containing universe α, you get evidence that favors h_M. For it is more probable on h_M than it is on $\neg h_M$ that one or more observer-containing universes should exist (one of which the messenger was then bound to bring you news about). Here, therefore, we have $P(h_M | T) > P(h_M)$.

What is grounding T's support for h_M? I think it is best answered by saying not that T makes it more probable that α should exist, but rather that T makes it more probable that at least one observer-containing universe should exist. It is nonetheless true that h_M makes it more probable that α should exist. But this is not by itself the reason why h_M is to be preferred given our knowledge of the existence of α. If it were, then since the same reason operates in Case 3a, we would have to have concluded that h_M were favored in that case as well. For even though it was guaranteed in Case 3a that some observer-containing universe would exist, it was not guaranteed that it would be α. In Case 3a as well as in Case 3b, the existence of α was made more likely by h_M than by $\neg h_M$. If this should not lead us to favor h_M in Case 3a then the fact that the existence of is made more likely by h_M cannot be the whole story about why h_M is to be preferred in Case 3b.

So what is the whole story about this? This will become clearer as we proceed, but we can give at least the outlines now. Subsequent chapters will fill in important details and supply arguments for the claims we make here.

In a nutshell: although h_M makes it more probable that α should exist, h_M also makes it more probable that there are other observer-containing universes. And the greater the number of observer-containing universes, the smaller the probability that we should observe any particular one of them. These two effects balance each other. The result is that the messenger's tidings are evidence in favor of theories on which it is probable that at least one observer-containing universe would exist. But this evidence does not favor theories on which it is probable that there are *many* observer-containing universes over theories on which it is probable that there are merely a *few* observer-containing universes.

We can get an intuitive grasp of this if we consider a two-step procedure. Suppose the messenger first tells you that some observer-containing universe x exists. This rules out all hypotheses on which there would be no such universes; it counts against hypotheses on which it would be very unlikely that there are any observer-containing universes; and it favors hypotheses on which it would be very likely or certain that there is one or more observer-containing universes. In the second step, the messenger tells you that $x = \alpha$. This should not change your beliefs as to how many observer-containing universes there are (assuming you don't think there is anything special about α). One might say that if God were equally likely to create any universe, then the probability that α should exist is proportional to the number of universes God created. True. But the full evidence you have is not only that α exists but also that the messenger told you about α. If the messenger selected the universe he reports on randomly from the class of all actual observer-containing universes, then the probability that he would select α, given that α is an actual observer-containing universe, is *inversely* proportional to the number of actual observer-containing universes. The messenger's report therefore does not allow you to discriminate between general hypotheses[6] that imply that at least one observer-containing universe exists.

In our actual situation, our knowledge is not mediated by a messenger. But the idea is that the data we get about the world is subjected to observation selection effects that mimic the reporting biases present in Case 3. (Not quite, though. A better analogy yet would be one in which (*Case 4*) the messenger selects a random observer from among the observers that God has created, thus biasing the universe-selection in favor of those universes that have relatively large populations. But more on this in a later chapter. To keep things simple here, we can imagine all the observer-containing universes as having the same number of observers.)

When stating that the finding that α exists does not give us reason to think that there are many rather than few observer-containing universes, we have kept inserting the proviso that α not be "special". This is an essential qualification. For there clearly are some features F such that if we knew that α has them then finding that α exists *would* support the claim that there are a vast number of observer-containing universes. For instance, if you know that α is a universe in which a message is inscribed in every rock, in the distribution of fixed stars seen from any life-bearing planet, and in the microstructure of common crystal lattices, spelling: "God created this uni-

---

[6] By "general hypotheses" we here mean: hypotheses that don't entail anything preferentially about α. For example, a hypothesis which says "There is exactly one life-containing universe and it's not α." will obviously be refuted by the messenger's report. But the point is that there is nothing about the messenger's report that gives reason to favor hypotheses only because they imply a greater number of observer-containing universes, assuming there is nothing special about α.

verse. He also created many other universes."—then the fact that the messenger tells you that α exists can obviously give you reason to think that there are many universes. In our actual universe, if we were to find inscriptions that we were convinced could only have been created by a divine being, this would count as support for whatever these inscriptions asserted (the degree of support being qualified by the strength of our conviction that the deity was being honest). Leaving aside such theological scenarios, there are much more humdrum features our universe might have that could make it special in the sense here intended. It may be, for example, that the physics of our universe is such as to suggest a physical theory (because it's the simplest, most elegant theory that fits the facts) that entails the existence of vast numbers of observer-containing universes.

Fine-tuning may well be a "special" feature. This is so because fine-tuning seems to indicate that there is no simple, elegant theory which entails (or gives a high probability to) the existence our universe alone but not to the existence of other universes. If it were to turn out, present appearances notwithstanding, that there is such a theory, then our universe is not special. But in that case there would be little reason to think that our universe really is fine-tuned. For if a simple theory entails that precisely this universe should exist, then one could plausibly assert that no other boundary conditions than those implied by that theory are physically possible, and hence that physical constants and initial conditions could not have been different than they are—thus no fine-tuning. However, assuming that every theory fitting the facts and entailing that there is only one universe is a very ad hoc one involving many free parameters—as fine-tuning advocates argue—then the fine-tuning of our universe is a special feature that gives support to the hypothesis that there are many universes. There is nothing mysterious about this. Preferring simple theories that fit the facts to complicated ad hoc ones is just standard scientific practice. Cosmologists who work with multiverse theories are pursuing that inquiry because they think that multiverse theories represent a promising route forward to neat theories that are empirically adequate.

We can now answer the questions asked at the beginning of this chapter: Does fine-tuning cry out for explanation? Does it give support to the multiverse hypothesis? Beginning with the latter question, we should say: Yes, to the extent that multiverse theories are simpler, more elegant (and therefore able to claim a higher prior probability) than any rival theories that are compatible with what we observe. In order to be more precise about the magnitude of support, we need to determine the conditional probability that a multiverse theory gives to the observations we make. We have said something about how such conditional probabilities are determined: the conditional probability is greater—ceteris paribus—the greater the probability that the multiverse theory gives to the existence of a universe exactly like ours; it is smaller—ceteris paribus—the greater the number of observer-containing universes it entails. These two factors balance each other to the effect that if we are comparing various multiverse theories, what matters, generally speaking, is the likelihood they assign to at least some observer-containing universe existing. If two multiverse theories both do that, then there is no general reason to favor or disfavor the one that entails the larger number of observer-containing universes. All this will become clearer in subsequent chapters where the current hand-waving will be replaced by mathematically precise models.

The answer to the question whether fine-tuning cries out for explanation follows from this. If something's "crying out for explanation" means that it would be unsatisfactory to leave it unexplained or to dismiss it as a chance event, then fine-tuning cries out for explanation at least to the extent that we have reason to believe in some theory that would explain it. At present, multiverse theories look like reasonably promising candidates. For the theologically inclined, the Creator-hypothesis is also a candidate. And there remains the possibility that fine-tuning could turn out to be an illusion—if some neat single-universe theory that fits the data were to be discovered in the future.[7]

Finally, we may also ask whether there is anything surprising about our observation of fine-tuning. Let's assume, as the question presupposes, that the universe really is fine-tuned, in the sense that there is no neat single-universe theory that fits the data (but not in a sense that excludes our universe being one in an ensemble that is itself not fine-tuned). Is such fine-tuning surprising on the chance-hypothesis? It is, per assumption, a low-probability event if the chance-hypothesis is true; and it would tend to disconfirm the chance-hypothesis if there is some other hypothesis with reasonably high prior probability that assigns a high conditional probability to fine-tuning. For it to be a surprising event then (invoking Horwich's analysis) there has to be some alternative to the chance-hypothesis that meets conditions (iii) and (iv). Some would hold that the design hypothesis satisfies these criteria. But if we bracket the design hypothesis, does the multiverse hypothesis fit the bill? We can suppose, for the sake of the argument at least, that the prior probability of the multiverse hypothesis is not too low, so that (iv) is satisfied. The sticky point is condition (iii), which requires that $P(E \mid h_M) \approx 1$. According to the discussion above, the conditional probability of us observing a fine-tuned universe is greater given a suitable multiverse than given the existence of a single random universe. If the multiverse hypothesis is of a suitable kind—such that it entails (or makes it highly likely) that at least one observer-containing universe exists—then the conditional probability, given that hypothesis, of us observing an observer-containing universe

---

[7] If there is a sense of "explanation" in which a multiverse theory would not explain why we observe a fine-tuned universe, then the prospect of a multiverse theory would not add to the need for explanation in that sense.

should be set equal (or very close) to one. It then comes down to whether on this hypothesis representative[8] observer-containing universes would be fine-tuned.[9] If they would, it follows that this multiverse hypothesis should be taken to give a very high likelihood to our observing a fine-tuned universe; so Horwich's condition (iii) would be satisfied, and our observing fine-tuning would count as a surprising event. If, on the other hand, representative observer-containing universes in the multiverse would not be fine-tuned, then condition (iii) would not be satisfied, and the fine-tuning would not qualify as surprising.[10]

Note that in answering the question whether fine-tuning is surprising, we focused on E' (the statement that there is a fine-tuned universe) rather than E (the statement that α is fine-tuned). I suggest that what is primarily surprising is E', and E is surprising only in the indirect sense of implying E'. If E is independently surprising, then on Horwich's analysis, it has to be so owing to some other alternative[11] to the chance-hypothesis than the multiverse hypothesis, since it is not the case that $P(E \mid h_M) \approx 1$. But I find it quite

---

[8] The meaning of "representative" is *not* equivalent here to "most numerous type of universe in the multiverse" but rather "the type of universe with the greatest expected fraction of all observers".

[9] One can easily imagine multiverse theories on which this would not necessarily be the case. A multiverse theory could for example include a physics that allowed for two distinct regions in the space of possible boundary conditions to be life-containing. One of these regions could be very broad so that most universes in that region would not be fine-tuned—they would still have contained life even if the values of their physical constants had been slightly different. The other region could be very narrow. Universes in this region would be fine-tuned: a slight perturbation of the boundary conditions would knock a universe out of the life-containing region. If the universes in the two life-containing regions in parameter space are equivalent in other respects, this cosmos would be an instance of a multiverse where representative observer-containing universes would not be fine-tuned. If a multiverse theory assigns a high probability to the multiverse being of this kind, then on the hypothesis that that theory is true, representative observer-containing universes would not be fine-tuned.

[10] It may intuitively seem as if our observing a fine-tuned universe would be even *more* surprising if the only multiverse theory on the table implied that representative observer-containing universes were *not* fine-tuned, because it would then be even more improbable that we should live in a fine-tune universe. This intuition most likely derives from our not accepting the assumptions we made. For instance, the design hypothesis (which we ruled out by fiat) might be able to fit the four criteria and thus account for why we would find the fine-tuning surprising even in this case. Alternatively, we might think it implausible that we would be sufficiently convinced that the only available multiverse hypotheses would be ones in which representative universes would not be fine-tuned. So this represents a rather artificial case where our intuitions could easily go astray. I mention it only in order to round out the argument and to more fully illustrate how the reasoning works. The point is not very important in itself.

[11] It's not clear whether there is an alternative that would work here. There would be if, for instance, one assigned a high prior probability to a design hypothesis on which the designer was highly likely to create only α and to make it fine-tuned.

intuitive that what would be surprising on the chance-hypothesis is not that *this* universe (understood rigidly) should be fine-tuned but rather that there should be a fine-tuned universe at all if there is only one universe and fine-tuning was highly improbable.

PRELIMINARY CONCLUSIONS

It may be useful to summarize our main findings in this chapter. We set out to investigate whether fine-tuning needs explaining and whether it gives support to the multiverse hypothesis. We found:

• There is an easy part of the answer: Leaving fine-tuning unexplained is epistemically unsatisfactory to the extent that it involves accepting complicated, inelegant theories with many free parameters. If a neater theory can account for available data, it is to be preferred. This is just an instance of the general methodological principle that one should prefer simpler theories, and it has nothing to do with fine-tuning as such. I.e., this point is unrelated to the fact that observers would not have existed if boundary conditions had been slightly different.

• Ian Hacking's argument that multiverse theories such as Wheeler's oscillating universe model cannot receive any support from fine-tuning data, while multiverse theories such as the one Hacking ascribes to Brandon Carter can receive such support, is flawed. So are the more recent arguments by Roger White and Phil Dowe purporting to show that multiverse theories *tout court* would not be supported by fine-tuning.

• Those who think fine-tuning gives some support to the multiverse hypothesis have typically tried to argue for this by appealing to the surprisingness of fine-tuning. We examined van Inwagen's straw lottery example, refuted some objections by Carlson and Olsson, and suggested a variant of van Inwagen's example that is more closely analogous to our epistemic situation regarding fine-tuning. In this variant, the verdict seems to favor the multiverse advocates, although there appears to be room for opposing intuitions. In order to give the idea that an appeal to the surprisingness of fine-tuning could settle the issue a full run for its money, we considered Paul Horwich's analysis of what makes the truth of a statement surprising. This analysis may provide the best available explication of what multiverse advocates mean when they talk about surprise. We found, however, that applying Horwich's analysis to the fine-tuning situation doesn't settle the issue of whether fine-tuning is surprising. We concluded that in order to determine whether fine-tuning cries out for explanation or gives support for the multiverse hypothesis, it is not enough to appeal to the surprisingness or amazingness of fine-tuning. One has to dig deeper.

• What is needed is a way of determining the conditional probability $P(E|h_M)$. In order to get this right, it is essential to take into account observation selection effects. We created an informal model of how to think about such effects in the context of fine-tuning. Some of the consequences of this model are as follows:

• Suppose there exists a universe-generating mechanism such that each universe it produces has an equal probability of being observer-containing. Then fine-tuning favors (other things equal) theories on which the mechanism has operated enough times to make it probable that at least one observer-containing universe would result.

• However, if two competing general theories with equal prior probability each implies that the mechanism operated sufficiently many times to (nearly) guarantee that at least one observer-containing universe would be produced, then our observing an observer-containing universe is (nearly) no ground for favoring the theory which entails the greater number of observer-containing universes. Nor does it matter how many observerless universes the theories say exist.

• If two competing general theories with equal prior probability, T_1 and T_2, each entails the same number of observer-containing universes (and we assume that each observer-containing universe contains the same number of observers), but T_1 makes it more likely than does T_2 that a large fraction of all the observers live in universes that have those properties that we have observed that our universe has (e.g. the same values of physical constants), then our observations favor T_1 over T_2.

• Although $P(E|h_M)$ may be much closer to zero than to one, this conditional probability could nonetheless easily be large enough (taking observation selection effects into account) for E to favor the multiverse hypothesis.

• Here is the answer to the "tricky part" of the question about whether fine-tuning needs explanation or supports the multiverse hypothesis: Yes, there is something about fine-tuning as such that adds to the need for explanation and to the support for the multiverse hypothesis over and above what is accounted for by the general principle that simplicity is epistemically attractive. The ground for this is twofold: first, the availability of a potential rival explanation for why the universe is observer-containing. The design hypothesis, presumably, can more plausibly be invoked to explain a world that contains observers than one that doesn't. Second (theology apart), the capacity of the multiverse hypothesis to give a high conditional probability to E (and thereby in some sense to explain E), and to gain support from E, depends essentially on observation selection effects. Fine-tuning is therefore *not* just like any other way in which a theory may require a delicate setting of various free parameters to fit the data. The presumption that observers would not be so likely to exist if the universe were not fine-tuned is crucial. For that presumption entails that if a multiverse theory implies that there is an ensemble of universes, only a few of which are fine-tuned, then what the theory predicts that we should observe is still one of those exceptional universes that are fine-tuned. The observation selection effect enables the theory to give our observing a fine-tuned universe a high conditional probability even though such a universe may be very atypical of the cosmos as a whole. If there were no observation selection effect restricting our observation to an atypical proper part of the cosmos, then postulating a bigger cosmos would not in general give a higher conditional probability to us observing some particular feature. (It may make it more probable that that feature should be instantiated somewhere or other, but it would also make it less probable that we should happen to be at any particular place where it was instantiated.) Fine-tuning, therefore, involves issues additional to the ones common to all forms of scientific inference and explanation.

• On Horwich's analysis of what makes the truth of a statement surprising, it would be surprising against the background of the chance-hypothesis that only one universe existed and it happened to be fine-tuned. By contrast, that *this* universe should be fine-tuned would not contain any additional surprise factor (unless the design hypothesis could furnish an explanation for this datum satisfying Horwich's condition (iii) and (iv)).

CHAPTER 3

Anthropic Principles
The Motley Family

We have seen how observation selection effects are relevant in assessing the implications of cosmological fine-tuning, and we have outlined a model for how they modulate the conditional probability of us making certain observations given certain hypotheses about the large-scale structure of the cosmos. The general idea that observation selection effects need to be taken into account in cosmological theorizing has been recognized by several authors and there have been many attempts to express this idea in the form of an "anthropic principle". None of these attempts quite hits the mark, however, and some seem not even to know what they are aiming at.

The first section of this chapter reviews some of the more helpful formulations of the anthropic principle found in the literature and considers how far these can take us. Section two briefly discusses a set of very different "anthropic principles" and explains why they are misguided or at least irrelevant for our present purposes. A thicket of confusion surrounds the anthropic principle and its epistemological status. We shall need to clear that up. Since a main thrust of this book is that anthropic reasoning merits serious attention, we shall want to explicitly disown some associated ideas that are misguided. The third section continues where the first section left off. It argues that the formulations found in the literature are inadequate. A forth section proposes a new methodological principle to replace them. This principle forms the core of the theory of observation selection effects that we will develop in subsequent chapters.

THE ANTHROPIC PRINCIPLE AS EXPRESSING AN OBSERVATION SELECTION EFFECT

The term "anthropic principle" was coined by Brandon Carter in a paper of 1974, wherein he defined it thus:

> . . . what we can expect to observe must be restricted by the conditions
> necessary for our presence as observers. (Carter 1974), p. 126

Carter's notion of the anthropic principle, as evidenced by the uses to which he put it, is appropriate and productive. Yet his definitions and explanations of it are rather vague. While Carter himself was never in doubt about how to understand and apply the principle, he did not explain it a philosophically transparent enough manner to enable all his readers to do the same.

The trouble starts with the name. Anthropic reasoning has nothing in particular to do with homo sapiens. Calling the principle "anthropic" is therefore misleading and has indeed misled some authors (e.g. (Gale 1981; Gould 1985; Worrall 1996)). Carter has expressed regrets about not using a different name (Carter 1983), suggesting that maybe "the psychocentric principle", "the cognizability principle" or "the observer self-selection principle" would have been better. The time for terminological reform has probably passed, but emphasizing that the anthropic principle concerns intelligent observers in general and not specifically human observers should help to prevent misunderstandings.

Carter introduced two versions of the anthropic principle, one strong (SAP) and one weak (WAP). WAP states that:

> . . . we must be prepared to take account of the fact that our location in
> the universe is *necessarily* privileged to the extent of being compatible
> with our existence as observers. (p. 127)

And SAP:

> . . . the Universe (and hence the fundamental parameters on which it
> depends) must be such as to admit the creation of observers within it at
> some stage. (p. 129)

Carter's formulations have been attacked alternatively for being mere tautologies (and therefore incapable of doing any interesting explanatory work whatever) and for being widely speculative (and lacking any empirical support). Often WAP is accused of the former and SAP of the latter. I think we have to admit that both these readings are possible, since the definitions of WAP and SAP are very vague. WAP says that we have to "be prepared to take into account" the fact that our location is privileged, but it does not say *how* we are to take account of that fact. SAP says that the universe "must" admit the creation of observers, but we get very different meanings depending how we interpret the "must". Does it serve merely to underscore an implication of available data ("the universe must be life-admitting—present evidence about our existence implies that!")? Or is the "must" instead to be understood in some stronger sense, for example as alleging some kind of prior metaphysical or theological necessity? On the former alternative, the principle is indisputably true; but then the difficulty is to explain how this trivial statement can be useful or important. On the second alternative, we can see how it could be contentful (provided we can make sense of the intended notion of necessity), the difficulty now being to provide some reason for why we should believe it.

John Leslie (Leslie 1989) argues that AP, WAP and SAP can all be understood as tautologies and that the difference between them is often purely verbal. In Leslie's explication, AP simply says that:

> *Any intelligent living beings that there are can find themselves only where intelligent life is possible.* (Leslie 1989), p. 128

WAP then says that, within a universe, observers find themselves only at spatiotemporal locations where observers are possible. SAP states that observers find themselves only in universes that allow observers to exist. "Universes" means roughly: huge spacetime regions that might be more or less causally disconnected from other spacetime regions. Since the definition of a universe is not sharp, neither is the distinction between WAP and SAP. WAP talks about where within a life-permitting universe we should expect to find ourselves, while SAP talks about in what kind of universe in an ensemble of universes we should expect to find ourselves. On this interpretation the two principles are fundamentally similar, differing in scope only.

For completeness, we may also mention Leslie's (Leslie 1989) "Superweak Anthropic Principle", which states that:

> *If intelligent life's emergence, NO MATTER HOW HOSPITABLE THE ENVIRONMENT, always involves very improbable happenings, then any intelligent living beings that there are evolved where such improbable happenings happened."* (Leslie 1989), p. 132; emphasis and capitals as in the original.

The implication, as Michael Hart (Hart 1982) has stressed, is that we shouldn't assume that the evolution of life on an earth-like planet might not well be extremely improbable. Provided there are enough Earth-like planets, as there almost certainly are in an infinite universe, then even a chance lower than 1 in $10^{3,000}$ would be enough to ensure (i.e. give an arbitrarily great probability to the proposition) that life would evolve somewhere[1]. Naturally,

---

[1]The figure 1 in $10^{3,000}$ is Hart's most optimistic estimate of how likely it is that the right molecules would just happen to bump into each other to form a short DNA string capable of self-replication. As Hart himself recognizes, it is possible that there exists some as yet unknown abiotic process bridging the gap between amino acids (which we know can form spontaneously in suitable environments) and DNA-based self-replicating organisms. Such a bridge could

what we would observe would be one of the rare planets where such an improbable chance-event had occurred. The Superweak AP can be seen as special case of WAP. It doesn't add anything to what is already contained in Carter's principles.

The question that immediately arises is: Has not Leslie trivialized anthropic reasoning with this definition of AP?—Not necessarily. Whereas the principles he defines are tautologies, the invocation of them to do explanatory work is dependent on nontrivial assumptions about the world. Rather than the truth of AP being problematic, its *applicability* is problematic. That is, it is problematic whether the world is such that AP can play a role in interesting explanations and predictions. For example, the anthropic explanation of fine-tuning requires the existence of an ensemble of universes differing in a wide range of parameters and boundary conditions. Without the assumption that such an ensemble actually exists, the explanation doesn't get off the ground. SAP, as Leslie defines it, would be true even if there were no other universe than our own, but it would then be unable to help explain the fine-tuning. Writes Leslie:

> It is often complained that the anthropic principle is a tautology, so can explain nothing. The answer to this is that while tautologies cannot by themselves explain anything, they can *enter into* explanations. The tautology that three fours make twelve can help explaining why it is risky to visit the wood when three sets of four lions entered it and only eleven exited. (Leslie 1996), pp. 170–1

I would add that there is a lot more to anthropic reasoning than the anthropic principle. We discussed some of the non-trivial issues in anthropic reasoning in chapter 2, and in later chapters we shall encounter even greater mysteries. Anyhow, as we shall see shortly, the above anthropic principles are too weak to do the job they are supposed to do. They are best viewed as special cases of a more general principle, the Self-Sampling Assumption, which itself seems to have the status of a methodological and epistemological prescription rather than that of a tautology pure and simple.

ANTHROPIC HODGEPODGE

The "anthropic principles" are multitudinous—I have counted over thirty in

---

dramatically improve the odds of life evolving. Some suggestions have been given for what it could be: self-replicating clay structures, perhaps, or maybe some simpler chemicals isomorphic to Stuart Kaufmann's autocatalytic sets (such as thioesters?). But we are still very much in the dark about how life got started on Earth or what the odds are of it happening on a random Earth-like planet.

the literature. They can be divided into three categories: those that express a purported observation selection effect, those that state some speculative empirical hypothesis, and those that are too muddled or ambiguous to make any clear sense at all. The principles discussed in the previous section are in the first category. Here we will briefly review some members of the other two categories.

Among the better-known definitions are those of physicists John Barrow and Frank Tipler, whose influential 700-page monograph of 1986 has served to introduce anthropic reasoning to a wide audience. Their formulation of WAP is as follows:

> (WAP$_{B\&T}$) The observed values of all physical and cosmological quantities are not equally probable but they take on values restricted by the require-ment that there exist sites where carbon-based life can evolve and by the requirement that the Universe be old enough for it to have already done so. (Barrow and Tipler 1986), p. 16[2]

The reference to "carbon-based life" does not appear in Carter's original definition. Indeed, Carter has explicitly stated that he intended the principle to be applicable "not only by our human civilization, but also by any extra-terrestrial (or non-human future-terrestrial) civilization that may exist" (Carter 1989, p. 18). It is infelicitous to introduce a restriction to carbon-based life, and misleading to give the resulting formulation the same name as Carter's.

Restricting the principle to carbon-based life forms is a particularly bad idea for Barrow and Tipler, because it robs the principle of its tautological status, thereby rendering their position inconsistent, since they claim that WAP is a tautology. To see that WAP as defined by Barrow and Tipler is not a tautology, it is suffices to note that it is not a tautology that all observers are carbon-based. It is no contradiction to suppose that there are observers who are built of other elements, and thus that there may be observed values of physical and cosmological constants that are not restricted by the requirement that carbon-based life evolves.[3] Realizing that the anthropic principle must not be restrict-ed to carbon-based creatures is not a mere logical nicety. It is paramount if we

---

[2] A similar definition was given by Barrow in 1983:

[The] observed values of physical variables are not arbitrary but take values $V(x,t)$ restricted by the spatial requirement that $x \in L$, where L is the set of sites able to sustain life; and by the tem-poral constraint that t is bound by time scales for biological and cosmological evolution of liv-ing organisms and life-supporting environments. (Barrow 1983), p. 147

[3] There is also no contradiction involved in supposing that we might discover that *we* are not carbon-based.

want to apply anthropic reasoning to hypotheses about other possible life forms that may exist or come to exist in the cosmos. For example, when we discuss the Doomsday argument in chapter 6, this becomes crucial.

Limiting the principle to carbon-based life also has the side effect of encouraging a common type of misunderstanding of what anthropic reasoning is all about. It makes it look as if it were part of a project to restitute Homo sapiens into the glorious role of Pivot of Creation. For example, Stephen Jay Gould's criticism (Gould 1985) of the anthropic principle is based on this misconception. It's ironic that anthropic reasoning should have been attacked from this angle. If anything, anthropic reasoning could rather be said to be *anti*-theological and *anti*-teleological, since it holds up the prospect of an alternative explanation for the appearance of fine-tuning—the puzzlement that forms the basis for the modern version of the teleological argument for the existence of a creator.

Barrow and Tipler also provide a new formulation of SAP:

> (SAP$_{B\&T}$) The Universe must have those properties which allow life to develop within it at some stage in its history. (Barrow and Tipler 1986), p. 21

On the face of it, this is rather similar to Carter's SAP. The two definitions differ in one obvious but minor respect. Barrow and Tipler's formulation refers to the development of *life*. Leslie's version improves this to *intelligent life*. But Carter's definition speaks of *observers*. "Observers" and "intelligent life" are not the same concept. It seems possible that there could be (and might come to be in the future) intelligent, conscious observers who are not part of what we call life—for example by lacking such properties as being self-replicating or having a metabolism, etc. For reasons that will become clear later, Carter's formulation is superior in this respect. Not *being alive*, but *being an (intelligent) observer* is what matters for the purposes of anthropic reasoning.

Barrow and Tipler have each provided their own personal formulations of SAP. These definitions turn out to be quite different from SAP$_{B\&T}$:

> Tipler: . . . intelligent life must evolve somewhere in any physically realistic universe. (Tipler 1982), p. 37

> Barrow: The Universe must contain life. (Barrow 1983), p. 149

These definitions state that life must exist, which implies that life exists. The other formulations of SAP we looked at, by Carter, Barrow & Tipler, and Leslie, all stated that the universe must *allow* or *admit* the creation of life (or observers). This is most naturally read as saying only that the laws and parameters of the universe must be *compatible* with life—which does not imply that life exists. The propositions are not equivalent.

We are also faced with the problem of how to understand the "must". What is its modal force? Is it logical, metaphysical, epistemological or nomological? Or even theological or ethical? The definitions remain highly ambiguous until this is specified.

Barrow and Tipler list three possible interpretations of $SAP_{B\&T}$ in their monograph:

> (A) There exists one possible Universe 'designed' with the goal of generating and sustaining 'observers'.
> (B) Observers are necessary to bring the Universe into being.
> (C) An ensemble of other different universes is necessary for the existence of our Universe.

Since none of these is directly related to idea of about observation selection effects, I shall not discuss them further (except for some brief remarks relegated to this footnote[4]).

---

[4] (A) points to the teleological idea that the universe was designed with the goal of generating observers (spiced up with the added requirement that the "designed" universe be the only possible one). Yet, anthropic reasoning is counter-teleological in the sense described above; taking it into account *diminishes* the probability that a teleological explanation of the nature of the universe is correct. And it is hard to know what to make of the requirement that the universe be the only possible one. This is definitely not part of anything that follows from Carter's original exposition.

(B) is identical to what John Wheeler had earlier branded the *Participatory Anthropic Principle* (PAP) (Wheeler 1975, 1977). It echoes Berkelian idealism, but Barrow and Tipler want to invest it with physical significance by considering it in the context of quantum mechanics. Operating within the framework of quantum cosmology and the many-worlds interpretation of quantum physics, they state that, at least in its version (B), SAP imposes a boundary condition on the universal wave function. For example, all branches of the universal wave function have zero amplitude if they represent closed universes that suffer a big crunch before life has had a chance to evolve, from which they conclude that such short-lived universes do not exist. "SAP requires a universe branch which does not contain intelligent life to be non-existent; that is, branches without intelligent life cannot appear in the Universal wave function." ((Barrow and Tipler 1986), p. 503). As far as I can see, this speculation is totally unrelated to anything Carter had in mind when he introduced the anthropic principle, and PAP is irrelevant to the issues we discuss in this book. (For a critical discussion of PAP, see e.g. (Earman 1987).

Barrow and Tipler think that statement (C) receives support from the many-worlds interpretation and the sum-over-histories approach to quantum gravity "because they must unavoidably recognize the existence of a whole class of *real* 'other worlds' from which ours is selected by an optimizing principle." ((Barrow and Tipler 1986), p. 22). (Notice, by the way, that what Barrow and Tipler say about (B) and (C) indicates that the necessity to which these formulations refer should be understood as nomological: physical necessity.) Again, this seems to have little do to with observation selection effects. It is true that there is a connection between SAP and the existence of multiple worlds. From the standpoint of Leslie's explication, this connection can be stated as follows: SAP is applicable (non-vacuously) only if there is a suitable world ensemble; only then can SAP be involved in doing explanatory work. But in no way does anthropic reasoning presuppose that our universe could not have existed in the absence of whatever other universes there might be.

A "Final Anthropic Principle" (FAP) has been defined by Tipler (Tipler 1982), Barrow (Barrow 1983) and Barrow & Tipler (Barrow and Tipler 1986) as follows:

> Intelligent information-processing must come into existence in the universe, and, once it comes into existence, it will never die out.

Martin Gardner charges that FAP is more accurately named CRAP, the *Completely Ridiculous Anthropic Principle* (Gardner 1986). The spirit of FAP is antithetic to Carter's anthropic principle (Leslie 1985; Carter 1989). FAP has no claim on any special methodological status; it is pure speculation. The appearance to the contrary, created by affording it the honorary title of a Principle, is what prompts Gardner's mockery.

It may be possible to interpret FAP simply as a scientific hypothesis, and that is indeed what Barrow and Tipler set out to do. In a later book (Tipler 1994), Tipler considers the implications of FAP in more detail. He proposes what he calls the "Omega Point Theory". This theory assumes that our universe is closed, so that at some point in the future it will recollapse in a big crunch. Tipler tries to show that it is physically possible to perform an infinite number of computations during this big crunch by using the shear energy of the collapsing universe, and that the speed of a computer in the final moments can be made to diverge to infinity. Thus there could be an infinity of subjective time for beings that were running as simulations on such a computer. This idea can be empirically tested, and if present data suggesting that our universe is open or flat are confirmed, then the Omega Point Theory will indeed have been falsified (as Tipler himself acknowledges).[5] The point to emphasize here is that FAP is not in any way an application or a consequence of anthropic reasoning (although, of course, anthropic reasoning may have a bearing on how hypotheses such as FAP should be evaluated).

If one does want to treat FAP as an empirical hypothesis, it helps if one charitably deletes the first part of the definition, the part that says that intelligent information processing *must* come into existence. If one does this, one gets what Milan C. Ćirković and I have dubbed the *Final Anthropic Hypothesis* (FAH). It simply says that intelligent information processing will never cease, making no pretenses to being anything other than an interesting empirical question that one may ask. We find (Ćirković and Bostrom 2000) that the current balance of evidence tips towards a negative answer. For instance, the recent evidence for a large cosmological constant (Perlmutter, Aldering et al. 1998; Reiss 1998, 2000)[6] only makes things worse

---

[5] For further critique of Tipler's theory, see (Sklar 1989).

[6] A non-zero cosmological constant has been considered desirable from several points of view in recent years, because it would be capable of solving the cosmological age problem and because it would arise naturally from quantum field processes (see e.g. (Klapdor and Grotz 1986; Singh 1995; Martel, Shapiro et al. 1998)). A universe with a cosmological density parameter $\Omega \approx 1$ and a cosmological constant of about the suggested magnitude $\Lambda \approx 0.7$ would allow the formation of galaxies (Weinberg 1987; Efstathiou 1995) and would last long enough for life to have a chance to develop.

for FAH. There are, however, some other possible ways in which FAH may be true which cannot be ruled out at the present time, involving poorly understood mechanisms in quantum cosmology.

FREAK OBSERVERS AND WHY EARLIER FORMULATIONS ARE INADEQUATE

The relevant anthropic principles for our purposes are those that describe observation selection effects. The formulations mentioned in the first section of this chapter are all in that category, yet they are insufficient. They cover only a small fraction of the cases that we would want to have covered. Crucially, in all likelihood they don't even cover the actual case: they cannot be used to make interesting inferences about the world we are living in. This section explains why that is so, and why it constitutes serious gap in earlier accounts of anthropic methodology and a fortiori in scientific reasoning generally.

Space is big. It is very, *very* big. On the currently most favored cosmological theories, we are living in an infinite world, a world that contains an infinite number of planets, stars, galaxies, and black holes. This is an implication of most multiverse theories. But it is also a consequence of the standard big bang cosmology, if combined with the assumption that our universe is open, as recent evidence suggests it is. An open universe—assuming the simplest topology[7]—is spatially infinite at every point in time and contains infinitely many planets etc.[8]

---

[7] I.e. that space is singly connected. There is a recent spate of interest in the possibility that our universe might be multiply connected, in which case it could be both finite and hyperbolic. A multiply connected space could lead to a telltale pattern consisting of a superposition of multiple images of the night sky seen at varying distances from Earth (roughly, one image for each lap around the universe that the light has traveled). Such a pattern has not been found, although the search continues. For an introduction to multiply connected topologies in cosmology, see (Lachièze-Rey and Luminet 1995). There is an obvious methodological catch in trying to gain high confidence about the global topology of spacetime—if it is so big that we observe but a tiny, tiny speck of it, then how can we be sure that the whole resembles this particular part that we are in? A large sphere, for example, appears flat if you look at a small patch of it.

[8] A widespread misconception is that the open universe in the standard big bang model becomes spatially infinite only in the temporal limit. The *observable* universe is finite, but only a small part of the whole is observable (by us). One fallacious intuition that might be responsible for this misconception is that the universe came into existence at some spatial point in the big bang. A better way of picturing things is to imagine space as an infinite rubber sheet, and gravitationally bound groupings such as stars and galaxies, as buttons glued on. As we move forward in time, the sheet is stretched in all directions so that the separation between the buttons increases. Going backwards in time, we imagine the buttons coming closer together until, at "time zero", the density of the (still spatially infinite) universe becomes infinite everywhere. See e.g. (Martin 1995).

Until recently, it appeared that the mass density of the universe fell far short of the critical density and thus that the universe is open (Coles and Ellis 1994). Recent evidence, however, suggests that the missing mass might be in the form of vacuum energy, a cosmological constant (Zehavi and Dekel 1999; Freedman 2000). This is supported by studies of supernovae and the

Most modern philosophical investigations relating to the vastness of the cosmos have focused on the fine-tuning of our universe. As we saw in chapter 2, a philosophical cottage industry has sprung up around controversies over issues such as whether fine-tuning is in some sense "improbable", whether it should be regarded as surprising, whether it calls out for explanation and if so whether a multiverse theory could explain it, whether it suggests ways in which current physics is incomplete, or whether it is evidence for the hypothesis that our universe resulted from design.

Here we shall turn our attention to a more fundamental problem: How can vast-world cosmologies have *any* observational consequences *at all?* We shall show that these cosmologies imply, or give a very high probability to, the proposition that every possible observation is in fact made. This creates a challenge: if a theory is such that for any possible human observation that we specify, the theory says that that observation will be made, then how do we test the theory? What could possibly count as negative evidence? And if all theories that share this feature are equally good at predicting the data we will get, then how can empirical evidence distinguish between them?

I call this a "challenge" because cosmologists are constantly modifying and refining theories in light of empirical findings, and they are surely not irrational in doing so. The challenge is explain how that is possible, i.e. to find the missing methodological link that enables a reliable connection to be established between cosmological theories and astronomic observation.

Consider a random phenomenon, for example Hawking radiation. When black holes evaporate, they do so in a random manner[9] such that for any given physical object there is a finite (although, typically, astronomically small) probability that it will be emitted by any given black hole in a given time interval. Such things as boots, computers, or ecosystems have some finite probability of popping out from a black hole. The same holds true, of course, for human bodies, or human brains in particular states.[10] Assuming that mental states supervene on brain states, there is thus a finite probabili-

---

microwave background radiation. If this is confirmed, it would bring the actual density very close to the critical density, and it may thus be hard to tell whether the universe is open, flat, or closed.

Some additional backing for the infinite-universe hypothesis can be garnered if we consider models of eternal inflation, in which an infinite number of galaxies are produced over time.

[9] Admittedly, a complete understanding of black holes probably requires new physics. For example, the so-called information loss paradox is a challenge for the view that black hole evaporation is totally random (see e.g. (Belot, Earman et al. 1999) for an overview). But even pseudo-randomness, like that of the trajectories of molecules in gases in a deterministic universe, would be sufficient for the present argument.

[10] See e.g. (Hawking and Israel 1979): "[I]t is possible for a black hole to emit a television set or Charles Darwin" (p. 19). (To avoid making a controversial claim about personal identity, Hawking and Israel ought perhaps to have weakened this to ". . . an exact replica of Charles Darwin".) See also (Garriga and Vilenkin 2001).

ty that a black hole will produce a brain in a state of making any given observation. Some of the observations made by such brains will be illusory, and some will be veridical. For example, some brains produced by black holes will have the illusory of experience of reading a measurement device that does not exist. Other brains, with the same experiences, will be making veridical observations—a measurement device may materialize together with the brain and may have caused the brain to make the observation. But the point that matters here is that any observation we could make has a finite probability of being produced by any given black hole.

The probability of *anything* macroscopic and organized appearing from a black hole is, of course, minuscule. The probability of a given conscious brain-state being created is even tinier. Yet even a low-probability outcome has a high probability of occurring if the random process is repeated often enough. And that is precisely what happens in our world, if the cosmos is very vast. In the limiting case where the cosmos contains an infinite number of black holes, the probability of any given observation being made is one.[11]

There are good grounds for believing that our universe is infinite and contains an infinite number of black holes. Therefore, we have reason to think that any possible human observation is in fact instantiated in the actual world.[12] Evidence for the existence of a multiverse would only add further support to this proposition.

It is not necessary to invoke black holes to make this point. Any random physical phenomenon would do. It seems we don't even have to limit the argument to quantum fluctuations. Classical thermal fluctuations could, presumably, in principle lead to the molecules in a gas cloud containing the right elements to bump into each other so as to form a biological structure such as a human brain.

The problem is that it seems impossible to get any empirical evidence that could distinguish between different Big World theories. For any observation we make, *all* such theories assign a probability of one to the hypothesis that that observation be made. That means that the fact that the observation is made gives us no reason whatever for preferring one of these theories to the others. Experimental results appear totally irrelevant.[13]

We can see this formally as follows. Let *B* be the proposition that we are

---

[11] In fact, there is a probability of unity that infinitely many tokens of each observation-type will appear. But one of each suffices for our purposes.

[12] I restrict the assertion to *human* observations in order to avoid questions as to whether there may be other kinds of possible observations that perhaps could have infinite complexity or be of some alien or divine nature that does not supervene on stuff that is emitted from black holes—such stuff is physical and of finite size and energy.

[13] Some cosmologists are recently becoming aware of the problematic that this section describes, e.g. (Linde and Mezhlumian 1996; Vilenkin 1998). See also (Leslie 1992).

in a Big World, defined as one that is big enough and random enough to make it highly probable that every possible human observation is made. Let *T* be some theory that is compatible with *B*, and let *E* be some proposition asserting that some specific observation is made. Let P be an epistemic probability function. Bayes' theorem states that

$$P(T|E\&B) = P(E|T\&B)P(T|B) / P(E|B).$$

In order to determine whether *E* makes a difference to the probability of *T* (relative to the background assumption *B*), we need to compute the difference $P(T|E\&B) - P(T|B)$. By some simple algebra, it is easy to see that

$$P(T|E\&B) - P(T|B) \approx 0 \text{ if and only if } P(E|T\&B) \approx P(E|B).$$

This means that *E* will fail to give empirical support to *E* (modulo *B*) if *E* is about equally probable given *T&B* as it is given *B*. We saw above that $P(E|T\&B) \approx P(E|B) \approx 1$. Consequently, whether *E* is true or false is irrelevant for whether we should believe in *T*, given that we know that *B*.

Let T_2 be some perverse permutation of an astrophysical theory T_1 that we actually accept. T_2 differs from the T_1 by assigning a different value to some physical constant. To be specific, let us suppose that T_1 says that the current temperature of the cosmic microwave background radiation is about 2.7 degrees Kelvin (which is the observed value) whereas T_2 says it is, say, 3.1 K. Suppose furthermore that both T_1 and T_2 say that we are living in a Big World. One would have thought that our experimental evidence favors T_1 over T_2. Yet, the above argument seems to show that this view is mistaken. Our observational evidence supports T_2 just as much as T_1. We really have no reason to think that the background radiation is 2.7 K rather than 3.1 K.

At first blush, it could seem as if this simply rehashes the lesson, made familiar by Duhem and Quine, that it is always possible to rescue a theory from falsification by modifying some auxiliary assumption, so that strictly speaking no scientific theory ever implies any observational consequences. The above argument would then merely have provided an illustration of how this general result applies to cosmological theories. But that would be to miss the point.

If the argument given above is correct, it establishes a much more radical conclusion. It purports to show that all Big World theories are not only logically compatible with any observational evidence, but they are also *perfectly probabilistically compatible*. They all give the same conditional probability (namely one) to every observation statement *E* defined as above. This entails that no such observation statement can have *any* bearing, whether logical or probabilistic, on whether the theory is true. If that were the case, it would not be worthwhile to make astronomical observations if what we are interested in is determining which Big World theory to accept. The only reasons we could have for choosing between such theories would be either a priori (simplicity, elegance etc.) or pragmatic (such as ease of calculation).

Nor is the argument making the ancient statement that human epistemic faculties are fallible, that we can never be certain that we are not dreaming or that we are not brains in a vat. No, the point here is not that such illusions *could* occur, but rather that we have reason to believe that they *do* occur, not just some of them but all possible ones. In other words, we can be fairly confident that the observations we make, along with all possible observations we could make in the future, are being made by brains in vats and by humans who have spontaneously materialized from black holes or from thermal fluctuations. The argument would entail that this abundance of observations makes it impossible to derive distinguishing observational consequences from contemporary cosmological theories.

I trust that most readers will find this conclusion unacceptable. Cosmologists certainly appear to be doing experimental work and to modify their theories in light of new empirical findings. The COBE satellite, the Hubble Space Telescope, and other devices are showering us with a wealth of data that is causing a renaissance in the world of astrophysics. Yet the argument described above would show that the empirical import of this information could never go beyond the limited role of providing support for the hypothesis that we are living in a Big World, for instance by showing that the universe is open. Nothing apart from this one fact could be learnt from such observations. Once we have established that the universe is open and infinite, then any further work in observational astronomy would be a waste of time and money.

Worse still, the leaky connection between theory and observation in cosmology spills over into other domains. Since nothing hinges on how we defined *T* in the derivation above, the argument can easily be extended to prove that observation does not have a bearing on any empirical scientific question so long as we assume that we are living in a Big World.

This consequence is absurd, so we should look for a way to fix the methodological pipeline and restore the flow of testable observational consequences from Big World theories. How can we do that?

Taking into account the selection effects expressed by SAP, much less those expressed by WAP or the Superweak AP, will not help us. It isn't true that we couldn't have observed a universe that wasn't fine-tuned for life. For even "uninhabitable" universes can contain the odd, spontaneously materialized "freak observer", and if they are big enough or if there are sufficiently many such universes, then it is indeed highly likely that they contain infinitely many freak observers making all possible human observations. It is even logically consistent with all our evidence that *we* are such freak observers.

It may appear as if this is a fairly superficial problem. It is based on the technical point that some infrequent freak observers will appear even in non-tuned universes. Couldn't it be thought that this shouldn't really matter because it is still true that the overwhelming majority of all observers are regular observers, not freak observers? While we cannot interpret "the majority" in the straightforward cardinal sense, since the class of freak observers may well be of the same cardinality as the class of regular observers, nonetheless, in some natural sense, "almost all" observers in a multiverse live in the fine-tuned parts and have emerged via ordinary evolutionary processes, not from Hawking radiation or bizzare thermal fluctuations. So if we modify SAP slightly, to allow for a small proportion of observers living in non-tuned universes, maybe we could repair the methodological pipeline and make the anthropic fine-tuning explanation (among other useful results) go through?

In my view, this response suggests the right way to proceed. The presence of the odd observer in a non-tuned universe changes nothing essential. SAP should be modified or strengthened to make this clear. Let's set aside for the moment the complication of infinite numbers of observers and assume that the total number is finite. Then the idea is that so long as the vast majority of observers are in fine-tuned universes, and the ones in non-tuned universes form a small minority, then what the multiverse theory predicts is that we should *with overwhelming probability* find ourselves in one of the fine-tuned universes. That we observe such a universe is thus what such a multiverse theory predicts, and our observations, therefore, tend to confirm it to some degree. A multiverse theory of the right kind, coupled with this ramified version of the anthropic principle, can potentially account for the apparent fine-tuning of our universe and explain how our scientific theories are testable even when conjoined with Big World hypotheses. (In chapter 5 we shall explain how this idea works in more detail.)

How to formulate the requisite kind of anthropic principle? Astrophysicist Richard Gott III has taken one step in the right direction with his "Copernican anthropic principle":

> [T]he location of your birth in space and time in the Universe is privileged (or special) only to the extent implied by the fact that you are an intelligent observer, that your location among intelligent observers is not special but rather picked at random from the set of all intelligent observers (past, present and future) any one of whom you could have been. (Gott 1993), p. 316

This definition comes closer than any of the others we have examined to giving an adequate expression of the basic idea behind anthropic reasoning. It introduces a notion of randomness that can be applied to the Big World theories. Yes, you could have lived in a non-tuned universe; but if the vast majority of observers live in fine-tuned universes, then the multiverse theory predicts that you should (very probably) find yourself in a fine-tuned universe.

One drawback with Gott's definition is that it makes problematic claims which are not be essential to anthropic reasoning. It says your location was "picked at random". But who or what did the picking? Maybe that reading is too naïve. Yet the expression does suggest that there is some kind of physical randomization mechanism at work, which, so to speak, picks out a birthplace for you. We can imagine a possible world where this would be a good description of what was going on. Suppose that God, after having created a multiverse, posts a world-map on the door to His celestial abode. He takes a few steps back and starts throwing darts at the map. Wherever a dart hits, He creates a body, and sends down a soul to inhabit it. Alternatively, maybe one could imagine some sort of physical apparatus, involving a time travel machine, that could putter about in spacetime and distribute observers in a truly random fashion. But of course, there is no evidence that any such randomization mechanism exists. Perhaps some less farfetched story could be spun to the same end, but anthropic reasoning would be tenuous indeed had it to rely on such suppositions—which, thankfully, it doesn't.

Further, the assertion that "you could have been" any of these intelligent observers who will ever have existed is also problematic. Ultimately, we *may* have to confront this problem. But it would be nicer to have a definition that doesn't preempt that debate.

Both these points are relatively minor quibbles. I think one could reasonably explicate Gott's definition so that it comes out right in these regards.[14] There is, however, a much more serious problem with Gott's approach which we shall discuss during the course of our examination of the Doomsday argument in chapter 6. We will therefore work with a different principle, which sidesteps these difficulties.

THE SELF-SAMPLING ASSUMPTION

The preferred explication of the anthropic principle that we shall use as a starting point for subsequent investigations is the following, which we term the *Self-Sampling Assumption*:

> (SSA) One should reason as if one were a random sample from the set of all observers in one's reference class.

This is a *preliminary* formulation. Anthropic reasoning is about taking observation selection effects into account, which tend to creep in when we evaluate evidence that has an indexical component. In chapter 10 we shall replace SSA with another principle that takes more indexical information into account. That principle will show that only under certain special conditions is SSA a permissible simplification. However, in order to get to the

---

[14] In his work on inflationary cosmology, Alexander Vilenkin has proposed a "Principle of Mediocrity" (Vilenkin 1995), which is similar to Gott's principle.

point where we can appreciate the more general principle, it is necessary to start by thoroughly examining SSA—both the reasons for accepting it, and the consequences that flow from its use. Wittgenstein's famous ladder, which one must first climb and then kick away, is a good metaphor for how to view SSA. Thus, rather than inserting qualifications everywhere, let it simply be declared here that we will revisit and reassess SSA when we reach chapter 10.

SSA as stated leaves open what the appropriate reference class might be and what sampling density should be imposed over this reference class. Those are crucial issues that we will need to examine carefully, an enterprise we shall embark on in the next chapter.

The other observational selection principles discussed above are special cases of SSA. Take first WAP (in Carter and Leslie's rendition). If a theory *T* says that there is only one universe and some regions of it contain no observers, then WAP says that *T* predicts that we don't observe one of those observerless regions. (That is, that we don't observe them "from the inside". If the region is observable from a region where there are observers, then obviously, it could be observable by those observers.) SSA yields the same result, since if there is no observer in a region, then there is zero probability that a sample taken from the set of all observers will be in that region, and hence zero probability that you should observe that region given the truth of *T*.

Similarly, if *T* says there are multiple universes, only some of which contain observers, then SAP (again in Carter and Leslie's sense) says that *T* predicts that what you should observe is one of the universes that contain observers. SSA says the same, since it assigns zero sampling density to being an observer in an observerless universe.

The meaning, significance, and use of SSA will be made clearer as we proceed. We can already state, however, that SSA and its strengthenings and specifications are to be understood as *methodological prescriptions*. They state how reasonable epistemic agents ought to assign credence in certain situations and how we should make certain kinds of probabilistic inferences. As will appear from subsequent discussion, SSA is not (in any straightforward way at least) a restricted version of the principle of indifference. Although we will provide arguments for adopting SSA, it is not a major concern for our purposes whether SSA is strictly a "requirement of rationality". It suffices if many intelligent people do in fact—upon reflection—have subjective prior probability functions that satisfy SSA. If that much is acknowledged, it follows that investigating the consequences for important matters that flow from SSA can potentially be richly rewarding.

CHAPTER 4

Thought Experiments Supporting the Self-Sampling Assumption

This chapter and the next argue that we should accept SSA. In the process, we also elaborate on the principle's intended meaning and begin to develop a theory of how SSA can be used in concrete scientific contexts to guide us through the thorny issues of anthropic biases.

The case for accepting SSA has two separable parts. One part focuses on its applications. We will continue the argument begun in the last chapter, that a new methodological rule is needed in order to explain how observational consequences can be derived from contemporary cosmological and other scientific theories. I will try to show how SSA can do this for us. This part will be considered in the next chapter, where we'll also look at how SSA underwrites useful inferences in thermodynamics, evolutionary biology, and traffic analysis.

The present chapter deals with the other part of the case for SSA. It consists of a series of thought experiments designed to demonstrate that it is rational to reason in accordance with SSA in a rather wide range of circumstances. While the application-part can be likened to field observations, the thought experiments we shall conduct in this chapter are more like laboratory research. We here have full control over all relevant variables and can stipulate away inessential complications in order to hopefully get a more accurate measurement of our intuitions and epistemic convictions regarding SSA itself.

THE DUNGEON GEDANKEN

Our first thought experiment is *Dungeon*:

> The world consists of a dungeon that has one hundred cells. In each cell there is one prisoner. Ninety of the cells are painted blue on the outside and the other ten are painted red. Each prisoner is asked to guess whether he is in a blue or a red cell. (Everybody knows all

this.) You find yourself in one of the cells. What color should you think it is?—Answer: Blue, with 90% probability.

Since 90% of all observers are in blue cells, and you don't have any other relevant information, it seems you should set your credence of being in a blue cell to 90%. Most people I've talked to agree that this is the correct answer. Since the example does not depend on the exact numbers involved, we have the more general principle that in cases like this, your credence of having property P should be equal to the fraction of observers who have P, in accordance with SSA.[1] Some of our subsequent investigations in this chapter will consider arguments for extending this class in various ways.

While many accept without further argument that SSA is applicable to the *Dungeon* gedanken, let's consider how one might seek to defend this view if challenged to do so.

One argument we may advance is the following. Suppose everyone accepts SSA and everyone has to bet on whether they are in a blue or a red cell. Then 90% of all prisoners will win their bets; only 10% will lose. Suppose, on the other hand, that SSA is rejected and the prisoners think that one is no more likely to be in a blue cell than in a red cell; so they bet by flipping a coin. Then, on average, 50% of the prisoners will win and 50% will lose. It seems better that SSA be accepted.

This argument is incomplete as it stands. That one betting-pattern A leads more people to win their bets than does another pattern B does not necessarily make it rational for anybody to prefer A to B. In *Dungeon*, consider the pattern A which specifies that "If you are Harry Smith, bet you are in a red cell; if you are Geraldine Truman, bet that you are in a blue cell; . . ."— such that for each person in the experiment, A gives the advice that will lead him or her to be right. Adopting rule A will lead to more people winning their bets (100%) than any other rule. In particular, it outperforms SSA which has a mere 90% success rate.

Intuitively it is clear that rules like A are cheating. This is best seen by putting A in the context of its rival permutations A', A'', A''' etc., which map the captives' names to recommendations about betting red or blue in different ways than does A. Most of these permutations do rather badly. On average, they give no better advice than flipping a coin, which we saw was inferior

---

[1] This does not rule out that there could be other principles of assigning probabilities that would also provide plausible guidance in *Dungeon*, provided their advice coincides with that of SSA. For example, a relatively innocuous version of the Principle of Indifference, formulated as "*Assign the same credence to any two hypotheses if you don't have any reason to prefer one to the other*", would also do the trick in *Dungeon*. But subsequent thought experiments impose additional constraints. For reasons that will become clear, it doesn't seem that any straightforward principle of indifference would suffice to express the needed methodological rule.

to accepting SSA. Only if the people in the cells could pick the right A-permutation would they benefit. In *Dungeon,* they don't have any information enabling them to do this. If they picked A and consequently benefited, it would be pure luck.

What allows the people in *Dungeon* to do better than chance is that they have a relevant piece of empirical information regarding the distribution of observers over the two types of cells. They have been informed that 90% of them are in blue cells and it would be irrational of them not to take this information into account. We can imagine a series of thought experiments where an increasingly large fraction of observers are in blue cells—91%, 92%, . . . , 99%. The situation gradually degenerates into the 100%-case where they are told, "You are all in blue cells", from which each can deductively infer that she is in a blue cell. As the situation approaches this limiting case, it is plausible to require that the strength of participants' beliefs about being in a blue cell should gradually approach probability 1. SSA has this property.

One may notice that while it is true that if the detainees adopt SSA, 90% of them would win their bets, yet there are even simpler methods that produce the same result, for instance: "Set your probability of being in a blue cell equal to 1 if most people are in blue cells; and to 0 otherwise." Using this epistemic rule will also result in 90% of the people winning their bets. Such a rule, however, would not be attractive. When the participants step out of their cells, some of them will find that they were in red cells. Yet if their prior probability of that were zero, they could never learn that by Bayesian belief updating. A second and more generic problem is that when we consider rational *betting quotients,* rules like this are revealed to be inferior. A person whose probability for finding herself in a blue cell was 1 would be willing to bet on that hypothesis at any odds.[2] The people following this simplified rule would thus risk losing arbitrarily great sums of money for an arbitrarily small and uncertain gain—an uninviting strategy. Moreover, collectively they would be *guaranteed* to lose an arbitrarily large sum.

Suppose we agree that all the participants should assign the same probability to being in a blue cell (which is quite plausible since their evidence does not differ in any relevant way). It is then easy to show that out of all possible probabilities they could assign to finding themselves in blue cells, a probability of 90% is the only one which would make it impossible to bet against them in such a way that they were collectively guaranteed to lose money. And in general, if we vary the numbers of the example, their degree of belief would in each case have to be what SSA prescribes in order to save them from being a *collective sucker.*

On an individual level, if we imagine the experiment repeated many

---

[2] Setting aside, as is customary in contexts like this, any risk aversion or aversion against gambling, or computational limitations that the person might have.

times, the only way a given participant could avoid having a negative expected outcome when betting repeatedly against a shrewd outsider would be by setting her odds in accordance with SSA.

All these considerations support what seems to be most persons' initial intuition about *Dungeon*: that it is a situation where one should reason in accordance with SSA. Any plausible principle of the epistemology of information that has an indexical component would have to agree with SSA's verdicts in this particular case.

Another thing to notice about *Dungeon* is that we didn't specify how the prisoners arrived in their cells. The prisoners' ontogenesis is irrelevant so long as they don't know anything about it that gives them clues about the color of their abodes. They may have been allocated to their respective cells by some objectively random process such as drawing tickets from a lottery urn, after which they were blindfolded and led to their designated locations. Or they may have been allowed to choose cells for themselves, and a fortune wheel subsequently spun to determine which cells should be painted blue and which red. But the gedanken doesn't depend on there being a well-defined randomization mechanism. One may just as well imagine that prisoners have been in their cells since the time of their birth or indeed since the beginning of the universe. If there is a possible world where the laws of nature dictate which individuals are to appear in which cells, without any appeal to initial conditions, then the inmates would still be rational to follow SSA, provided only that they did not have knowledge of the laws or were incapable of deducing what the laws implied about their own situation. Objective chance, therefore, is not an essential part of the thought experiment. It runs on low-octane subjective uncertainty.

Two thought experiments by John Leslie

We shall now look at an argument for extending the range of cases where SSA can be applied. We shall see that the synchronous nature of *Dungeon* is inessential: you can in some contexts legitimately reason as if you were a random sample from a reference class that includes observers who exist at different times. Also, we will find that one and the same reference class can contain observers who differ in many respects, including their genes and gender. To this effect, consider an example due to John Leslie, which we shall refer to as *Emeralds*:

> Imagine an experiment planned as follows. At some point in time, three humans would each be given an emerald. Several centuries afterwards, when a completely different set of humans was alive, five thousand humans would each be given an emerald. Imagine next that you have yourself been given an emerald in the experiment. You have no knowledge, however, of whether your century is the earlier century in which just three

people were to be in this situation, or in the later century in which five thousand were to be in it. . . .

Suppose you in fact betted that you lived [in the earlier century]. If every emerald-getter in the experiment betted in this way, there would be five thousand losers and only three winners. The sensible bet, therefore, is that yours is instead the later century of the two. (Leslie 1996), p. 20

The arguments that were made for SSA in *Dungeon* can be recycled in *Emeralds*. Leslie makes the point about more people being right if everyone bets that they are in the later of the two centuries. As we saw in the previous section, this point needs to be supplemented by additional arguments before it yields support for SSA. (Leslie gives the emeralds example as a response to one objection against the Doomsday argument. He never formulates SSA, but parts of his arguments in defense of the Doomsday argument and parts of his account of anthropic reasoning in cosmology are relevant to evaluating SSA.)

As Leslie notes, we can learn a second lesson if we consider a variant of the emeralds example (*Two Batches*):

A firm plan was formed to rear humans in two batches: the first batch to be of three humans of one sex, the second of five thousand of the other sex. The plan called for rearing the first batch in one century. Many centuries later, the five thousand humans of the other sex would be reared. Imagine that you learn you're one of the humans in question. You don't know which centuries the plan specified, but you are aware of being female. You very reasonably conclude that the large batch was to be female, almost certainly. If adopted by every human in the experiment, the policy of betting that the large batch was of the same sex as oneself would yield only three failures and five thousand successes. . . . [Y]ou mustn't say: 'My *genes* are female, so I have to observe myself to be female, no matter whether the female batch was to be small or large. Hence I can have no special reason for believing it was to be large.' (Ibid. pp. 222–3)

If we accept this, we can conclude that members of both genders can be in the same reference class. In a similar vein, one can argue for the irrelevance of short or tall, black or white, rich or poor, famous or obscure, fierce or meek, etc. If analogous arguments with two batches of people with any of these property pairs are accepted, then we have quite a broad reference class already. We shall return in a moment to consider what limits there might be to the inclusiveness of the reference class, but first we want to look at another dimension in which one may seek to extend the applicability of SSA.

THE *INCUBATOR* GEDANKEN

All the examples so far have been of situations where all the competing hypotheses entail the same number of observers in existence. A key new element is introduced in cases where the total number of observers is different depending on which hypothesis is true. Here is a simple case where this happens.

Incubator, version I

Stage (a): In an otherwise empty world, a machine called "the incubator"[3] kicks into action. It starts by tossing a fair coin. If the coin falls tails then it creates one room and a man with a black beard inside it. If the coin falls heads then it creates two rooms, one with a black-bearded man and one with a white-bearded man. As the rooms are completely dark, nobody knows his beard color. Everybody who's been created is informed about all of the above. You find yourself in one of the rooms. *Question:* What should be your credence that the coin fell tails?

Stage (b): A little later, the lights are switched on, and you discover that you have a black beard. *Question:* What should your credence in Tails be now?

Consider the following three models of how you should reason:

Model 1 (Naïve)

Neither at stage (*a*) nor at stage (*b*) do you have any relevant information as to how the coin (which you know to be fair) landed. Therefore, in both instances, your credence of Tails should be 1/2.

Answer: At stage (a) your credence of Tails should be 1/2 and at stage (b) it should be 1/2.

Model 2 (SSA)

If you had had a white beard, you could have inferred that there were two rooms, which entails Heads. Knowing that you have a black beard does not allow you to rule out either possibility but it is still relevant information. This can be seen by the following argument. The prior probability of Heads is one half, since the coin was fair. If the

---

[3] We suppose the incubator to be a mindless automaton that doesn't count as an observer.

coin fell heads, then the only observer in existence has a black beard; hence by SSA, the conditional probability of having a black beard given Heads is one. If the coin fell tails, then one out of two observers has a black beard; hence, also by SSA, the conditional probability of a black beard given Tails is one half. That is, we have

P(Heads) = P(¬Heads) = ½

P(Black | Heads) = ½

P(Black | ¬Heads) = 1

By Bayes' theorem, the posterior probability of Heads, after conditionalizing on Black, is

P(Heads | Black)

$$= \frac{P(Black \mid Heads)P(Heads)}{P(Black \mid Heads)P(Heads) + P(Black \mid \neg Heads)P(\neg Heads)} = 1/3.$$

Answer: At stage (a) your credence of Tails should be ½ and at stage (b) it should be ⅔.

Model 3 (SSA & SIA)

It is twice as likely that you should exist if two observers exist than if only one observer exists. This follows if we make the Self-*Indication* Assumption (SIA), to be explained shortly. The prior probability of Heads should therefore be ⅔, and of Tails, ⅓. As in Model 2, the conditional probability of a black beard given Heads is 1 and the conditional probability of black beard given Tails is ½.

P(Heads) = ⅔

P(¬Heads) = ⅓

P(Black | Heads) = ½

P(Black | ¬Heads) = 1

By Bayes' theorem, we get

P (Heads | Black) = ½.

Answer: At stage (a) your credence of Tails should be ⅓ and at stage (b) it should be ½.

The last model uses something that we have dubbed the Self-Indication Assumption, according to which you should conclude from the fact that you came into existence that probably quite a few observers did:

> (SIA) Given the fact that you exist, you should (other things equal) favor hypotheses according to which many observers exist over hypotheses on which few observers exist.

SIA may seem *prima facie* implausible, and we shall argue in chapter 7 that it is no less implausible *ultimo facie*. Yet some of the more profound criticisms of specific anthropic inferences rely implicitly on SIA. In particular, adopting SIA annihilates the Doomsday argument. It is therefore good to put it on the table so that we can consider what reasons there are for accepting or rejecting it. To give SIA the best chance it can get, we will postpone this evaluation until we have discussed the Doomsday argument and have seen why a range of more straightforward objections against the Doomsday argument fail. The fact that SIA could seem to be the only coherent way (but later we'll show that it only *seems* that way!) of resisting the Doomsday argument is possibly the strongest argument that can be made in its favor.

For the time being, we put SIA to one side (i.e. we assume that it is false) and focus on comparing Model 1 and Model 2. The difference between these models is that Model 2 uses SSA and Model 1 doesn't. By determining which of these models is correct, we get a test of whether SSA should be applied in epistemic situations where hypotheses implying different numbers of observers are entertained. If we find that Model 2 (or, for that matter, Model 3) is correct, we have extended the applicability of SSA beyond what was established in the previous sections, where the number of observers did not vary between the hypotheses under consideration.

In Model 1 we are told to consider the objective chance of 50% of the coin falling heads. Since you know about this chance, you should according to Model 1 set your subjective credence equal to it.

The step from knowing about the objective chance to setting your credence equal to it follows from the *Principal Principle*[4]. This is not the place to delve into the details of the debates surrounding this principle and the connection between chance and credence (see Skyrms 1980; Kyburg, Jr. 1981; Bigelow, Collins et al. 1993; Hall 1994; Halpin 1994; Thau 1994; Strevens 1995; Hoefer 1997, 1999; Black 1998; Sturgeon 1998; Vranas 1998; Bostrom 1999). Suffice it to point out that the Principal Principle does not say that you should always set your credence equal to the corresponding objective chance if you know it. Instead, it says that you should do this

---

[4] David Lewis (Lewis 1986, 1994). A similar principle had earlier been formulated by Hugh Mellor (Mellor 1971).

unless you have other relevant information that should be taken into account. There is some controversy about how to specify which types of such additional information will modify reasonable credence when the objective chance is known, and which types of additional information will leave the identity intact. But there is general agreement that the proviso is needed. For example, no matter how objectively chancy a process is, and no matter how well you know the chance, if you have actually seen what the outcome was, your credence in that observed outcome should of course be one (or extremely close to one) and your credence in any other outcome the process could have had should be (very close to) zero. This is so quite independently of what the objective chance was. None of this is controversial.

Now, the point is that in *Incubator* you do have such extra relevant information that you need to take into account, and Model 1 fails to do that. The extra information is that you have a black beard. This information is relevant because it bears probabilistically on whether the coin fell heads or tails. We can see this as follows. Suppose you are in a room but you don't know what color your beard is. You are just about to look in the mirror. If the information that you have a black beard were not probabilistically relevant to how the coin fell, there would be no need for you to change your credence about the outcome after looking in the mirror. But this is an incoherent position. For there are two things you may find when looking in the mirror: that you have a black beard or that you have a white beard. Before the light comes on and you see the mirror, you know that if you find that you have a white beard then you will have conclusively refuted the hypothesis that the coin fell tails. So the mirror *might* give you information that would increase your credence of Heads (to 1). But that entails that making the other possible finding (that you have a black beard) must *decrease* your credence in Heads. In other words, your conditional credence of Heads given black beard must be less than your unconditional credence of Heads.

If your conditional probability of Heads given a black beard were not lower than the probability you assign to Heads, while also your conditional probability of Heads given a white beard equals one, then you would be incoherent. This is easily shown by a standard Dutch book argument, or more simply as follows:

Write h for the hypothesis that the coin fell heads, and e for the evidence that you have a black beard. We can assume that $P(e|h) < 1$. Then we have

and

$$P(h\,|\,e) = \frac{P(e\,|\,h)P(h)}{P(e)}$$

$$P(\neg h\,|\,e) = \frac{P(e\,|\,\neg h)P(\neg h)}{P(e)}.$$

Dividing these two equations and using $P(e \mid \neg h) = 1$, we get

$$\frac{P(h \mid e)}{P(\neg h \mid e)} = \frac{P(e \mid h)\Pr(h)}{P(\neg h)} < \frac{P(h)}{P(\neg h)}.$$

So the quotients between the probabilities of *h* and *¬h* is less *after e* is known than *before*. In other words, learning *e* decreases the probability of *h* and increases the probability of *¬h*.

So the observation that you have a black beard gives you relevant information that you need to take into account and it should lower your credence of Tails to below your unconditional credence of Tails, which (provided we reject SIA) is 50%. Model 1, which fails to do this, is therefore wrong.

Model 2 does take the information about your beard color into account and sets your posterior credence of Heads to ⅓, lower than it would have been had you not seen your beard. This is a consequence of SSA. The exact figure depends on the assumption that your conditional probability of a black beard equals that of a white beard, *given* Heads. If you knew that the coin landed heads but you hadn't yet looked in the mirror, you would know that there was one man with a white beard and one with black. Provided these men were sufficiently similar in other respects (so that from your present position of ignorance about your beard color you didn't have any evidence as to which one of them you are), these conditional credences should both be 50% according to SSA.

If we agree that Model 2 is the correct one for *Incubator,* then we have seen how SSA can be applied to problems where the total number of observers in existence is not known. In chapter 10, we will reexamine *Incubator* and argue for adoption of a fourth model, which conflicts with Model 2 in subtle but important ways. The motivation for doing this, however, will become clear only after detailed investigations into the consequences of accepting Model 2. So for the time being, we will adopt Model 2 as our working assumption in order to explore the implications of the way of thinking it embodies.

If we combine this with the lessons of the previous thought experiments, we now have a very wide class of problems where SSA can be applied. In particular, we can apply it to reference classes that contain observers who live at different times and who are different in many substantial ways including genes and gender, and to reference classes that may be of different sizes depending on which hypothesis under consideration is true.

One may wonder if there are any limits at all to how much we can include in the reference class. *There are.* We shall now see why.

THE REFERENCE CLASS PROBLEM

The reference class in the SSA is the class of entities such that one should reason as if one were randomly selected from it. We have seen examples of things that must be included in the reference class. In order to complete the specification of the reference class, we also have to determine what things must be excluded.

In many cases, where the total number of observers is the same on any of the hypotheses assigned non-zero probability, the problem of the reference class appears irrelevant. For instance, take *Dungeon* and suppose that in ten of the blue cells there is a polar bear instead of a human observer. Now, whether the polar bears count as observers who are members of the reference class makes no difference. Whether they do or not, you know you are not one of them. Thus you know that you are not in one of the ten cells they occupy. You therefore recalculate the probability of being in a blue cell to be $\frac{80}{90}$, since 80 out of the 90 observers whom you—for all you know—might be, are in blue cells. Here you have simply eliminated the ten polar-bear cells from the calculation. But this does not rely on the assumption that polar bears aren't included in the reference class. The calculation would come out the same if the bears were replaced with human observers who were very much like yourself, provided you knew you were not one of them. Maybe you are told that ten people who have a birthmark on their right calves are in blue cells. After verifying that you yourself don't have such a birthmark, you adjust your probability of being in a blue cell to $\frac{80}{90}$. This is in agreement with SSA. According to SSA (given that the people with the birthmarks are in the reference class), P(Blue cell | Setup) = $\frac{90}{100}$. But also by SSA, P(Blue cell | Setup & Ten of the people in blue cells have birth marks of a type you don't have) = $\frac{80}{90}$.

Where the definition of the reference class becomes an issue is when the total number of observers is unknown and is correlated with the hypotheses under consideration. Consider the following schema for producing *Incubator*-type experiments: There are two rooms. Whichever way the coin falls, a person with a black beard is created in Room 1. If and only if it falls heads, then one other thing *x* is created in Room 2. You find yourself in one of the rooms and you are informed that it is Room 1. We can now ask, for various choices of *x*, what your credence should be that the coin fell heads.

The original version of *Incubator* was one where *x* is a man with white beard:

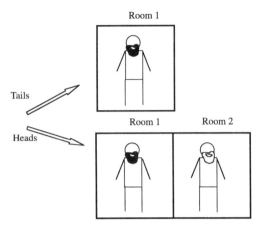

Figure 1: *Incubator*, version I

As we saw above, on Model 2 ("SSA and not SIA"), your credence of Heads is ⅓. But now consider a second case (version II) where we let *x* be a rock:

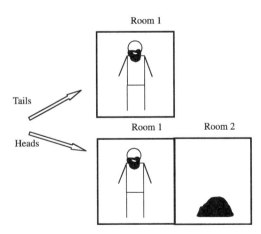

Figure 2: *Incubator*, version II

In version II, when you find that you are the man in Room 1, it is evident that your credence of Heads should be ½. The conditional probability of you observing what you are observing (i.e. your being the man in Room 1) is unity on both Heads and Tails, because with this setup you couldn't possibly have found yourself observing being in Room 2. (We assume, of course, that the rock does not have a soul or a mind.) Notice that the arguments used to argue for SSA in the previous examples cannot be used in version II. A rock cannot bet and cannot be wrong, so the fraction of observers who are right or would win their bets is not improved here by including rocks in the reference class. Moreover, it seems impossible to conceive of a situation where you are ignorant as to whether you are the man in Room 1 or the rock in Room 2.

If this is right then the probability you should assign to Heads depends on what you know would be in Room 2 if the coin fell heads, even though you know that you are in Room 1. The reference class problem can be relevant in cases like this, where the size of the population depends on which hypothesis is true. What you should believe depends on whether the object x that would be in Room 2 would be in the reference class or not. It makes a difference to your rational credence whether x is rock or an observer like yourself.

Rocks, consequently, are not in the reference class. In a similar vein we can rule out armchairs, planets, books, plants, bacteria, and other such non-observer entities. It gets trickier when we consider possible borderline cases such as a gifted chimpanzee, a Neanderthal, or a mentally disabled human. It is not clear whether the earlier arguments for including things in the reference class could be used to argue that these entities should be admitted. Can a severely mentally disabled person bet? Could you have found yourself as such a person? (Although anybody could of course in one sense become severely mentally disabled, it could be argued that the being that results would not in any real sense still be "you," if the damage is sufficiently severe.)

That these questions arise seems to suggest that something beyond a plain version of the principle of indifference is involved. The principle of indifference is primarily about what your credence should be when you are ignorant of certain facts (Castell 1998; Strevens 1998). SSA purports to determine conditional probabilities of the form P("*I'm* an observer with such and such properties" | "The world is such and such"), and it applies even when you were never ignorant of who you are and what properties you have.[5]

---

[5] An additional problem with the principle of indifference is that it balances precariously between vacuity and inconsistency. Starting from the generic formulation suggested earlier, "*Assign equal credence to any two hypotheses if you don't have any reason to prefer one to the other*", one can make it go either way depending on how a strong an interpretation one gives of "reason". If reasons can include any subjective inclination, the principle loses most if not all of its content. But if having a reason requires one to have objectively significant statistical data, then the principle can be shown to be inconsistent.

Intellectual insufficiency might not be the only source of vagueness or indeterminacy of the reference class. Here is a list of possible borderlines:

- *Intellectual limitations* (e.g. chimpanzees; persons with brain damage; Neanderthals; persons who can't understand SSA and the probabilistic reasoning involved in using it in the application in question)

- *Insufficient information* (e.g. persons who don't know about the experimental setup)

- *Lack of some occurrent thoughts* (e.g. persons who, as it happens, don't think of applying SSA to a given situation although they have the capacity to do so)

- *Exotic mentality* (e.g. angels; superintelligent computers; posthumans)

No claim is made that all of these dimensions are such that one can exit the reference class by going to a sufficiently extreme position along them. For instance, maybe an intellect cannot by disqualified for being too smart. The purpose of the list is merely to illustrate that the exact way of delimiting the reference class has not been settled by the preceding discussion and that in order to so one would have to address at least these four points.

We will return to the reference class problem in the next chapter, where we'll see that an attempted solution by John Leslie fails, and yet again in chapters 10 and 11, where we will finally resolve it.

For many purposes, however, the details of the definition of the reference class may not matter much. In thought experiments, we can usually avoid the problem by stipulating that no borderline cases occur. And real-world applications will often approximate this ideal closely enough that the results one derives are robust under variations of the reference class within the zone of vagueness we have left open.

CHAPTER 5

The Self-Sampling Assumption in Science

We turn to the second strand of arguments for SSA. Here we show that many important scientific fields implicitly rely on SSA and that it (or something much like it) constitutes an indispensable part of scientific methodology.

SSA IN COSMOLOGY

Recall our earlier hunch that the trouble in deriving observational consequences from theories that were coupled to some Big World hypothesis might originate in the somewhat "technical" point that while in a large enough cosmos, every observation will be made by *some* observers here and there, it is notwithstanding true that those observers are exceedingly rare and far between. For every observation made by a freak observer spontaneously materializing from Hawking radiation or thermal fluctuations, there are trillions and trillions of observations made by regular observers who have evolved on planets like our own, and who make veridical observations of the universe they are living in. Maybe we can solve the problem, then, by saying that although all these freak observers exist and are suffering from various illusions, it is highly unlikely that *we* are among their numbers? In this case we should think, rather, that we are very probably one of the regular observers whose observations reflect reality. We could safely ignore the freak observers and their illusions in most contexts when doing science. Because the freak observers are in such a tiny minority, their observations can usually be disregarded. It is *possible* that we are freak observers. We should assign to that hypothesis some finite probability—but such a tiny one that it doesn't make any practical difference.

To see how SSA enables us to cash in on this idea, it is first of all crucial that we construe our evidence differently than we did when originally stating the conundrum. If our evidence is simply "Such and such an observation is made" then the evidence has probability one given any Big World theory—and we ram our heads straight into the problem that all Big World theories become empirically impotent. But if we construe our evidence in the more specific form "*We* are making such and such observations." then we have a way out. For we can then say that although Big World theories make it probable ($P \approx 1$) that some such observations be made, they need not make it probable that we should be the ones making them.

Let us therefore define:

$E' :=$ "Such and such observations are made by us."

E' contains an indexical component that the original evidence-statement we considered, E, did not. E' is logically stronger than E. The rationality requirement that one should take all relevant evidence into account dictates that in case E' leads to different conclusions than does E, it is E' that determines what we ought to believe.

A question that now arises is how to determine the evidential bearing that statements of the form of E' have on cosmological theories. Using Bayes' theorem, we can turn the question around and ask, how do we evaluate $P(E' | T\&B)$, the conditional probability that a Big World theory gives to us making certain observations? The argument in chapter 3 showed that if we hope to be able to derive any empirical implications from Big World theories, then $P(E' | T\&B)$ should not generally be set to unity or close to unity. $P(E' | T\&B)$ must take on values that depend on the particular theory and the particular evidence that we are we are considering. Some theories T are supported by some evidence E'; for these choices $P(E' | T\&B)$ is relatively large. For other choices of E' and T, the conditional probability will be relatively small.

To be concrete, consider the two rival theories T_1 and T_2 about the temperature of the cosmic microwave background radiation. (T_1 was the theory that says that the temperature of the cosmic microwave background radiation is about 2.7 K (the observed value); T_2 says it is 3.1 K.) Let E' be the proposition that we have made those observations that cosmologists innocently take to support T_1. E' includes readouts from radio telescopes, etc. Intuitively, we want $P(E' | T_1\&B) > P(E' | T_2\&B)$. That inequality must be the reason why cosmologists believe that the background radiation is in accordance with T_1 rather than T_2, since a priori there is no ground for assigning T_1 a substantially greater probability than T_2.

A natural way in which we can achieve this result is by postulating that we should think of ourselves as being in some sense "random" observers. Here we use the idea that the essential difference between T_1 and T_2 is that the *fraction* of observers who would be making observations in agreement with E' is enormously greater on T_1 than on T_2. If we reason as if we were randomly selected samples from the set of all observers, or from some suitable subset thereof, then we can explicate the conditional probability

P(E'| T&B) in terms of the expected fraction of all observers in the reference class that the conjunction of T and B says would be making the kind of observations that E' says that we are making. This will enable us to conclude that P(E'| T_1&B) > P(E'| T_2&B).

In order to spotlight basic principles, we can make some simplifying assumptions. In the present application, we can think of the reference class as consisting of all observers who will ever have existed. We can also assume a uniform sampling density over this reference class. Moreover, it simplifies things if we set aside complications arising from assigning probabilities over infinite domains by assuming that B entails that the number of observers is finite, albeit such a large finite number that the problems described earlier obtain.

Here is how SSA supplies the missing link needed to connect theories like T_1 and T_2 to observation. On T_2, the only observers who observe an apparent temperature of the cosmic microwave background CMB ≈ 2.7 K are those who have various sorts of rare illusions (for example because their brains have been generated by black holes and are therefore not attuned to the world they are living in) or happen to be located in extremely atypical places (where e.g. a thermal fluctuation has led to a locally elevated CMB temperature). On T_1, by contrast, almost every observer who makes the appropriate astronomical measurements and is not deluded will observe CMB ≈ 2.7 K. A much greater fraction of the observers in the reference class observe CMB≈2.7 K if T_1 is true than if T_2 is true. By SSA, we consider ourselves as random observers; it follows that on T_1 we would be more likely to find ourselves as one of those observers who observe CMB ≈ 2.7 K than we would on T_2. Therefore, P(E'| T_1&B) >> P(E'| T_2&B). Supposing that the prior probabilities of T_1 and T_2 are roughly the same, P(T_1) ≈ P(T_2), it is then trivial to derive via Bayes' theorem that P(T_1 |E&B) > P(T_2 |E&B). This vindicates the intuitive view that we do have empirical evidence that favors T_1 over T_2.

The job that SSA is doing in this derivation is to enable the step from propositions about fractions of observers to propositions about corresponding probabilities. We get the propositions about fractions of observers by analyzing T_1 and T_2 and combining them with relevant background information B; from this, we conclude that there would be an extremely small fraction of observers observing CMB ≈ 2.7 K given T_2 and a much larger fraction given T_1. We then consider the evidence E', which is that *we* are observing CMB ≈ 2.7 K. SSA authorizes us to think of the "we" as a kind of random variable ranging over the class of actual observers. From this it then follows that E' is more probable given T_1 than given T_2. But without assuming SSA, all we can say is that a greater fraction of observers observe CMB ≈ 2.7 K if T_1 is true; at that point the argument would grind to a halt. We could not reach the conclusion that T_1 is supported over T_2. Therefore, SSA, or something like it, must be adopted as a methodological principle.

SSA IN THERMODYNAMICS

Here we'll examine Ludwig Boltzmann's famous attempt to explain why entropy is increasing in the forward time-direction. We will show that a popular and intuitively very plausible objection against Boltzmann relies on an implicit appeal to SSA.

The outlines of Boltzmann's[1] explanation can be sketched roughly as follows. The direction of time's arrow appears to be connected to the fact that entropy increases in the forward time-direction. Now, if one assumes, as is commonly done, that low entropy corresponds in some sense to low probability, then one can see that if a system starts out in a low-entropy state then it will probably evolve over time into a higher entropy state, a more probable state of the system. The problem of explaining why entropy is increasing is thus reduced to the problem of explaining why entropy is currently so low. The world's being in such a low-entropy state would appear a priori improbable. Boltzmann points out, however, that in a sufficiently large system (and the universe may well be such a system) there are, with high probability, local regions of the system—let's call them "subsystems"—which are in low-entropy states even if the system as a whole is in a high-entropy state. Think of it like this: In a sufficiently large container of gas, there will be some places where all the gas molecules in that local region are lumped together in a small cube or some other neat pattern. That is probabilistically guaranteed by the random motion of the gas molecules together with the fact that there are so many of them. Hence, Boltzmann argued, in a large-enough universe there will be some places and some times at which, just by chance, the entropy happens to be exceptionally low. Since life can only exist in a region if it has very low entropy, we would naturally find that in our part of the universe entropy is very low. And since low-entropy subsystems are overwhelmingly likely to evolve towards higher-entropy states, we thus have an explanation of why entropy is currently low here and increasing. An observation selection effect guarantees that we observe a region where that is the case, even though such regions are enormously sparse in the bigger picture.

Lawrence Sklar has remarked about Boltzmann's explanation that it has been "credited by many as one of the most ingenious proposals in the history of science, and disparaged by others as the last, patently desperate, ad hoc attempt to save an obviously failed theory" ((Sklar 1993), p. 44). I think that the ingenuity of Boltzmann's contribution should be fully granted, especially considering that writing this in 1895, he was nearly seventy years ahead of his time in reckoning with observation selection effects when reasoning about the large-scale structure of the world. But the idea, nonetheless, is flawed.

The standard objection is that Boltzmann's datum—that the observable

---

[1] Boltzmann attributes the idea to his assistant, Dr. Schuetz.

universe is a low-entropy subsystem—turns out on a closer look to be in conflict with his explanation. Low-entropy regions that are as huge as the one we observe are *very* sparsely distributed if the universe as a whole is in a high-entropy state. A much smaller low-entropy region would have sufficed to permit intelligent life to exist. Boltzmann's theory fails to account for why the observed low-entropy region is so large and so grossly out of equilibrium.

This plausible objection can be fleshed out with the help of SSA. Let us follow Boltzmann and suppose that we are living in a very vast, perhaps infinite, universe which is in thermal equilibrium, and that observers can exist only in low-entropy regions. Let *T* be the theory that asserts this. According to SSA, what *T* predicts we should observe depends on where *T* says that the bulk of observers tend to be. Since *T* is a theory of thermodynamic fluctuations, it implies that smaller fluctuations (low-entropy regions) are *vastly* more frequent than larger fluctuations, and hence that most observers will find themselves in rather small fluctuations. This is so because the infrequency of larger fluctuations increases rapidly enough to ensure that even though a given large fluctuation will typically contain more observers than a given small fluctuation, the vast majority of observers will nonetheless be in small fluctuations. By SSA, *T* assigns a probability to us observing what we actually observe that is proportional to the fraction of all observers *T* says would make that kind of observations. Since an extremely small fraction of all observers will observe a low entropy region as large as ours if *T* is true, it follows that *T* gives an extremely small probability to the hypothesis that we should observe such a large low-entropy region. Hence *T* is heavily disfavored by our evidence and should be rejected unless its a priori probability is so extremely high as to compensate for its empirical implausibility. For instance, if we compare *T* with a rival theory *T** which asserts that the average entropy in the universe as a whole is about the same as the entropy of the region we observe, then in light of the preceding argument we have to acknowledge that *T** is much more likely to be true, unless our prior probability function were severely skewed towards *T*. (The bias would have to be truly extreme. It would not suffice, for example, if one's prior probabilities were P(*T*) = 99.999999% and P(*T**) = 0.000001%.) This validates the standard objection against Boltzmann. His anthropic explanation is refuted—probabilistically but with extremely high probability—by a more careful application of the anthropic principle.

A contemporary philosopher, Lawrence Sklar, writes that a Boltzmannian has a "reasonable reply" (ibid. p. 299) to this objection, namely that in Boltzmann's picture there will be *some* large regions where entropy is low, so our observations are not really incompatible with his proposal. However, while there is no logical incompatibility, the *probabilistic incompatibility* is of a very high degree. This can, for all practical purposes, be just as decisive as a logical deduction of a falsified empirical consequence, making it totally unreasonable to accept this reply.

Sklar goes on to state what he sees as the real problem for Boltzmannians:

> The major contemporary objection to Boltzmann's account is its apparent failure to do justice to the observational facts . . . as far as we can tell, the parallel direction of entropic increase of systems toward what we intuitively take to be the future time direction that we encounter in our local world seems to hold throughout the universe." (Ibid. p. 300)

It is easy to see that this is but a veiled reformulation of the objection discussed above. If there were a "reasonable reply" to the former objection, the same reply would work equally well against this reformulated version. An unreformed Boltzmannian could simply retort: "Hey, even on my theory there are some regions and some observers in those regions to whom, as far as they can tell, entropy seems to be on the increase throughout the universe—they see only their local region of the universe, after all. Hence our observations are compatible with my theory!" If we are not impressed by this reply, it is because we are willing to take probabilistic entailments seriously. Failing to do so would spell methodological disaster for any theory that postulates a sufficiently big cosmos, since according to such theories there will always be some observer somewhere who observes what we are observing, so the theories would be logically compatible with any observation we could make.[2] But that is clearly not how such theories work. Rational belief is constrained not only by the chains of deduction but also by the rubber bands of probabilistic inference.

SSA IN EVOLUTIONARY BIOLOGY

Anthropic reasoning has been applied to estimate probabilistic parameters in evolutionary biology. For example, we may ask how difficult it was for intelligent life to evolve on our planet.[3] Naively, one may think that since intelligent life evolved on the only planet we have closely examined, evolution of intelligent life seems quite easy. Science popularizer Carl Sagan appears to have held this view: "the origin of life must be a highly probable circumstance; as soon as conditions permit, up it pops!" (Sagan 1995). A moment's reflection reveals that this inference is incorrect, since no matter how unlikely it was for intelligent life to develop on any given planet, we should still expect to have originated from a planet where such an improb-

---

[2] The only observational consequence such theories would have on that view is that we don't make observations that are logically incompatible with the laws of nature which that theory postulates. That is too weak to be of any use. Any finite sequence of sensory stimulation we could have seems to be logically compatible with the laws of nature, both in the classical mechanics framework used in Boltzmann's time and in a contemporary quantum mechanical setting.

[3] A natural way of explicating this question is by construing it as asking about what fraction of all Earth-like planets actually develop intelligent life, provided they are left untouched by alien civilization.

able sequence of events took place. As we saw in chapter 2, the theories that are disconfirmed by the fact that intelligent life exists here are those according to which the difficulty of evolving intelligent life is so great that they give a small likelihood to there being even a single planet with intelligent life in the whole world.

Brandon Carter combined this realization with some additional assumptions and argued that the chances of intelligent life evolving on any particular Earth-like planet are in fact very small (Carter 1983, 1989). His argument is summarized in this footnote.[4]

Carter has also suggested a clever way of estimating the number of improbable "critical" steps in the evolution of humans. A princess is locked in a tower. Suitors have to pick five combination locks to get to her. They can do this only through random trial and error, i.e. without memory of which combinations have been tried. A suitor gets one hour to pick all five

---

[4] Let us make use of a little story to convey the idea.

Define three time intervals: $\bar{t}$, "the expected average time . . . which would be intrinsically most likely for the evolution of a system of 'intelligent observers', in the form of a scientific civilization such as our own" (Carter 1983), p. 353); t_e, which is the time taken by biological evolution on this planet $\approx 0.4 \times 10^{10}$ years; and τ_0, the lifetime of the main sequence of the sun $\approx 10^{10}$ years.

The argument in outline runs as follows: Since at the present stage of understanding in biochemistry and evolutionary biology we have no way of making even an approximate calculation of how likely the evolution of intelligent life is on a planet like ours, we should use a very broad prior probability distribution for this. We can partition the range of possible values of $\bar{t}$ roughly into three regions: $\bar{t} \ll \tau_0$, $\bar{t} \approx \tau_0$, or $\bar{t} \gg \tau_0$. Of these three possibilities we can, according to Carter, "rule out" the second one a priori, with fairly high probability, since it represents a very narrow segment of the total hypothesis space, and since a priori there is no reason to suppose that the expected time to evolve intelligent life should be correlated with the duration of the main sequence of stars like the sun. But we can also rule out, with great probability, the first alternative, since if the expected time to evolve intelligent life were much smaller than τ_0, then we would have expected life to evolve much earlier than it in fact did. This leaves us with $\bar{t} \gg \tau_0$, meaning that life was very unlikely to evolve as fast as it did, within the lifetime of the main sequence of the sun.

What drives this conclusion is the near coincidence between t_e and τ_0. A priori, there is no reason to suppose that these two quantities would be within an order of magnitude (or even within a factor of about two) from each other. This fact, combined with an observation selection effect, yields the prediction that the evolution of intelligent life is very unlikely to happen on a given planet within the main sequence of its star. The contribution that the observation selection effect makes is that it prevents observations of intelligent life taking *longer* than τ_0 to evolve. Whenever intelligent life evolves on a planet, we must find that it evolved before its sun went extinct. Were it not for the fact that the only evolutionary processes that are observed firsthand are those which gave rise to intelligent observers in a shorter time than τ_0, then the observation that $t_e \approx \tau_0$ would have disconfirmed the hypothesis that $\bar{t} \gg \tau_0$ just as much as it disconfirmed $\bar{t} \gg \tau_0$. But thanks to this selection effect, $t_e \approx \tau_0$ is precisely what one would expect to observe even if the evolutionary process leading to intelligent life were intrinsically very unlikely to take place in as short a time as τ_0.

Patrick Wilson (Wilson 1994) advances some objections against Carter's reasoning, but as these objections do not concern the basic anthropic methodology that Carter uses, they don't need to be addressed here.

A corollary of Carter's conclusion is that there very probably aren't any extraterrestrial civilizations anywhere near us, maybe not even in our galaxy.

locks. If he doesn't succeed within the allotted time, he is beheaded. However, the princess' charms are such that there is an endless line of hopeful suitors waiting their turn.

After the deaths of some unknown number of suitors, one of them finally passes the test and marries the princess. Suppose that the numbers of possible combinations in the locks are such that the expected time to pick each lock is .01, .1, 1, 10, and 100 hours respectively. Suppose that pick-times for the suitor who got through are (in hours) {.00583, .0934, .248, .276, .319}. By inspecting this set you could reasonably guess that .00583 hour was the pick-time for the easiest lock and .0934 hour the pick-time for the second easiest lock. However, you couldn't really tell which locks the remaining three pick-times correspond to. This is a typical result. When conditioning on success before the cut-off (in this case 1 hour), the average completion time of a step is nearly independent of its expected completion time, provided the expected completion time is much longer than the cut-off. Thus, for example, even if the expected pick-time of one of the locks had been a million years, you would still find that its average pick-time *in successful runs* is closer to .2 or .3 than to 1 hour, and you wouldn't be able to tell it apart from the 1, 10, and 100 hours locks.

If we don't know the expected pick-times or the number of locks that the suitor had to break, we can obtain estimates of these parameters if we know the time it took him to reach the princess. The less surplus time left over before the cut-off, the greater the number of difficult locks he had to pick. For example, if the successful suitor took 59 minutes to get to the princess, that would favor the hypothesis that he had to pick a fairly large number of locks. If he reached the princess in 35 minutes, that would strongly suggest that the number of difficult locks was small. The relation also works the other way around so that if we are not sure what the maximum allowed time is we can estimate it from information about the number of difficult locks and their combined pick-time in a random successful trial. Monte Carlo simulations confirming these claims have been performed by Robin Hanson, who has also derived some useful analytical expressions (Hanson 1998).

Carter applies these mathematical ideas to evolutionary theory by noting that an upper bound on the cut-off time after which intelligent life could not have evolved on Earth is given by the duration of the main sequence of the sun—about $10*10^9$ years. It took about $4*10^9$ years for intelligent life to develop. From this (together with some other assumptions which are problematic but not in ways relevant for our purposes), Carter concludes that the number of critical steps in human evolution is likely very small—not much greater than two.

One potential problem with Carter's argument is that the duration of the main sequence of the sun gives only an upper bound on the cut-off. Maybe climate change or some other event would have made Earth unconducive to evolution of complex organisms long before the sun becomes a red giant. Recognizing this possibility, Barrow and Tipler apply Carter's reasoning in the opposite direction and seek to infer the true cut-off by directly estimating the number of critical steps (Barrow and Tipler 1986).[5] In a recent paper, Robin Hanson scrutinizes Barrow and Tipler's alleged critical steps and argues that their model does not fit the evidence very well when considering the relative time the steps actually took to complete (Hanson 1998).

Our concern here is not which estimate is correct or even whether at the current state of biological science enough empirical data and theoretical understanding are available to supply the substantive premises needed to derive any specific conclusion from this sort of considerations.[6] My contention, rather, is twofold. Firstly, if one wants to argue about or make a claim regarding such things as the improbability of intelligent life evolving, or the probability of finding extraterrestrial life, or the number of critical steps in human evolution, or the planetary window of opportunity during which evolution of intelligent life is possible, then one needs to be careful to make sure that one's position is probabilistically coherent. The works by Carter and others have revealed subtle ways in which some views on these things are untenable. Secondly, underlying the basic constraints appealed to in Carter's reasoning (and this is quite independent of the specific empirical assumptions he needs to get any concrete results) is an application of SSA. WAP and SAP are inadequate in these applications. SSA makes its entrée when we realize that in a large universe there are actual evolutionary histories of most any sort. On some planets, life evolves swiftly; on others, it will uses up all the time available before the cut-off.[7] On some planets, difficult

---

[5] For example, the step from prokaryotic to eukaryotic life is a candidate for being a critical step, since it seems to have happened only once and appears to be necessary for intelligent life to evolve. By contrast, there is evidence that the evolution of eyes from an "eye precursor" has occurred independently at least forty times, so this step does not seem to be difficult. A good introduction to some of the relevant biology is (Schopf 1992).

[6] There are complex empirical issues that would need to be confronted were one to the seriously investigate these questions. For instance, if a step takes a very long time, that *may* suggest that the step was very difficult (perhaps requiring simultaneous muli-loci mutations or other rare occurrences). But there can be other reasons for a step taking long to complete. For example, oxygen breathing took a long time to evolve, but this is not a ground for thinking that it was a difficult step. For oxygen breathing became adaptive only after there were significant levels of free oxygen in the atmosphere, and it took anaerobic organisms hundreds of millions of years to produce enough oxygen to satiate various oxygen sinks and increase atmospheric oxygen to the required levels. This process was slow but virtually guaranteed eventually to run to completion, so it would be a mistake to infer that the evolution of oxygen breathing and the concomitant Cambrian explosion represent a hugely difficult step in human evolution.— Likewise, that a step took only a short time (as, for instance, did the transition from our ape ancestors to homo sapiens) *can* be evidence suggesting it was relatively easy, but it need not be if we suspect that there was only a small window of opportunity for the step to occur (so that if it occurred at all, it would have to happen within that time-interval).

[7] In case of an infinite (or extremely large finite) cosmos, intelligent life would also evolve after the "cut-off". Normally we may feel quite confident in stating that intelligent life cannot evolve on Earth after the swelling sun has engulfed it. Yet the freak-observer argument made in chapter

steps are completed more quickly than easy steps. Without some probabilistic connection between the distribution of evolutionary histories and
our own observed evolutionary past, none of the above considerations
would even make sense.

SSA is not the only methodological principle that would establish such a
connection. For example, we could formulate a principle stating that every
civilization should reason as if it were a random sample from the set of all
civilizations.[8] For the purposes of the above anthropic arguments in evolution theory, this principle would amount to the same thing as the SSA, provided that all civilizations contain the same number of observers. However,
when considering hypotheses on which certain types of evolutionary histories are correlated with the evolved civilizations containing a greater or
smaller number of observers, this principle is not valid. We then need to
have recourse to the more generally applicable principle given by SSA.

SSA IN TRAFFIC ANALYSIS

When driving on the motorway, have you ever wondered about (or cursed!)
the phenomenon that cars in the other lane appear to be getting ahead faster
than you? Although one may be inclined to account for this by invoking
Murphy's Law[9], a recent paper in *Nature* (Redelmeier and Tibshirani 1999),
further elaborated in (Redelmeier and Tibshirani 2000), seeks a deeper
explanation. According to this view, drivers suffer from systematic illusions
causing them to mistakenly think they would have been better off in the
next lane. Here we show that their argument fails to take into account an
important observation selection effect. Cars in the next lane actually do go
faster.

In their paper, Redelmeier and Tibshirani present some evidence that
drivers on Canadian roadways (which don't have an organized laminar
flow) think that the next lane is typically faster. The authors seek to explain
this phenomenon by appealing to a variety of psychological factors. For
example, "a driver is more likely to glance at the next lane for comparison
when he is relatively idle while moving slowly"; "Differential surveillance
can occur because drivers look forwards rather than backwards, so vehicles
that are overtaken become invisible very quickly, whereas vehicles that
overtake the index driver remain conspicuous for much longer"; and

---

3 can of course be extended to show that in an infinite universe there would, with probability
one, be some red giants that enclose a region where—because of some ridiculously improbable statistical fluke—an Earth-like planet continues to exist and develop intelligent life. Strictly
speaking, it is not impossible but only highly improbable that life will evolve on any given
planet after its orbit has been swallowed by an expanding red giant.

[8] Such a principle would be very similar to what Alexander Vilenkin has (independently) called
the "principle of mediocrity" (Vilenkin 1995).

[9] "If anything can go wrong, it will." (Discovered by Edward A. Murphy, Jr., in 1949.)

"human psychology may make being overtaken (losing) seem more salient than the corresponding gains". The authors recommend that drivers be educated about these effects and encouraged to resist small temptations to switch lanes, thereby helping to reduce the risk of accidents.

While all these illusions may indeed occur[10], there is a more straightforward explanation of the phenomenon. It goes as follows. One frequent cause of why a lane (or a segment of a lane) is slow is that there are too many cars in it. Even if the ultimate cause is something else, such as road work, there is nonetheless typically a negative correlation between the speed of a lane and how densely packed are the vehicles driving in it. That suggests (although it doesn't logically imply) that a disproportionate fraction of the average driver's time is spent in slow lanes. And by SSA, that means that there is a greater than even prior probability of that holding true about you in particular.

The last explanatory link can be tightened up further if we move to a stronger version of the SSA replaces "observer" with "observer-moment", i.e. time-segment of an observer. (We will discuss this stronger principle, "SSSA", in depth in chapter 10; the invocation of it here is an aside.) If you think of your present observation, when driving on the motorway, as a random sample from all observations made by drivers, then chances are that your observation will be made from the viewpoint that most observers have, which is the viewpoint of the slow-moving lane. In other words, appearances are faithful: more often than not, the "next" lane *is* faster!

Even when two lanes have the same average speed, it can be advantageous to switch lanes. For what is relevant to a driver who wants to reach her destination quickly is not the average speed of the lane as a whole, but rather the speed of some segment extending maybe a couple of miles forwards from the driver's current position. More often than not, the next lane has a higher average speed, at this scale, than does the driver's present lane. On average, there is therefore a benefit to switching lanes (which of course has to be balanced against the costs of increased levels of effort and risk).

Adopting a thermodynamics perspective, it is easy to see that (at least in the ideal case) increasing the "diffusion rate" (i.e. the probability of lane-switching) will speed the approach to "equilibrium" (i.e. equal velocities in both lanes), thereby increasing the road's throughput and the number of vehicles that reach their destinations per unit time.

The mistake to avoid is ignoring the selection effect residing in the fact that when you randomly select a driver and ask her whether she thinks the next lane is faster, more often than not you will have selected a driver in the lane which is in fact slower. And if there is no random selection of a driver, but it is just you yourself wondering why you are so unlucky as to be in the

---

[10] For some relevant empirical studies, see e.g. (Feller 1966; Tversky and Kahnemann 1981, 1991; Gilovich, Vallone et al. 1985; Larson 1987; Angrilli, Cherubini et al. 1997; Snowden, Stimpson et al. 1998; Walton and Bathurst 1998).

slow lane, then the selection effect is an observational one. Once we realize this, we see that no case has been made for recommending that drivers change lanes less frequently.

SSA IN QUANTUM PHYSICS

One of the fundamental problems in the interpretation of quantum physics is how to understand the probability statements that the theory makes. On one kind of view, the "single-history version", quantum physics describes the "propensities" or physical chances of a range of possible outcomes, but only one series of outcomes actually occurs. On an alternative view, the "many-worlds version", all possible sequences of outcomes (or at least all that have nonzero measure) actually occur. These two kinds of views are often thought to be observationally indistinguishable (Wheeler 1957; DeWitt 1970; Omnès 1973), but, depending on how they are fleshed out, SSA may provide a method of telling them apart experimentally. What follows are some sketchy remarks about how such an observational wedge could be inserted. We're sacrificing rigor and generality in this section in order to keep things brief and simple.

The first problem faced by many-worlds theories is how to connect statements about the measure of various outcomes with statements about how probable we should think it is that we will observe a particular outcome. Consider first this simpleminded way of thinking about the many-worlds approach: When a quantum event E occurs in a quantum system in state S, and there are two possible outcomes A and B, then the wavefunction of S will after the event contain two components or "branches", one were A obtains and one where B obtains, and these two branches are in other respects equivalent. The problem with this view is that it fails to give a role to the amplitude of the wavefunction. If nothing is done with the fact that one of the branches (say A) might have a higher amplitude squared (say ⅔) than does the other branch, then we've lost an essential part of quantum theory, namely that it specifies not just what *can* happen but also the probabilities of the various possibilities. In fact, if there are equally many observers on the branch were A obtains as on the branch were B obtains, and if there is no other relevant difference between these branches, then by SSA the probability that you should find yourself on branch A is ½, rather than ⅔ as asserted by quantum physics. This simpleminded interpretation must therefore be rejected.

One way of trying to improve the interpretation is by postulating that when the measurement occurs, the wavefunction splits into more than two branches. Suppose, for example, that there are two branches where A obtains and one branch were B obtains (and that these branches are otherwise equivalent). Then, by SSA, you'd have a ⅔ probability of observing A— the correct answer. If one wanted to adopt this interpretation, one would have to stipulate that there are lots of branches. One could represent this interpretation pictorially as a tree, where a thick bundle of fibers in the trunk gradually split off into branches of varying degrees of thickness. Each fiber would represent one "world". When a quantum event occurs in one branch, the fibers it contains would divide into smaller branches, with the number of fibers going into each sub-branch being proportional to the amplitude squared of the wave function. For example, ⅔ of all the fibers on a branch where the event E occurs in system S would go into a sub-branch where A obtains, and ⅓ into a sub-branch where B obtains. In reality, if we wanted to hold on to the exact real-valued probabilities given by quantum theory, we'd have to postulate a continuum of fibers, so it wouldn't really make sense to speak of different fractions of fibers going into different branches. But something of the underlying ontological picture could possibly be retained so that we could speak of the more probable outcomes as obtaining in "more worlds" in some generalized sense of that expression.

Alternatively, a many-worlds interpretation could simply decide to take the correspondence between quantum mechanical measure and the probability of one observing the correlated outcome as a postulated primitive. It would then be assumed that, as a brute fact, you are more likely to find yourself on one of the branches of higher measure. (Maybe one could speak of such higher-measure branches as having a "higher degree of reality".)

On either of these alternatives, there are observational consequences that diverge from those one gets if one accepts the single-history interpretation. These consequences come into the light when one considers quantum events that lead to different numbers of observers. This was recently pointed out by Don N. Page (Page 1999). The point can be made most simply by considering a quantum cosmological toy model:

World 1: Observers; measure or probability 10^{-30}

World 2: No observers; measure or probability $1-10^{-30}$

The single-history version predicts with overwhelming probability ($P = 1-10^{-30}$) that World 2 would be the (only) realized world. If we exist, and consequently World 1 has been realized, this gives us strong reasons for rejecting the single-history version, given this particular toy model. By contrast, on the many-worlds version, both World 1 and World 2 exist, and since World 2 has no observers, what is predicted (by SSA) is that we should observe World 1, notwithstanding its very low measure. In this example, if the choice is between the single-history version and the many-worlds version, we should therefore accept the latter.

Here's another toy model:

World A: 10^{10} observers; measure or probability $1-10^{-30}$

World B: 10^{50} observers; measure or probability 10^{-30}

In this model, finding that we are in World B does not logically refute the single-history version, but it does make it extremely improbable. For the single-history version gives a conditional probability of 10^{-30} to us observing World B. The many-worlds version, on the other hand, gives a conditional probability of approximately 1 to us observing World B.[11] Provided, then, that our subjective prior probabilities for the single-history and the many-worlds versions are in the same (very big) ballpark, we should in this case again accept the latter. (The opposite would hold, of course, if we found that we are living in World A.)

These are toy models, sure. In practice, it will no doubt be hard to get a good grip on the measure of "worlds". A few things should be noted though. First, the "worlds" to which we need assign measures needn't be temporally unlimited. We could instead focus on smaller "world-parts" that arose from, and got their measures from, some earlier quantum event whose associated measures or probabilities we think we know. Such an event could, for instance, be a hypothetical symmetry-breaking event in an early inflationary epoch of our universe, or it could be some later occurrence that influences how many observers there will be (we'll study in depth some cases of this kind in chapter 9). Second, the requisite measures may be provided by other theories so that the conjunction of such theories with either the single-history or the many-worlds versions may be empirically testable. For example, Page performs some illustrative calculations using the Hartle-Hawking "no-boundary" proposal and some other assumptions. Third, since in many quantum cosmological models, the difference in the number of observers existing in different worlds can be quite huge, we might get results that are robust for a rather wide range of plausible measures that the component worlds might have. And fourth, as far as our project is concerned, the important point is that our methodology ought to be able to make this kind of consideration intelligible and meaningful, whether or not at the present time we have enough data to put it into practice.[12]

SUMMARY OF THE CASE FOR SSA

In the last chapter, we argued through a series of thought experiments for reasoning in accordance with SSA in a wide range of cases. We showed that while the problem of the reference class is sometimes irrelevant when all

---

11

$$P = \frac{10^{50} \cdot 10^{-30}}{10^{50} \cdot 10^{-30} + 10^{10} \cdot (1 - 10^{-30})} \approx 1$$

[12] On some related issues, see especially (Leslie 1996; Page 1996, 1997) but also (Albert 1989; Papineau 1995, 1997; Tegmark 1996, 1997; Schmidhuber 1997; Olum 2002). Page has independently developed a principle he calls the "Conditional Aesthemic Principle", which is a sort of special-case version of SSSA applied to quantum physics.

hypotheses under consideration imply the same number of observers, the definition of the reference class becomes crucial when different hypotheses entail different numbers of observers. In those cases, what probabilistic conclusions we can draw depends on what sort of things are included in the reference class, even if the observer doing the reasoning knows that she is not one of the contested objects. We argued that many types of entities should be excluded from the reference class (rocks, bacteria, buildings, plants, etc.). We also showed that variations in regard to many quite "deep-going" properties (such as gender, genes, social status, etc.) are not sufficient grounds for discrimination when determining membership in the reference class. Observers differing in any of these respects can at least in some situations belong to the same reference class.

In this chapter, a complementary set of arguments was presented, focusing on how SSA caters to a methodological need in science by providing a way of connecting theory to observation. The scientific applications we looked at included:

• Deriving observational predictions from contemporary cosmological models.

• Evaluating a common objection against Boltzmann's proposed thermodynamic explanation of time's arrow.

• Identifying probabilistic coherence constraints in evolutionary biology. These are crucial in a number of contexts, such as when asking questions about the likelihood of intelligent life evolving on an Earth-like planet, the number of critical steps in human evolution, the existence of extraterrestrial intelligent life, and the cut-off time after which the evolution of intelligent life would no longer have been possible on Earth.

• Analyzing claims about perceptual illusions among drivers.

• Realizing a potential way of experimentally distinguishing between single-history and many-worlds versions of quantum theory.

Any proposed rival to SSA should be tested in all of the above thought experiments and scientific applications. Anybody who refuses to accept that something like SSA is needed, is hereby challenged to propose a simpler or more plausible method of reasoning that works in all these cases.

Our survey of applications is by no means exhaustive. We shall now turn to a purported application of SSA to evaluating hypotheses about humankind's prospects. Here we are entering controversial territory where it is not obvious whether or how SSA can be applied, or what conclusions to derive from it. Indeed, the ideas we begin to pursue at this point will eventually lead us (in chapter 10) to propose important revisions to SSA. But we have to take one step at a time.

CHAPTER 6

The Doomsday Argument

BACKGROUND

By now we have seen several examples where SSA gives intuitively plausible results. If SSA is applied to our actual situation and the future prospects of the human species, however, we get disturbing consequences. Coupled with a few seemingly quite weak empirical assumptions, SSA generates (given that we use the universal reference class) the Doomsday argument (DA), which purports to show that the life expectancy of the human species has been systematically overestimated. That is a shocking claim. The prediction is derived from premises which one would have thought too weak to entail such a thing. Moreover, under some not-so-implausible empirical assumptions, the reduction in our species' life expectancy is quite drastic.

Most people who hear about DA at first think there must be something wrong with it. A small but significant minority think it is obviously right.[1] What everybody must agree is that if the argument works, it would be a momentous result, since it has major empirical consequences for an issue that we care a lot about, our survival.

Up until now, DA remains unrefuted. Not for a lack of trying; the attempts to refute it are legion. In the next chapter, we will analyze in detail some of the more recent objections and explain why they fail. In the present chapter, we shall spell out the Doomsday argument, identify its assumptions, and examine various related issues.

We can distinguish two forms of DA that have been presented in the literature, one due to Richard Gott and one to John Leslie. Gott's version is incorrect. Leslie's version, while a great improvement on Gott's, also falls

---

[1] The ranks of distinguished supporters of DA include among others: J.J.C. Smart, Anthony Flew, Michael Lockwood, John Leslie, Alan Hàjek (philosophers); Werner Israel, Brandon Carter, Stephen Barr, Richard Gott, Paul Davis, Frank Tipler, H.B. Nielsen (physicists); and Jean-Paul Delahaye (computer scientist). (John Leslie, personal communication.)

short on several points. Correcting these shortcomings does not, however, destroy the basic idea of the argument. So we shall try to fill in some of the gaps and set forth DA in a way that gives it a maximum run for its money. But to my cards on the table, I think DA ultimately fails. However, it is crucial that it not be dismissed for the wrong reasons.

DA has been independently discovered many times over. Brandon Carter was first, but did not publish on the issue. John Leslie gets the credit for being the first to clearly enunciate it in print (Leslie 1989). Leslie, who had heard rumors of Carter's discovery from Frank Tipler, has been the most prolific writer on the topic, with one monograph and over a dozen academic papers. Richard Gott III independently discovered and published a version of DA in 1993 (Gott 1993). The argument also appears to have been conceived by H.B. Nielsen (Nielsen 1981) (although Nielsen might have been influenced by Tipler), and again more recently by Stephen Barr. Saar Wilf (personal communication) has convinced me that he, too, independently discovered the argument a few years ago.

Although Leslie has the philosophically most sophisticated exposition of DA, it is instructive to first take a look at the version expounded by Gott.

Doomsayer Gott

Gott's version of DA[2] is based on a more general argument-type which he calls the "delta t argument". Notwithstanding its extreme simplicity, Gott reckons it can be used to make predictions about most everything in heaven and on earth. It goes as follows.

Suppose we want to estimate how long some series of observations (or "measurements") is going to last. Then,

> Assuming that whatever we are measuring can be observed only in the interval between times t_{begin} and t_{end}, if there is nothing special about t_{now} we expect t_{now} to be randomly located in this interval. (Gott 1993), p. 315

Using this randomness assumption, we can make the estimate

$$t_{future} = (t_{end} - t_{now}) \approx t_{past} = (t_{now} - t_{begin}).$$

t_{future} is the estimated value of how much longer the series will last. What

---

[2] Gott's version of DA is set forth in a paper in *Nature* dating from 1993 (Gott 1993); see also the responses (Buch 1994; Goodman 1994; Mackay 1994), and Gott's replies (Gott 1994). A popularized exposition by Gott appeared (Gott 1997). In the original article, Gott not only sets forth a version of DA but also pursues its implications for the search of extraterrestrial life project and for the prospects of space travel. Further elaborations by Gott can be found in (Gott 1996, 2001).

this means is that we make the estimate that the series will continue for roughly as long as it has already lasted when we make the random observation. This estimate will overestimate the true value half of the time and underestimate it half of the time. It also follows that a 50% confidence interval is given by

$$\tfrac{1}{3} t_{past} < t_{future} < 3 t_{past},$$

and a 95% confidence interval is given by

$$\tfrac{1}{39} t_{past} < t_{future} < 39 t_{past}.$$

Gott gives some illustrations of how this reasoning can be applied:

> [In] 1969 I saw for the first time Stonehenge ($t_{past} \approx 3,868$ years) and the Berlin Wall ($t_{past} \approx 8$ years). Assuming that I am a random observer of the Wall, I expect to be located randomly in the time between t_{begin} and t_{end} (t_{end} occurs when the Wall is destroyed or there are no visitors left to observe it, whichever comes first). (Gott 1993), p. 315

At least in the case of the Berlin Wall, the delta *t* argument seems to have worked! (We may have to wait a while for the results to come in on Stonehenge, though.) A popular exposition that Gott wrote for *New Scientist* article also features a sidebar inviting the reader to use the arrival date of that issue of the magazine to predict how long their current romantic relationship will last. Presumably you can use this book for the same purpose. How long has your present relationship lasted? Use that value for t_{past} and you get your prediction from the expressions above, complete with an exact confidence interval.

Wacky? Yes, but all this does indeed follow from the assumption that t_{now} is randomly (and uniformly) sampled from the interval t_{begin} to t_{end}. Gott admits that this imposes some restrictions on the applicability of the delta *t* argument:

> [At] a friend's wedding, you couldn't use the formula to forecast the marriage's future. You are at the wedding precisely to witness its beginning. Neither can you use it to predict the future of the Universe itself—for intelligent observers emerged only long after the Big Bang, and so witness only a subset of its timeline. (Gott 1997), p. 39

Unfortunately, Gott does not discuss in any more detail the all-important question of when, in practice, the delta *t* argument is applicable. Yet it is clear from his examples that he thinks it should be applied in a very broad range of real-world situations.

In order to apply the delta *t* argument to estimate the life-expectancy of the human species, we must measure time on a "population clock" where one unit of time corresponds to the birth of one human. This modification is necessary because the human population is not constant. Thanks to population growth, most humans who have been born so far find themselves later rather than earlier in the history of our species. According to SSA, we should consequently assign a higher prior probability to finding ourselves at these later times. By measuring time as the number of humans who have come into existence, we obtain a scale where we can assign a uniform sampling density to all points of time.

There has been something like 60 billion humans so far. Using this value as t_{past}, the delta t argument gives the 95% confidence interval

$$1.5 \; billion < t_{future} < 2.3 \; trillion.$$

The units are human births. To convert this into years, we would have to estimate what the future population figures will be at different times given that a total of N humans will have existed. Absent such an estimate, DA leaves room for alternative interpretations. If the world population levels out at 12 billion and human life-expectancy stabilizes at approximately 80 years, then disaster is likely to put an end to our species fairly soon (within 1200 years with 75% probability). If population grows larger, the prognosis is even worse. But if population decreases drastically, or individual human life-spans get much longer, then the delta t argument would be compatible with survival for millions of years.

The probability of space colonization looks dismal in the light of Gott's version of DA. Reasoning via the delta t argument, Gott concludes that the probability that we will colonize the galaxy is about $p \leq 10^{-9}$, because if we did, we would expect there to be at least a billion times more humans in the future than have been born to date.

THE INCORRECTNESS OF GOTT'S ARGUMENT

A crucial flaw in Gott's argument is that it fails to take into account our empirical prior probability of the hypotheses under consideration. Even granting that SSA is applicable to all the situations and in the manner that Gott suggests (and we shall argue in a later chapter that that is not generally the case, because the "no-outsider requirement" is not satisfied), the conclusion would not necessarily be the one intended by Gott once this omission is rectified.

And it is clear, once we focus our attention on it, that our prior probabilities must be considered. It would be foolish when estimating the future duration of Stonehenge or the Berlin Wall not to take into account any other information you might have. Say you are part of a terrorist organization that is planning to destroy Stonehenge. Everything has been carefully plotted. The explosives are in the truck, the detonators are in your suitcase; tonight at 11 P.M. your confederates will to pick you up from King's Cross St. Pancras... Knowing this, surely the odds of Stonehenge lasting another year are different from, and much lower than, what a straightforward application of the delta *t* argument would suggest. In order to save the delta *t* argument, Gott would have to restrict its applicability to situations where we in fact lack other relevant information. But then the argument cannot be used to estimate the future longevity of the human species, for we certainly have plenty of extraneous information that is relevant to that. So Gott's version of DA fails.

That leaves open the question whether the delta *t* argument might not perhaps provide interesting guidance in some other estimation problems. Suppose we are trying to guess the future duration of some phenomenon, and that we have a "prior" probability distribution (after taking into account all other empirical information available) that is uniform for total duration T in the interval $0 \leq T \leq T_{max}$, and is zero for $T > T_{max}$:

$$P(T) = \begin{cases} \dfrac{T}{T_{max}} & \text{for } 0 \leq T \leq T_{max} \\[2ex] 0 & \text{otherwise} \end{cases}$$

Suppose you make an observation at time t_0 and find that the phenomenon at that time has lasted for $(t_0 - 0)$ and is still ongoing. Let us assume, further, that there is nothing "special" about the time you choose to make the observation. That is, we assume that the case is not like using the delta *t* argument to forecast the prospects of a friend's marriage at his wedding. We have made quite a few assumptions here, but if the argument could be shown to work under these conditions it might still find considerable practical use. Some real-world cases at least approximate this ideal setting.

Even under these favorable conditions, however, the argument is inconclusive, because it neglects a potentially important observation selection effect. The probability of your observation occurring at a time when the phenomenon is taking place may be positively correlated with the duration of the phenomenon. We will discuss this in more detail in the next chapter, in the context of what we shall call the "no-outsider" requirement. For now, it suffices to note that if your observation is sampled from a time interval that is longer than the minimum guaranteed duration of the phenomenon—so that you could have made your observation before the phenomenon started or after it ended—then finding that the phenomenon is still in progress when you make your observation gives you some reason to think that the phenomenon probably lasts relatively long. The delta *t* argument fails to take account of this effect. The argument, hence, is flawed, unless we make the additional assumption (not made by Gott) that your observation point is sampled from a time interval that does not exceed the duration of the phenomenon. And this entails that in order to legitimately apply Gott's method, you must be convinced that your observation point's sampling interval covaries with durations of the phenomenon. That is to say, you must be convinced that *given* the phenomenon lasts from t_a to t_b, *then* your observation point is sampled from the interval $[t_a, t_b]$; and that *given* that the phenomenon lasts from $t_{a'}$ to $t_{b'}$, *then* your observation point is sampled from the interval $[t_{a'}, t_{b'}]$; and similarly for any other start- and end-points that you assign a non-zero prior probability. This imposes a strong additional constraint on the situations where the delta *t* argument can be applied.[3]

The failure of Gott's approach to take into account the empirical prior probabilities and to respect the no-outsider requirement constitute the more serious difficulties with the "Copernican Anthropic Principle" alluded to in chapter 3 and are part of the reason why we replaced that principle with SSA.

DOOMSAYER LESLIE

Leslie's presentation of DA differs in several respects from Gott's. Stylistically, Leslie's writing is more informal and his arguments often take the form of analogies. But he is much more explicit than Gott about the philosophical underpinnings and he places the argument in a Bayesian framework. Leslie also devotes considerable attention to the empirical considerations that determine the priors, as well as to the ethical imperative of working to reduce the risk of human extinction.

Leslie presents DA through a loosely arranged series of thought experiments and analogies, and a large part of the argumentation consists in refuting various objections that could be advanced against his preferred way of reasoning. This makes it hard to do justice to Leslie's version of DA in a brief summary, but a characteristic passage runs as follows:

> One might at first expect the human race to survive, no doubt in evolutionary much modified form, for millions or even billions of years, perhaps just on Earth but, more plausibly, in huge colonies scattered through the galaxy and maybe even through many galaxies. Contemplating the entire history of the race—future as well as past history—I should in that case see myself as a very unusually early human. I might well be among the first 0.00001 per cent to live their lives. But what if the race is instead about to die out? I am then a fairly typical human. Recent population growth has been so rapid that, of all human lives lived so far, anything up to about 30 per cent . . . are lives which are being lived at this very moment. Now, whenever lacking evidence to the contrary one should prefer to think of one's own position as fairly typical rather than highly untypical. To promote the reasonable aim of making it quite ordinary that I exist where I do in human history, let me therefore assume that the human race will rapidly die out. (Leslie 1990), pp. 65f.

---

[3] I made these two points—that Gott's argument fails to take into account the empirical prior and that it ignores the selection effect just described—in a paper of 1997 (Bostrom 1997). More recently, Carlton Caves has independently rediscovered these two objections and presented them elegantly in (Caves 2000). See also (Ledford, Marriott, et al. 2001; Olum 2002), and for a reply by Gott, see (Gott 2000).

Leslie emphasizes that DA does not show that doom *will* strike soon. It only argues for a probability shift. If we started out being extremely confident that the humans will survive for a long time, we might still be fairly confident after having taken DA into account—though less confident than before. Also, it is possible for us to improve our prospects. Leslie hopes that having been convinced that the risks are greater than we previously thought, we will become more willing to take steps to diminish them. This could perhaps be done by pushing for nuclear disarmament, setting up an early-warning system for meteors on collision course with Earth, being careful with future very-high-energy particle physics experiments (which might, conceivably, knock our cosmic region out of a metaunstable vacuum state and destroy the world), and developing workable strategies for dealing with the weapons potential of future nanotechnology (Drexler 1985, 1992; Freitas, Jr. 1999). So we should not take DA as a ground for despair but as a call for greater caution and concern about potential species-annihilating disasters.

A major advantage over Gott's version of Leslie's is that it stresses that the empirical priors must be taken into account. Bayes' theorem tells us how to do that. Suppose we are entertaining two hypotheses about how many humans there will have been in total:

> H_1: There will have been a total of 200 billion humans.
> H_2: There will have been a total of 200 trillion humans.

For simplicity, let us assume that these are the only possibilities. The next step is to assign prior probabilities to these hypotheses on the basis of available empirical information (but ignoring, for the moment, information about your birth rank). For example, you might think that:

> $P(H_1) = 5\%$
> $P(H_2) = 95\%$

All that remains now is to factor in the information about your birth rank, which is in the neighborhood of 60 billion (R) for those of us who are alive at the beginning of the 21st century.

$$P(H_1|R) = \frac{P(R|H_1)P(H_1)}{P(R|H_1)P(H_1) + P(R|H_2)P(H_2)} \qquad (\#)$$

$$= \frac{\dfrac{1}{200 \cdot 10^9} \times .05}{\left(\dfrac{1}{200 \cdot 10^9} \times .05\right) + \left(\dfrac{1}{200 \cdot 10^{12}} \times .95\right)}$$

$$\approx .98$$

In this example, the prior probability of Doom soon (H_1) of 5% is increased to about 98% when you take into account your birth rank.

This is how calculations are to be made on Leslie's version of DA. The calculation is not the argument, however. Rather, the calculation is a derivation of a specific prediction from assumptions which DA seeks to justify. Let's look in more detail at what these assumptions are and whether they can be supported.

THE PREMISES OF DA, AND THE OLD EVIDENCE PROBLEM

Leslie talks of the principle that, lacking evidence to the contrary, one should think of one's position as "fairly typical rather than highly untypical". SSA can be viewed as an explication of this rather vague idea. The crucial question now is whether SSA can be applied in the context of DA in the way the above calculation presupposes.

Let's suppose for a moment that it can. What other assumptions does the argument use? Well, an assumption was made about the prior probabilities of H_1 and H_2. This assumption is no doubt incorrect, since there are other hypotheses that we want to assign non-zero probability. However, it is clear that choosing different values of the prior will not change the fact that hypotheses that postulate fewer observers will gain probability relative to hypotheses that postulate more observers.[4] The absolute posterior probabilities depend on the precise empirical prior, but the fact that there is this probability shift does not. Further, (#) is merely a formulation of Bayes' theorem. So once we have the empirical priors and the conditional probabilities, the prediction follows mathematically.

The premise that bears the responsibility for the surprising conclusion is that SSA can be applied to justify these conditional probabilities. Can it?

Recall that we argued for Model 2 in version I of *Incubator* in chapter 4. If DA could be assimilated to this case, it would be justified to the extent that Model 2 is justified. The cases are in some ways similar, but there are also differences. The question is whether the differences are relevant. In this section, we shall examine whether the arguments that were made in favor of Model 2 can be adapted to support DA. We will find that there are significant disanalogies between the two cases. It might be possible to bridge these disanalogies, but until that is done the attempt to support the assumptions of DA by assimilating it to something like Model 2 remains inconclusive. This is not to say that the similarities between the two cases cannot be *persuasive* for some people. So this section is neither an attack on nor a defense of DA. (On the other hand, in chapter 9 we will find that the reasoning used in

---

[4] Provided, of course, that the prior probabilities are non-trivial, i.e. not equal to zero for all but one hypothesis. But that is surely a very reasonable assumption. The probabilities in questions are subjective probabilities, credences, and I for one am uncertain about how many humans there will have been in total; my prior is smeared out—non-zero—over a wide range of possibilities.

Model 2 leads to quite strongly counterintuitive results, and in chapter 10 we will develop a new way of thinking about cases like *Incubator* that need not lead to DA-like conclusions. Those results will suggest that even if we are persuaded that DA could be assimilated to Model 2, we may still not accept DA because we reject Model 2!)

One argument that was used to justify Model 2 for *Incubator* was that if you had at first been ignorant of the color of your beard, and you had assigned probabilities to all the hypotheses in this state of ignorance, and you then received information about your beard color and updated your beliefs using Bayesian conditionalization, then you would end up with the probability assignments that Model 2 prescribes. This line of reasoning does not presuppose that you actually were, at some point in time, ignorant of your beard color. Rather, considering what you would have thought if you had been once ignorant of your beard color is merely a way of clarifying your current conditional probabilities of being in a certain room given a certain outcome of the coin flip in *Incubator*.

I hasten to stress that I'm not suggesting a counterfactual analysis as a general account of conditional degrees of belief. I am not saying that $P(e|h)$ should in general be indentified with the credence you would have assigned to e had you not known whether e but known that h. A solution to the so-called Old evidence problem (see e.g. (Eells 1990; Howson 1991; Schlesinger 1991; Earman 1992; Achinstein 1993)) no doubt requires a much more complicated account than that. Nonetheless, thinking in terms of such counterfactuals can in *some* cases be a useful way of getting clearer about what your subjective probabilities are. Take the following case.

> Two indistinguishable urns are placed in front of Mr. Simpson. He is credibly informed that one of them contains ten balls and the other a million balls, but he is ignorant as to which is which. He knows the balls in each urn are numbered consecutively 1, 2, 3, 4… and so on. Simpson flips a coin, which he is convinced is fair, and based on the outcome he selects one of the urns—as it happens, the left one. He picks a ball at random from this urn. It is ball number 7. Clearly, this is a strong indication that the left urn contains only ten balls. If originally the odds were fifty-fifty (which is reasonable given that the urn was selected randomly), a swift application of Bayes' theorem gives the posterior probability: P(Left urn contains 10 balls | Sample ball is #7) = 99.999%.
>
> Simpson, however, had never much of a proclivity for cognitive exertions. When he picks the ball number 7 and is asked to give his odds for that urn being the one with only ten balls, he says: "D'oh, fifty-fifty!"

Before Mr. Simpson stakes his wife's car on these inclement odds, what can we say to him to help him come to his senses? When we start explaining about conditional probabilities, Simpson decides to stick to his guns rather than admit that his initial response is incorrect. He accepts Bayes' theorem, and he accepts that the probability that the ten-ball urn would be selected by the coin toss was 50%. What he refuses to accept is that the conditional probability of selecting ball number 7 is one in ten (one in a million), given that the urn contains ten (one million) balls. Instead he thinks that there was a 50% probability of selecting ball number 7 on each hypothesis about the total number of balls in the urn. Or maybe he declares that he simply doesn't have any such conditional credence.

One way to proceed from here is to ask Simpson, "What probability would you have assigned to the sample you have just drawn being number 7 if you hadn't yet looked at it but you knew that it had been picked from the urn with ten balls?" Suppose Simpson says, "One in ten." We may then appropriately ask, "So why then does not your conditional probability of picking number 7 given that the urn contains ten balls equal one in ten?"

There are at least two kinds of reasons that one could give to justify a divergence of one's conditional probabilities from what one thinks one would have believed in a corresponding counterfactual situation. First, one may think that one would have been irrational in the counterfactual situation. What one thinks one would have believed in a counterfactual situation in which one was drugged into a state of irrationality is usually irrelevant for the purpose of determining one's current conditional credences.[5] In the case of Simpson, this response is unavailable, because Simpson does not believe he would have been irrational in the counterfactual situation where he hadn't yet observed the number on the selected ball; in fact (let's suppose) Simpson thinks that in the counterfactual situation, he would have believed precisely that which it would have been rational for him to believe.

A second reason for divergence is if the counterfactual situation (where one doesn't know that *e*) doesn't exactly "match" the conditional probability $P(h \mid e)$ being assessed. The corresponding counterfactual situation might contain features—other than one's not knowing that *e*—that would rationally influence one's degree of belief in *h*. For instance, suppose we add the following feature to the example: Simpson has been credibly informed at the beginning of the experiment that *if* there is a gap in time (*"Delay"*) between the selection of the ball and his observing what number it is (so that he has the opportunity to be for a while in a state of ignorance as to the number of the selected ball), *then* the experiment has been rigged in such a way that he was bound to have selected either ball number 6 or 7. Then in the counterfactual situation where Simpson is ignorant of the number on the selected ball, *Delay* would be true; and Simpson would have known that. In the counterfactual situation he would therefore have had the additional information that the experiment was rigged (an event to which, we can

---

[5] One obvious exception is in evaluating hypotheses *about how one would behave if one were drugged,* etc.

assume, he assigned a low prior probability). Clearly, what he would have thought in that counterfactual situation does not determine the value that he should, in the actual case, assign to the conditional probability $P(h \mid e)$, since in the actual case (where *Delay* is false) he does not have that extra piece of information. (What he thinks he would have thought in the counterfactual situation would rather be relevant to what value he should now give to the conditional probability $P(h \mid e\&Delay)$; but that is not what he needs to know in the present case.)

This second source of divergence suggests a more general limitation of the counterfactual-test of what your current conditional probabilities should be. In many cases, there is no clearly defined, unique situation that would have obtained if you had not known some data that you in fact know. There are many ways of not knowing something. Take "the counterfactual situation" where you don't know whether there have ever been any clouds in the sky. Is that a situation where you have never been outdoors and don't know whether there is a sky? Or is it a situation where you don't know what condensation is? Or perhaps a situation where you are unsure about whether the fluffy things you see up there are really clouds rather than, say, large chunks of cotton candy? It seems clear that we have not specified the hypothetical state of "you not knowing whether clouds have ever existed in the sky" sufficiently to get an unambiguous answer to what else you would or would not believe if you were in that situation.

In *some* cases, however, the counterfactual situation *is* sufficiently specified. Take the original case with Mr. Simpson again (where there is no complication such as the selection potentially being rigged). Is there a counterfactual situation that we can point to as the counterfactual situation that Simpson would be in if he didn't know the number on the selected ball? It seems there is. Suppose that in the actual course of the experiment there was a one-minute interval of ignorance between Simpson's selecting a ball and his looking to see what number it was. Suppose that during this minute Simpson contemplated his probability assignments to the various hypotheses and reached a reflective equilibrium. Then one can plausibly maintain that, at the later stage when Simpson has looked at the ball and knows its number, what he *would have* rationally believed if he didn't know its number is what he *did* in fact believe a moment earlier before he learned what the number was. Moreover, even if, in fact, there never was an interval of ignorance where Simpson didn't know that *e*, it can still make sense to ask what he would have thought if there *had* been one. At least in this kind of example, there is a suitably definite counterfactual from which we can read off the conditional probability $P(h \mid e)$ that Simpson was once implicitly committed to.

If this is right, then there are at least some cases where $P(h \mid e)$ can be meaningfully assigned a non-trivial probability even if there never was any time when *e* was not known. The "Old evidence problem" retains its bite in the general case, but in some special cases it can be tamed. This is indeed what one should have expected, since otherwise the Bayesian method could never be applied except in cases where one had *in advance* contemplated and assigned probabilities to all relevant hypotheses and possible evidence. That would fly in the face of the fact that we are often able to plausibly model the evidential bearing of old evidence on new hypotheses within in the Bayesian framework.

Returning now to the *Incubator* (version I) gedanken, recall that it was not assumed that there actually was a point in time when the people created in the rooms were ignorant about the color of their beards. They popped into existence, we could suppose, right in front of the mirror and gradually formed a system of beliefs as they reflected on their circumstances.[6] Nonetheless, we can use an argument involving a counterfactual situation where they were ignorant about their beard color to motivate a particular choice of conditional probability.

Let's look more closely at how this can be done. Let I be the set of all information that you have received up to the present time. I can be decomposed in various ways. For example, if I is logically equivalent to $I_1\&I_2$ then I can be decomposed into I_1 and I_2. You currently have some credence function that specifies your present degree of belief in various hypotheses (conditional or otherwise), and this credence is conditionalized on the background information I. Call this credence function C_I. But although this is the credence function you have, it may not be the credence function you ought to have. You may have failed to understand all the probabilistic connections among the facts that you have learnt. Let C_I^* be a rival credence function, conditionalized on the same information I. The task is now to determine whether on reflection you ought to switch to C_I^* or stick with C_I.

The relation to DA should be clear. C_I can be thought of as your credence function before you heard about DA; C_I^*, the credence function that the proponent of DA (the "doomsayer") seeks to persuade you to adopt. Both these functions are based on the same background information I, which includes everything you have learnt up until now. What the doomsayer argues is not that she can give you some new piece of relevant information that you didn't have before, but rather that she can point out a probabilistic implication of information you already have that you hitherto has failed to fully realize or take into account—in other words, that you have been in error in your assessment of the probabilistic bearing of your evidence on hypotheses about how long the human species will last. How can she go about that? Since, presumably, you haven't made any explicit calculations to decide what credence to attach to these hypotheses, she cannot point to any mistakes that you've made in some mathematical derivation.

---

[6] That this is possible is not entirely uncontroversial. Some hold the view that knowledge requires that the knower and her epistemic faculties have a particular kind of causal origin. For the purposes of the present investigation, we can set such scruples aside.

But here is one method she *can* use. She can specify some decomposition of your evidence into I_1 and I_2. She can then ask you what you think you ought to have rationally believed if all the information you had were I_1 (and you didn't know I_2). (This thought operation involves reference to a counterfactual situation, and, as we saw above, whether such a procedure is legitimate depends on the particulars; sometimes it works, sometimes it doesn't. Let's assume for the moment that it works in the present case.) What she is asking for, thus, is what credence function C_{I1} you think you ought to have had if your total information were I_1. In particular, C_{I1} assigns values to certain conditional probabilities of the form $C_{I1}(*|I_2)$. This means we can then use Bayes' theorem to conditionalize on I_2 and update the credence function. If the result of this updating is C_I^*, then she will have shown that you are committed to jettisoning your present credence function C_I and replacing it with C_I^* (provided you choose to adhere to $C_{I1}(*|I_2)$ even after realizing that this obligates you to change C_I). For C_I and C_I^* are based on the same information, and you have just acknowledged that you think that if you were ignorant of I_2 you should set your credence equal to C_{I1}, which results in C_I^* when conditionalized on I_2. One may summarize this, roughly, by saying that the order in which you choose to consider the evidence should not make any difference to the probability assignment you end up with.[7]

This method can be applied to the case of Mr. Simpson. I_1 is all the information he would have had up to the time when the ball was selected from the urn. I_2 is the information that this ball is number 7. If Simpson firmly maintains that what would have been rational for him to believe had he not known the number of the selected ball (i.e. if his information were I_1) is that the conditional probability of the selected ball being number 7 given that the selected urn contains ten balls (a million balls) is one in ten (one in a million), then we can show that his present credence function ought to assign a 99.999% credence to the hypothesis that the left urn, the urn from which the sample was taken, contains only ten balls.

In order for the doomsayer to use the same method to convince somebody who resists DA on the grounds that the conditional probabilities used in DA do not agree with his actual conditional probabilities, she'd have to define some counterfactual situation S such that the following holds:

(1) In S he does not know his birth rank.
(2) The probabilities assumed in DA are the probabilities he now thinks that it would be rational for him to have in S.

---

[7] Subject to the obvious restriction that none of the hypotheses under consideration is about the order in which you consider the evidence. For instance, the probability you assign to the hypothesis "I considered evidence e_1 before I considered evidence e_2." is not independent of the order in which you consider the evidence!

(3) His present information is logically equivalent to the information he would have in *S* conjoined with information about his birth
rank (modulo information which he thinks is irrelevant to the case
at hand).

The probabilities referred to in (2) are of two sorts. There are the "empirical"
probabilities that DA uses—the ordinary kind of estimates of the risks of
germ warfare, asteroid impact, abuse of military nanotechnology, etc. And
then there are the conditional probabilities of having a particular birth rank
given a particular hypothesis about the total number of humans that will
have lived. The conditional probabilities presupposed by DA are the ones
given by applying SSA to that situation. *S* should therefore ideally be a situation where he possesses all the evidence he actually has which is relevant
to establishing the empirical prior probabilities, but where he lacks any indication as to what his birth rank is.

Can such a situation *S* be conceived? That is what is unclear. Spot the flaw
in the following beguiling but unworkable argument:

> *An erroneous argument*
> What if we in actual fact don't know our birth ranks, even approxi-
> mately? What if we actually *are* in a situation *S* that is characterized
> by precisely the sort of partial ignorance that the argument urging a
> DA-like choice of conditional probabilities presupposes? "But," you
> object, "didn't you say that our birth ranks are about 60 billion? If I
> know that this is (approximately) the truth, how can I be ignorant
> about my birth rank?"
>
> Well, what I said was that your birth rank *in the human species*
> is about 60 billion. Yet that does not imply that your birth rank *sim-
> pliciter* is anywhere near 60 billion. There could be other intelligent
> species in the universe, extraterrestrials who count as observers,
> and I presume you would not assert with any confidence that your
> birth rank *within this larger group* is about 60 billion. You presum-
> ably agree that you are highly uncertain about your relative tempo-
> ral position in the set of all observers in the cosmos, if there are
> many alien civilizations out there.
>
> Now, if you go back and re-examine the arguments that were
> given in chapters 4 and 5, you will find that they can be adapted to
> show that intelligent aliens should be included in the reference
> class to which SSA is applied, at least if they are not too different
> from human observers. Indeed, the arguments that were based on
> how SSA seems to be the most plausible way of deriving observa-
> tional predictions from multiverse theories and of making sense of
> the objection against Boltzmann's attempted explanation of the
> arrow of time *presuppose* such an inclusive reference class. And the
> arguments that were based on the thought experiments can easily

be adapted to include extraterrestrials—draw antennas on some of the people in the illustrations, adjust the terminology accordingly, and these arguments go through as before.

We should consequently propose for Mr. Simpson's consideration (who now plays the role of a skeptic about DA) the following hypothetical situation S (which might be a counterfactual situation or a situation that will actually occur in the future): Scientists report having obtained evidence strongly favoring the disjunction $h_1 \vee h_2$, where h_1 is the hypothesis that our species is the only intelligent life-form in the world, and h_2 is the hypothesis that our species is one out of a total of one million intelligent species throughout spacetime, each of which is pretty much like our own in terms of its nature and population size. Mr. Simpson knows what his birth rank would be given h_1, namely 60 billion; but he does not know, even approximately, what his birth rank would be given h_2.

By considering various sequences of additional incoming evidence favoring either h_1 or h_2, we can thus probe how Simpson does or does not take into account the information about his birth rank in evaluating hypotheses about how long the human species will last.

Suppose first that evidence comes in strongly favoring h_2. We then have a situation S satisfying the three criteria listed above. Mr. Simpson acknowledges that he is ignorant about his birth rank, and so he now thinks that in this situation it would be rational for him to apply SSA. This gives him the conditional probabilities required by DA. The empirical priors are, let us assume, not substantially affected by the information favoring h_2, so they are the same in S as they are in his actual situation.

Suppose, finally, that scientists a while later and contrary to expectation obtain new evidence that very strongly favors h_1. When Simpson learns about this, his evidence becomes equivalent to the information he has in the actual situation (where we assume that Simpson does not believe there are any extraterrestrials). All the input needed by the DA-calculation has now been supplied, and Bayes' theorem yields a posterior probability (that is properly conditionalized on all available information, including the indexical information about Simpson's birth rank). This posterior reflects the probability shift in favor of hypotheses of impending doom, which Simpson and other DA-skeptics had thought they could avoid.

It could seem as if this argument has successfully described a hypothetical situation S that satisfies criteria (1)–(3) and thus verifies DA. Not so.

The weakness of the scenario is that although Simpson doesn't know even approximately what his birth rank is in S, he still knows in S his *relative* rank within the human species: he knows that he is about the 60 billionth human.

Thus, the option remains for Simpson to maintain that when he applies SSA, he should assign probabilities that are invariant between various specifications of our species' position among all the extraterrestrial species—since he is ignorant about that—but that the probabilities should not be uniform over various positions within the human species—since he is not ignorant about that. For example, if we suppose that the various species are temporally non-overlapping so that they exist one after another, then he might assign a probability close to one that his absolute birth rank is either about 60 billion, or about 120 billion, or about 180 billion, or... Suppose this is what he now thinks it would be rational for him to do in *S*. Then the DA-calculation does not get the conditional probabilities it needs in order to produce the intended conclusion, and DA fails. For after conditioning on the strong evidence for b_1, the conditional probability of having a birth rank of roughly 60 billion will be the same given any of the hypotheses about the total size of the human species that he might entertain.

It might be possible to find some other hypothetical situation *S* that would really satisfy the three constraints, and that could thereby serve to compel a person like Simpson to adopt the conditional probabilities that DA requires.[8] But unless and until such a situation is described (or some other argument is provided for why we should accept those probabilities), this is a loose end to which those may gladly cling whose intuitions do not drive them to adopt the requisite probabilities without argument.

LESLIE'S VIEWS ON THE REFERENCE CLASS PROBLEM

Returning to problem of the reference class (the class from which one should reason as if one were randomly selected), let's consider what John Leslie has to say on the topic. As a first remark, Leslie suggests that "perhaps nothing too much hangs on it." ((Leslie 1996), p. 257):

> [DA] can give us an important warning even if we confine our attention to the human race's chances of surviving for the next few centuries. All the signs are that these centuries would be heavily populated if the race met with no disaster, and they are centuries during which there would presumably be little chance of transferring human thought-processes to machines in a way which would encourage people to call the machines 'human'. (Leslie 1996), p. 258

There are two problems with this reply. First, the premise that there is little chance of creating machines with human-level thought processes within the next few centuries is a claim that many of those who have thought seri-

---

[8] In order for *S* to do this, it would have to be the case that the subject decides to retain his initial views about *S* even after it is pointed out to him that those views commit him to accepting the DA-conclusion given he accepts Model 2 for *Incubator*. Some might elect to revise their views about a situation *S,* which *prima facie* satisfies the three conditions, rather than to change their minds about DA.

ously about these things disagree with. Many thinkers in this field believe that these developments will happen within the first half of the present century (e.g. (Drexler 1985; Moravec 1989, 1998, 1999; Minsky 1994; Bostrom 1998; Kurzweil 1999)). Second, the comment does nothing to allay the suspicion that the difficulty of determining an appropriate reference class might be symptomatic of an underlying ill in DA itself.

Leslie proceeds, however, to offer a positive proposal for how to settle the question of which reference class to choose. The first part of this proposal is best understood by expanding our urn analogy in which we previously made the acquaintance of Mr. Simpson. Suppose that the balls in the urns come in different colors (while still being numbered consecutively as before). Your task is to guess how many red balls there are in the left urn. Now, "red" is a vague concept; when does red become orange, brown, purple, or pink? This vagueness could be seen as corresponding to the vagueness about what to classify as an observer for the purposes of DA. So, if some vagueness like this is present in the urn example, does that mean that the Bayesian induction used in the original example can no longer be made to work?

By no means. The right response in this case is that you get to choose how you define the reference class. The choice depends on what hypothesis you are interested in testing. Suppose that you want to know how many balls there are in the urn of the color faint-pink-to-dark-purple. Then all you have to do is to classify the random sample you select as being either faint-pink-to-dark-purple or not faint-pink-to-dark-purple. Once the classification is made, the calculation proceeds as before. If instead you are interested in knowing how many faint-pink-to-medium-red balls there are, then you classify the sample according to whether it has *that* property, and proceed as before. The Bayesian apparatus is neutral as to how you define hypotheses. There is no right or wrong way, just different questions you might be interested in asking.

Applying this idea to DA, Leslie writes:

> The moral could seem to be that one's reference class might be made more or less what one liked for doomsday argument purposes. What if one wanted to count our much-modified descendants, perhaps with three arms or with godlike intelligence, as 'genuinely human'? There would be nothing wrong with this. Yet if we were instead interested in the future only of two-armed humans, or of humans with intelligence much like that of humans today, then there would be nothing wrong in refusing to count any others. (Leslie 1996), p. 260

This passage seems to suggest that if we are interested in the survival-prospects of just a special kind of observers, we are entitled to apply DA to this subset of the reference class. Suppose you are a person with hemophilia and you want to know how many hemophiliacs there will have been. Solution: Count the number of hemophiliacs that have existed before you and use the DA-style calculation to update your prior probabilities (given by ordinary empirical considerations) to take account of the fact that this random sample from the set of all hemophiliacs—*you*—turned out to be living when just so many hemophiliacs had already been born.

How far can one push this mode of reasoning though, before crashing into absurdity? If the reference class is defined to consist of all those people who were born on the same day as you or later, then you should expect doom to strike quite soon. Worse still, let's say you want to know how many people there will have been with the property of being born either on the day when you were born or after the year 2002. If humans continue to be sired after the year 2002, you will become "improbably early" in this "reference class" alarmingly soon. Should you therefore have to conclude that humankind is likely to go extinct in the first few months of 2003? Crazy!

How can the doomsayer avoid this conclusion? According to Leslie, by adjusting the prior probabilities in a suitable way, a trick that he says was suggested to him by Carter ((Leslie 1996), p. 262). Leslie thinks that defining the reference class as humans-born-as-late-as-you-or-later is fine and that ordinary inductive knowledge will make the priors so low that no absurd consequences will follow:

> No inappropriately frightening doomsday argument will result from narrowing your reference class . . . provided you adjust your prior probabilities accordingly. Imagine that you'd been born knowing all about Bayesian calculations and about human history. The prior probability of the human race ending in the very week you were born ought presumably to have struck you as extremely tiny. And that's quite enough to allow us to say the following: that although, if the human race had been going to last for another century, people born in the week in question would have been exceptionally early in the class of those-born-either-in-that-week-or-in-the-following-century, this would have been a poor reason for you to expect the race to end in that week, instead of lasting for another century. (Leslie 1996), p. 262

But alas, it is a vain hope that the prior will cancel out the distortions of a gerrymandered reference class. Suppose that you are convinced that the population of beings who know that Francis Crick and James Watson discovered the structure of DNA will go extinct no sooner and no later than the human species. You want to evaluate the hypothesis that this will occur before the year 2100. Based on ordinary empirical considerations, you assign, say, a 25% credence to this hypothesis. The doomsayer then presents you with DA. Now, should you use the reference class consisting of human beings, or the reference class consisting of human beings who know that Francis Crick and James Watson discovered the structure of DNA? You get a different posterior probability for the hypothesis depending on which of these reference classes you use. The problem is not that you have chosen the wrong prior probability, one giving "too frightening" a conclusion when used with the latter reference class. The problem is that for any prior probability, you get many different—incompatible—predictions depending on which reference class you use.

Of course, it is trivially true that given any non-trivial reference class one can always pick some numbers such that when one plugs them into Bayes' formula together with the conditional probabilities based on that chosen reference class, one gets any posterior probability function one pleases. But these numbers one plugs in will not in general be one's prior probabilities. They'll just be arbitrary numbers of no significance or relevance.

The example in which a hemophiliac applies DA to predict how many hemophiliacs there will have been may at first sight appear to work quite well and to be no more implausible than applying DA to predict the total number of observers. Yet it would be a mistake to take this as evidence that the reference class varies depending on what one is trying to predict. If the hemophiliac example has an air of plausibility, it is only because one tacitly assumes that the hemophiliac population constitutes a roughly constant fraction of the human population. Suppose one thinks otherwise. Genetic treatments for hemophilia being currently in clinical trial, one may speculate that one day a germ-line therapy will be used to eliminate the hemophiliac type from the human gene pool, long before the human species goes extinct. Does a hemophiliac reading these lines have especially strong reason for thinking that the speculation will come true, on grounds that it would make her position within the class of all hemophiliacs that will ever have lived more probable than the alternative hypothesis, that hemophilia will always be a part of the human condition? It would seem not.

So the idea that it doesn't matter how we define the reference class because we can compensate by adjusting the priors is misconceived. We saw in chapter 4 that your reference class must not be too wide. It can't include rocks, for example. Now we have seen that it must not be too narrow either, such as by excluding everybody born before yourself. We also know a given person at a given time cannot have multiple reference classes for the same application of DA-reasoning, on pain of incoherence. Between these constraints there is still ample space for divergent definitions, which further studies may or may not further restrict. (We shall suggest in chapter 10 that there is an ineludible subjective component in a thinker's choice of reference class, and moreover that the same thinker can legitimately use different reference classes at different times.)

ALTERNATIVE CONCLUSIONS OF DA

It should be pointed out that *even if* DA were basically correct, there would still be room for other interpretations of the result than that humankind is likely to go extinct soon. For example, one may think that:

• The priors are so low that even after a substantial probability shift in favor of earlier doom, we remain likely to survive for quite a while.

• The size of the human population will decrease in the future; this reconciles DA with even extremely long survival of the human species.

• Humans evolve (or we reengineer ourselves using advanced technology) into "posthumans", who belong in a different reference class than humans. All that DA would show in this case is that the posthuman transition is likely to happen before there have been vastly more humans than have lived to date.

• There will be infinitely many humans, in which case it is unclear what DA amounts to. In some sense, each observer would be "infinitely early" if there are infinitely many.[9]

A better way of expressing what DA aims to show is therefore as a disjunction of possibilities rather than as the simple statement "Doom will probably strike soon." Of course, even this more ambiguous prediction would be a remarkable result from both a practical and a philosophical perspective.

Bearing in mind that we understand by DA the general form of reasoning described in this chapter, one that is not necessarily wedded to the prediction that doomsday is impending, let us consider some objections from the recent literature.

---

[9] Further, John Leslie thinks that DA is seriously weakened if the world is indeterministic. I don't accept that that would be the case.

CHAPTER 7

Invalid Objections Against the Doomsday Argument[1]

It would probably not be an exaggeration to say that I have encountered over a hundred objections against DA in the literature and in personal communication, many of them mutually inconsistent. Even merging those objections that use the same basic idea would leave us with dozens of distinct and often incompatible explanations of what is wrong with DA. The authors of these refutations frequently seem extremely confident that they have discovered the true reason why DA fails, at least until a doomsayer gets an opportunity to reply. It is as if DA is so counterintuitive (or threatening?) that people reckon that *every* criticism must be valid.

Rather than aiming for completeness, we shall select a limited number of objections for critical examination. We want to choose those that seem currently alive, or have made their entrée recently, or that have a Phoenix-like tendency to keep reemerging from their own ashes. While the objections studied in this chapter are unsuccessful, they do have the net effect of forcing us to become clearer about what DA does and doesn't imply.[2]

DOESN'T THE DOOMSDAY ARGUMENT FAIL TO "TARGET THE TRUTH"?

Kevin Korb and Jonathan Oliver propose a minimalist constraint that any good inductive method should satisfy (Korb and Oliver 1999a):

---

[1] This chapter is partly based on a paper previously published in *Mind* (Bostrom 1999); those bits are reproduced here with permission.

[2] For some other objections against DA, see e.g. (Dieks 1992, 1999; Eckhardt 1992, 1993; Buch 1994; Goodman 1994; Kopf, Krtous et al. 1994; Mackay 1994; Tipler 1994; Delahaye 1996; Oliver and Korb 1997; Tännsjö 1997; Franceschi 1998; Smith 1998; Bartha and Hitchcock 1999; Franceschi 1999; Greenberg 1999; Caves 2000), and for replies to some of these, see e.g. (Leslie 1992, 1993, 1996; Gott 1994).

Targeting Truth (TT) Principle: No good inductive method should—in this world—provide no more guidance to the truth than does flipping a coin. (p. 404)

DA, they claim, violates this principle. In support of their claim they ask us to consider

a population of size 1000 (i.e., a population that died out after a total of 1000 individuals) and retrospectively apply the Argument to the population when it was of size 1, 2, 3 and so on. Assuming that the Argument supports the conclusion that the total population is bounded by two times the sample value . . . then 499 inferences using the Doomsday Argument form are wrong and 501 inferences are right, which we submit is a lousy track record for an inductive inference schema. Hence, in a perfectly reasonable metainduction we should conclude that there is something very wrong with this form of inference. (p. 405)

But in this purported counterexample to DA, the TT principle is *not* violated—501 right and 499 wrong guesses is strictly better than what one would expect from a random procedure such as flipping a coin. The reason why the track record is only marginally better than chance is simply that the above example assumes that the doomsayers bet on the most stringent hypothesis that they would be willing to bet on at even odds, i.e. that the total population is bounded by two times the sample value. This means, of course, that their expected gain is minimal. It is not remarkable, then, that *in this case,* a person who applies the Doomsday reasoning is only slightly better off than one who doesn't. If the bet were on the proposition not that the total population is bounded by two times the sample value but instead that it is bounded by, say, three times the sample value, the doomsayer's advantage would be more drastic. And the doomsayer can be even more confident that the total value will not exceed thirty times the sample value.

Additionally, Korb and Oliver's example assumes that the doomsayer doesn't take any additional information into account when making her prediction. But as we saw in the previous chapter, there is no basis for that assumption. All relevant information can and should be incorporated. (One of the failings of Gott's version of DA was that it failed to do so, but that's just a reason not to accept that version.) If the doomsayer has information about other things than her birth rank, she can do even better.

Therefore, Korb and Oliver have not shown that DA violates the TT principle, nor that the Doomsday reasoning at best improves the chances of being right only slightly.[3]

---

[3] In a response to criticism, Korb and Oliver make two comments. "(A) The minimal advantage over random guessing in the example can be driven to an arbitrarily small level simply by increasing the population in the example." (Korb and Oliver 1999b), p. 501. This misses the

THE "BABY-PARADOX"

As first noted by the French mathematician Jean-Paul Delahaye in an unpublished manuscript (Delahaye 1996), the basic Doomsday argument form can seem to be applicable not only to the survival of the human race but also to your own life span. A second objection by Korb and Oliver picks up on this idea:

> [I]f you number the minutes of your life starting from the first minute you were aware of the applicability of the Argument to your life span to the last such minute and if you then attempt to estimate the number of the last minute using your current sample of, say, one minute, then according to the Doomsday Argument, you should expect to die before you finish reading this article. (p. 405)

The claim is untrue. The Doomsday argument form, applied to your own life span, does not imply that you should expect to die before you have finished reading their article. DA says that in some cases you can reason as if you were a sample drawn randomly from a certain reference class. Taking into account the information conveyed by this random sample, you are to update your beliefs in accordance with Bayes' theorem. This may cause a shift in your probability assignments in favor of hypotheses that imply that your position in the human race will have been fairly typical—say among the middle 98% rather than in the first or the last percentile of all humans that will ever have been born. DA just says you should make this Bayesian shift in your probabilities; it does not by itself determine the absolute probabilities that you end up with. As we emphasized in the last chapter, what probability assignment you end up with depends on your prior, i.e. the probability assignment you started out with before taking DA into account.

---

point, which was that the doomsayer's gain was small because she was assumed to bet at the worst odds on which she is would be willing to bet—which per definition entails that she'd not expect to benefit significantly from the scheme but which is, of course, perfectly consistent with her doing much better than someone who doesn't accept the "DA" in this example.

I quote the second comment in its entirety:

> (B) Dutch book arguments are quite rightly founded on what happens to an incoherent agent who accepts any number of "fair" bets. The point in those arguments is not, as some have confusedly thought, that making such a series of bets is being assumed always to be rational; rather, it is that the subsequent guaranteed losses appear to be attributable only to the initial incoherence. In the case of the Doomsday Argument (DA), it matters not if Doomsayers can protect their interests by refraining from some bets that their principles advise them are correct, and only accepting bets that appear to give them a whopping advantage: the point is that their principles are advising them wrongly. (p. 501)

To the extent that I can understand this objection, it fails. Dutch book arguments are supposed to show that the victim is bound to lose money. In Korb and Oliver's example, the "victim" is expected to gain money.

In the case of the survival of the human race, your prior may be based on your estimates of the risk that we will be extinguished through nuclear war, germ warfare, self-replicating nanomachines, a meteor impact, etc. In the case of your own life expectancy, you will want to consider factors such as the average human life span, your state of health, and any hazards in your environment that may cause your demise before you finish the article. Based on such considerations, the probability that you will die within the next half-hour ought presumably to strike you as extremely small. If so, then even a considerable probability shift due to a DA-like inference should not make you expect to die before reaching the last line. Hence, contra Korb and Oliver, the doomsayer would not draw the absurd conclusion that she is likely to perish within half an hour, even should she think the Doomsday argument form applicable to her individual life span.

While this is enough to refute the objection, a more fundamental question here is whether (and if so, how) the Doomsday argument form is applicable to individual life spans at all. I think we concede too much if we grant even a modest probability shift in this case. There are two reasons for this.

First, Korb and Oliver's application of the Doomsday argument form to individual life spans presupposes a specific solution to the problem of the reference class. This is the problem, remember, of determining what class of entities from which one should consider oneself a random sample. As we are dealing with temporal parts of observers here, we have to invoke SSSA, the version of SSA adapted to observer-moments rather than observes that we alluded to in the section on traffic analysis and which we will discuss more fully in chapter 10. Korb and Oliver's objection presupposes a particular choice of reference class: the one consisting of those and only those observer-moments that are aware of DA. This may not be the most plausible choice. Certainly, Korb and Oliver do not seek to justify it in any way.

The second reason for the doomsayer not to grant a probability shift in the present case is that the *no-outsider requirement* is not satisfied. The no-outsider requirement states that in applying SSA there must be no outsiders—beings who are ignored in the reasoning but who really belong in the reference class. Applying SSA in the presence of such outsiders will in many cases yield erroneous results.[4]

Consider first the original application of DA (to the survival of the human species). Suppose you were certain that there is extraterrestrial intelligent life. You know that there are a million "small" civilizations that will have contained 200 billion persons each and a million "large" civilizations that will have

---

[4] John Leslie argues against the no-outsider requirement (e.g. (Leslie 1996), pp. 229-30). I believe that he is mistaken for the reasons given below. (I suspect that Leslie's thoughts on the no-outsider requirement derive from his views on the problem of the reference class, which we criticized in the previous chapter.)

contained 200 trillion persons each. You know that the human species is one of these civilizations but you don't know whether it is small or large.

To calculate the probability that doom will strike soon (i.e. that the human species is small), we can proceed in three steps:

Step 1. Estimate the empirical prior P(*Small*), i.e. how likely it seems that nanotech warfare etc. will put an end to our species before it gets large. At this stage you don't take into account any form of the Doomsday argument or anthropic reasoning.

Step 2. Now take account of the fact that most people find themselves in large civilizations. Let H be the proposition "I am a human.", and define the new probability function $P^*(\,.\,) = P(\,.\, \mid H)$, obtained by conditionalizing on H. By Bayes' theorem,

$$P^*(Small) = P(Small \mid H) = \frac{P(H \mid Small)P(Small)}{P(H)}.$$

A similar expression holds for ¬*Small*. By SSA, we have:

$$P(H \mid Small) = \frac{200billion}{(200billion + 200trillion) \times 1million},$$

and

$$P(H \mid \neg Small) = \frac{200trillion}{(200billion + 200trillion) \times 1million}.$$

(If we calculate $P^*(Small)$, we find that it is very small for any realistic prior. In other words, at this stage in the calculation, it looks as though the human species is very likely long-lasting.)

Step 3. Finally, we take account of DA. Let E be the proposition that you find yourself "early", i.e. that you are among the first 200 billion persons in your species. Conditionalizing on this evidence, we get the posterior probability function $P^{**}(\,.\,) = P^*(\,.\, \mid E)$. So

$$P^{**}(Small) = P^*(Small \mid E) = \frac{P^*(E \mid Small)P^*(Small)}{P^*(E)}.$$

Note that $P^*(E \mid Small) = 1$ and $P^*(E \mid \neg Small) = 1/1000$. By substituting back into the above expressions, it is then easy to verify that

$$\frac{P^{**}(Small)}{P^{**}(\neg Small)} = \frac{P(Small)}{P(\neg Small)} .$$

Thus we get back the empirical probabilities that we started from. DA (in Step 3) only served to cancel the effect that we took into account in Step 2, namely that you were more likely to turn out to be in the human species given that the human species is one of the large rather than one of the small civilizations. This shows that if we assume we know that there are both "large" and "small" extraterrestrial civilizations, and that we know their proportion—though the precise numbers in the above example don't matter—then the right probabilities are the ones given by the naïve empirical prior.[5] So in this instance, if we had ignored the extraterrestrials (thus violating the no-outsider requirement) and simply applied SSA with the human population as the reference class, we would have got an incorrect result.

It is worth emphasizing, however, that suspecting that there are extraterrestrial civilizations does *not* damage DA if we don't have any information about what fraction of these alien species are "small". What DA would do in this case (if the argument were sound in other respects) is give us reason to think that the fraction of small intelligent species is greater than was previously held on ordinary empirical grounds.

Returning to the case where you are supposed to apply DA to your own life span, we can now see that the no-outsider requirement is not satisfied. True, if you consider the epoch of your life during which you know about DA, and you partition this epoch into time-segments (observer-moments), then you might say that if you were to live for a long time then the present observer-moment would be extraordinary early in this class of observer-moments. You may thus be tempted to infer that you are likely to die soon (ignoring the difficulties pointed out earlier). But even if DA were applicable in that way, this would be the wrong conclusion. For in this case you have good reason for thinking there are many "outsiders". The outsiders are the observer-moments of other humans. What's more, you have detailed information about what fraction of these other humans are "short-lasting". Just as knowledge about the proportion of actually existing extraterrestrial civilizations that are small would annul the original DA, so in the present case does knowledge about the existence of other short-lived and long-lived

---

[5] This was first pointed out by Dieks in (Dieks 1992), and more explicitly in (Dieks 1999), and was later demonstrated by Kopf et al. (Kopf, Krtous et al. 1994). It appears to have been independently discovered by Bartha and Hitchcock (Bartha and Hitchcock 1999).

humans and about their approximate proportions cancel the probability shift favoring impending death. The fact that the present observer-moment belongs to you would indicate that you are an individual who will have contained many observer-moments rather than few, i.e. that you will be long-lived. It can then be shown (just as above) that this would counterbalance the fact that your present observer-moment would have been extraordinarily early among all your observer-moments were you to be long-lived.

To sum up, the "baby paradox"-objection fails to take prior probabilities into account. These would be extremely low for the hypothesis that you will die within the next thirty minutes. Therefore, contrary to what Korb and Oliver claim, even if the doomsayer thought DA applied to this case, she would not make the prediction that you will die within 30 minutes. However, the doomsayer should not apply DA to this case, for two reasons. First, it presupposes an arguably implausible solution to the reference class problem. Second, even if we accepted that only beings who know about DA should be in the reference class, and that it is legitimate to run the argument on time-segments of observers, the conclusion still does not follow, because the no-outsider requirement is violated.

ISN'T A SAMPLE SIZE OF ONE TOO SMALL?

Korb and Oliver have a third objection. It starts off with the claim that, in a Bayesian framework, a sample size of one is too small to make a substantial difference to one's rational beliefs.

> The main point . . . is quite simple: a sample size of one is "catastrophically" small. That is, whatever the sample evidence in this case may be, the prior distribution over population sizes is going to dominate the computation. The only way around this problem is to impose extreme artificial constraints on the hypothesis space. (p. 406)

They follow this assertion by conceding that in a case where the hypothesis space contains only two hypotheses, a substantial shift can occur:

> If we consider the two urn case described by Bostrom, we can readily see that he is right about the probabilities. (p. 406)

The probability in the example to which refer shifted from 50% to 99.999%, which is surely "substantial", and similar results would obtain for a broad range of prior distributions. But Korb and Oliver seem to think that such a substantial shift can only occur if we "impose extreme artificial constraints on the hypothesis space" by considering only two rival hypotheses rather than many more.

It is easy to see that this is false. Let $\{h_1, h_2, \ldots h_N\}$ be a hypothesis space and let P be any probability function that assigns a non-zero prior probability to all these hypotheses. Let h_i be the least likely of these hypotheses. Let e be the outcome of a single random sampling. Then it is easy to see, by inspecting Bayes' formula, that the posterior probability of h_i, $P(h_i|e)$, can be made arbitrarily big (≤ 1) by an appropriate choice of e:

$$P(h_i \mid e) = \frac{P(e \mid h_i)P(h_i)}{\sum_{1 \leq j \leq N} P(e \mid h_j)P(h_j)}.$$

Choosing e such that $P(e \mid h_j)$ is small for $j \neq i$, we have

$$P(h_i \mid e) \approx \frac{P(e \mid h_i)P(h_i)}{P(e \mid h_i)P(h_i)} = 1.$$

Indeed, we get $P(h_i|e) = 1$ if we choose e such that $P(e|h_j) = 0$ for $j \neq i$. This would, for example, correspond to the case where you discover that you have a birth rank of 200 billion and immediately give probability zero to all hypotheses according to which there would be less than 200 billion persons.

COULDN'T A CRO-MAGNON MAN HAVE USED THE DOOMSDAY ARGUMENT?

Indeed he could (provided Cro-Magnon minds could grasp the relevant concepts), and his predictions about the future prospects of his species would have failed. Yet it would be unfair to see this as an objection against DA. That a probabilistic method misleads observers in some exceptional circumstances does not mean that it should be abandoned. Looking at the overall performance of the DA-reasoning, we find that it does not do so badly. Ninety percent of all humans will be right if everybody guesses that they are not among the first tenth of all humans who will ever have lived (Gott's version). Allowing users to take into account additional empirical information can improve their guesses further (as in Leslie's version). Whether the resulting method is optimal for arriving at the truth is not something that we can settle trivially by pointing out that some people might be misled.

WE CAN MAKE THE EFFECT GO AWAY SIMPLY BY CONSIDERING A LARGER HYPOTHESIS SPACE

By increasing the number of hypotheses about the ultimate size of the human species that we choose to consider, we can, according to this objection, make the probability shift that DA induces arbitrarily small. Again, we can rely on Korb and Oliver for giving the idea a voice[6]:

> In any case, if an expected population size for homo sapiens … seems uncomfortably small, we can push the size up, and so the date of our collective extermination back, to an arbitrary degree simply by considering larger hypothesis spaces. (p. 408)

The argument is that if we use a uniform prior over the chosen hypothesis space $\{h_1, h_2, \ldots, h_n\}$, where h_i is the hypothesis that there will have existed a total of i humans, then the expected number of humans that will have lived will depend on n: the greater the value we give to n, the greater the expected future population. Korb and Oliver compute the expected size of the human population for some different values of n and find that the result does indeed vary.

Notice first of all that nowhere in this is there a reference to DA. If this argument were right it would work equally against *any* way of making predictions about how long the human species will survive. For example, if during the Cuba missile crisis you feared—based on obvious empirical factors—that humankind might soon go extinct, you really needn't have worried. You could just have considered a larger hypothesis space, thereby attaining an arbitrarily high degree of confidence that doom was not impending. If only saving the world were that easy!

What, then, is the right prior to use for DA? All we can say about this from a general philosophical point of view is that it is the same as the prior for people who don't believe in DA. The doomsayer does not face a special problem. The only legitimate way of providing the prior is through an empirical assessment of the potential threats to human survival. You need to base it on your best guesstimates about known hazards and dangers as yet unimagined.[7]

On a charitable reading, Korb and Oliver could perhaps be interpreted as saying not that DA fails because the prior is arbitrary, but rather that the uniform prior (with some big but finite cut-off) is as reasonable as any other prior, and that with such a prior, DA will not show that doom is likely to strike very soon. If this is all they mean then they are not saying something that the doomsayer could not agree with. The doomsayer is not committed to the view that doom is likely to strike soon[8], only to the view that the risk

---

[6] A similar objection had been made earlier by Dennis Dieks (Dieks 1992) and independently by John Eastmond (personal communication).

[7] For my views on what the most likely human extinction scenarios are and some suggestions for what could be done to reduce the risk, see (Bostrom 2002).

[8] To get the conclusion that doom is likely to happen soon (say within 200 years) you need to make additional assumptions about future population figures and the future risk profile for humankind.

that doom will strike soon is *greater* than was thought before we understood the probabilistic implications of our having relatively low birth ranks. DA (if sound) shows that we have systematically underestimated the risk of doom soon, but it doesn't directly imply anything about the absolute magnitude of the probability of that hypothesis. Even with a uniform prior probability, there will still be a *shift* in our credence in favor of earlier doom.

But don't Korb and Oliver's calculations at least show that this probability shift in favor of earlier doom is in reality quite *small*, so that DA isn't such a big deal after all? Not so.

As already mentioned, their calculations rest on the assumption of a uniform prior. Not only is this assumption gratuitous—no attempt is made to justify it—but it is also, I believe, highly implausible even as an approximation of the real empirical prior. To me it seems fairly obvious (quite apart from DA) that the probability that there will exist between 100 billion and 500 billion humans is much greater than the probability that there will exist between 10^{20} and $(10^{20} + 500$ billion) humans.[9]

Aren't we necessarily alive now?

> We are necessarily alive at the time we consider our position in human history, so the Doomsday Argument excludes from the selection pool everyone who is not alive now. (Greenberg 1999), p. 22

This objection, put forward by Mark Greenberg, is profiting from an ambiguity. Yes, it is necessary that if you are at time *t* considering your position in the human history then you are alive at time *t*. But no, it is not necessary that if you think "I am alive at time *t*" then you are alive at time *t*. You can be wrong about when you are alive, and hence you can also be ignorant about it.

The possibility of a state where one is ignorant about what time it is can be used as the runway for an argument showing that one's reference class can include observers existing at different times (cf. the Emeralds

---

[9] Even granting the uniform prior, it turns out that the probability shift is actually quite *big*. Korb and Oliver assume a uniform distribution over the hypothesis space $\{h_1, h_2, \ldots, h_{2,048}\}$ (where again h_i is the hypothesis that there will have been a total of *i* billion humans) and they assume that you are the 60 billionth human. Then the expected size of the human population, before considering, DA is $\frac{2,048 - 60}{2} \times 10^9 = 994$ billion. And Korb and Oliver's calculations show that, after applying DA, the expected population is 562 billion. The expected human population has been reduced by over 43% in their own example.

gedanken). Indeed, if the observers living at different times are in states that are subjectively indistinguishable from your own current state, so that you cannot tell which of these observers you are, then a strong case can be made that you are *rationally required* to include them all in your reference class. Leaving some out would mean assigning zero credence to a possibility (viz., your later discovering that you are one of the excluded observers) that you really have no ground for rejecting with such absolute conviction.

SLIDING REFERENCE OF "SOON" AND "LATE"?

> Even if someone who merely happens to live at a particular time could legitimately be treated as random with respect to birth rank, the Doomsday Argument would still fail, since, regardless of when that someone's position in human history is observed, he will always be in the same position relative to Doom Soon and Doom Delayed. (Greenberg 1999), p. 22

This difficulty is easily avoided by substituting specific hypotheses for "Doom Soon" and "Doom Delayed": e.g. "The total is 200 billions" and "The total is 200 trillions". (There are many more hypotheses we need to consider, but as argued above, we can simplify by focusing on two.) It is true that some DA-protagonists speak in terms of doom as coming "soon" or "late". This can cause confusion because under a non-rigid (incorrect) construal, which hypotheses are expressed by the phrases "Doom Soon" and "Doom Late" depends on whom they are uttered by. When there is doubt, speak in terms of specific numbers.

HOW COULD I HAVE BEEN A 16TH CENTURY HUMAN?

SSA does not imply that you could have been a 16th century human. We make no assumption as to whether there is a counterfactual situation or a possible world in which you are Leonardo da Vinci, or, for that matter, one of your contemporaries.

Even assuming that you take these past and present people to be in your reference class, what you are thereby committing yourself to is simply certain conditional credences. There is no obvious reason why this should compel you to hold as true (or even meaningful) counterfactuals about alternative identities that you could supposedly have had. The arguments for SSA didn't appeal to controversial metaphysics of personhood. We should therefore feel free to read it straightforwardly as a prescription for how to assign values to various conditional subjective probabilities—probabilities that must be given values *somehow* if the scientific and philosophical problems we have been discussing are to be modeled in a Bayesian framework.

DOESN'T YOUR THEORY PRESUPPOSE THAT WHAT HAPPENS IN CAUSALLY DISCONNECTED REGIONS AFFECTS WHAT HAPPENS HERE?

The theory of observation selection effects implies that your beliefs about distant parts of the universe—including ones that lie outside your past light cone—can in some cases influence what credence you should assign to hypotheses about events in your near surroundings. We can see this easily by considering, for example, that whether the no-outsider requirement is satisfied can depend on what is known about non-human observers elsewhere, including regions that are causally disconnected from ours. This, however, does *not* require that (absurdly) those remote galaxies and their inhabitants exert some sort of physical influence on you.[10] Such a physical effect would violate special relativity theory (and in any case it would be hard to see how it could help account for the systematic probabilistic dependencies that we are discussing).

To see why this "dependence on remote regions" is not a problem, it suffices to note that the probabilities our theory delivers are not physical chances but subjective credences. Those distant observers have zilch effect on the physical chances of events that take place on Earth. Rather, what holds is that under certain special circumstances, *your beliefs* about the distant observers could come to rationally affect *your beliefs* about a nearby coin toss, say.

We will see further (hypothetical) examples of this kind of epistemic dependencies in later thought experiments. In the real world, the most interesting dependencies of this kind are likely to emerge in scientific contexts, for instance when measuring cosmological theories against observation or when seeking to estimate the likelihood of intelligent life evolving on Earth-like planets.

The fact that our beliefs about the near are rationally correlated with our beliefs about the remote is itself utterly unremarkable. If it weren't so, you could never learn anything about distant places by studying your surroundings.

BUT WE KNOW SO MUCH MORE ABOUT OURSELVES THAN OUR BIRTH RANKS!

Here is one thought that frequently stands in the way of understanding of how observation selection effects work:

> "We know a lot more about ourselves than our birth ranks. Doesn't this mean that even though it may be correct to view oneself as a random sample from some suitable reference class if all one knows is one's birth rank, yet in the actual case, where we know so much more, it is not permissible to regard oneself as in any way random?"

---

[10] This objection is advanced in (Olum 2002).

This question insinuates that there is an incompatibility between being known and being random. That we know a lot about *x*, however, does not entail that *x* cannot be treated as a random sample.

A ball randomly selected from an urn with an unknown number of consecutively numbered balls remains random after you have looked at it and seen that it is ball number 7. If the sample ceased to be random when you looked at it, you wouldn't be able to make any interesting inferences about the number of balls remaining in the urn by studying the ball you've just picked out. Further, getting even more information about the ball, say by assaying its molecular structure under an atomic force microscope, would not in any way diminish its randomness. What you get is simply information *about* the random sample. Likewise, you can and do know much more about yourself than when you were born. This additional information should not obfuscate whatever you can learn from considering your birth rank alone.

Of course, as we have already emphasized, SSA does not assert that you are random in the objective sense of there being a physical randomization mechanism responsible for bringing you into the world. We don't postulate a time-travelling stochastic stork! SSA is simply a specification of certain types of conditional probabilities. The randomness heuristic is useful because it reminds us how to take into account both the information about your birth rank and any extra information that you might have. Unless this extra information has a direct bearing on the hypothesis in question, it won't make any difference to what credence you should assign to the hypothesis. The pertinent conditional probabilities will in that case be the same: P("A fraction f of all observers in my reference class have property P" | "I have property P") = P("A fraction f of all observers in my reference class have property P" | "I have properties P, Q_1, Q_2, and . . . Q_i").

Let us illustrate this with a concrete example. Suppose that Americans and Swedes are in the same reference class. SSA then specifies a higher prior probability of you being an American than of you being a Swede (given the difference in population size). SSA does *not* entail, absurdly, that you should think that you are probably an American even when knowing that you are reading *Svenska Dagbladet* on the Stockholm subway on your way to work at *Ericsson* with a Swedish passport in your pocket; for this evidence provides strong direct evidence for the hypothesis that you are a Swede. All the same, if you were uncertain about the relative population of the two countries, then finding that you a Swede would indeed be some evidence in favor of the hypothesis that Sweden is the larger country; and this evidence would not be weakened by learning a lot of other information about yourself, such as what your passport says, where you work, the sequence of your genome, your family tree seven generations back, or your complete physical constitution down to the atomic level. These additional pieces of information would be irrelevant.

THE SELF-INDICATION ASSUMPTION—IS THERE SAFETY IN NUMBERS?

We now turn to an idea that can be spotted in the background of several attacks on DA, namely the Self-Indication Assumption (SIA). We encountered it briefly in chapter 4. Framed as an objection against DA, the idea is that the probability shift in favor of Doom Soon that DA leads us to make is offset by another probability shift—which is overlooked by doomsayers—in favor of Doom Late. When both these probability shifts are taken into account, the net effect is that we end up with the naïve probability estimates that we made before we learnt about either DA or SIA. According to this objection, the more observers that will ever have existed, the more "slots" there are that you could have been "born into". Your existence is more probable if there are many observers than if there are few. Since you do in fact exist, the Bayesian rule has to be applied and the posterior probability of hypotheses that imply that many observers exist must be increased accordingly. The nifty thing is that the effects of SIA and DA cancel each other precisely. We can see this by means of a simple calculation[11]:

> Let $P(h_i)$ be the naive prior for the hypothesis that in total i observers will have existed, and assume that $P(h_i) = 0$ for i greater than some finite N (this restriction allows us to set aside the problem of infinities). Then we can formalize SIA as saying that
>
> $$P'(h_i) = P(h_i \mid I \text{ am an observer}) = iP(h_i)\alpha$$
>
> where α is a normalization constant. Let $r(x)$ be the rank of x, and let "I" denote a random sample from a uniform probability distribution over the set of all observers. By SSA, we have
>
> $$P'(r(I) = k \mid h_i) = \begin{cases} 0 \text{ if } k > i \\ \frac{1}{i} \text{ otherwise} \end{cases} .$$

---

[11] Something like using SIA as an objection against DA was first done—albeit not very transparently—by Dennis Dieks in 1992 (Dieks 1992); see also his more recent paper (Dieks 1999). That SIA and DA exactly cancel each other was first showed by Kopf et al. in 1994 (Kopf, Krtous et al. 1994). The objection seems to have been independently discovered by Paul Bartha and Chris Hitchcock (Bartha and Hitchcock 1999), and in variously cloaked forms by several other people (personal communications). Ken Olum has a clear treatment in (Olum 2002). John Leslie argues against SIA in (Leslie 1996), pp. 224-8.

Consider two hypotheses h_n and h_m. We can assume that $r(I) \leq \min(n, m)$. (If not, then the example simplifies to the trivial case where one of the hypotheses is conclusively refuted regardless of whether SIA is accepted.) Using Bayes' formula, we expand the quotient between the conditional probabilities of these two hypotheses:

$$\frac{P'(h_m \mid r(I) = k)}{P'(h_n \mid r(I) = k)} = \frac{\dfrac{P'(r(I) = k \mid h_m)P'(h_m)}{P'(r(I) = k)}}{\dfrac{P'(r(I) = k \mid h_n)P'(h_n)}{P'(r(I) = k)}} = \frac{\dfrac{1}{m}mP(h_m)\alpha}{\dfrac{1}{n}nP(h_n)\alpha} = \frac{P(h_m)}{P(h_n)}.$$

We see that after we have applied both SIA *and* DA, we are back to the probabilities that we started with.

But why accept SIA? The fact that SIA has the virtue of leading to a complete cancellation of DA (and some related inferences that we shall consider in chapter 9) may well be the most positive thing that can be said on its behalf. As an objection against DA, this argument would be unabashedly question-begging. It could still carry some weight if DA were sufficiently unacceptable and if there were no other coherent way of avoiding its conclusion. However, that is not the case. We shall describe another way of resisting DA in chapter 10.

SIA thus makes a charming appearance when arriving arm-in-arm with DA. The bad side emerges when SIA is on its own. In cases where we don't know our birth ranks, DA cannot be applied. There is then no subsequent probability shift to cancel out the original boost that SIA gives to many-observer hypotheses. The result is a raw bias towards populous worlds that is very hard to justify.

In order for SIA always to be able to cancel DA, you would have to subscribe to the principle that, other things equal, a hypothesis that implies that there are 2N observers should be assigned twice the credence of a hypothesis that implies that there are only N observers. In the case of the Incubator gedanken, this means that before learning about the color of your beard, you should think it likely that the coin fell heads (so that two observers rather than just one were created). If we modify the gedanken so that Heads would lead to the creation of a million observers, you would have to be virtually certain that the coin fell heads (P=99.9999%) without knowing anything directly about the outcome and before learning about your beard-color. Even if you knew that the prior probability of Heads was just one-in-a-thousand (imagine a huge fortune wheel instead of a coin), SIA still tells you to be extremely sure that the outcome was Heads. This seems wrong. Think yourself into the situation. What you know and observe at stage (*a*) in *Incubator* is perfectly harmonious with the Tails hypothesis—there is nothing that strains your belief in supposing that the coin fell tails and one observer was created and you are that observer. Especially if the prior probability of Tails was a thousand times greater than that of Heads, it would be weird to insist that it would be irrational of you not to be cocksure that the coin fell heads (on the alleged ground that there would be lots of other observers if that were true).

It is not only in fictional toy examples that we would get counterintuitive results if we accepted SIA. For, as a matter of fact, we may well be radically ignorant of our birth ranks, namely if there are intelligent extraterrestrial species. Consider the following scenario:

> *The Presumptuous Philosopher*
> It is the year 2100 and physicists have narrowed down the search for a theory of everything to only two remaining plausible candidate theories, T_1 and T_2 (using considerations from super-duper symmetry). According to T_1 the world is very, very big but finite and there are a total of a trillion trillion observers in the cosmos. According to T_2, the world is very, very, *very* big but finite and there are a trillion trillion trillion observers. The super-duper symmetry considerations are indifferent between these two theories. Physicists are preparing a simple experiment that will falsify one of the theories. Enter the presumptuous philosopher: "Hey guys, it is completely unnecessary for you to do the experiment, because I can already show to you that T_2 is about a trillion times more likely to be true than T_1! (whereupon the philosopher runs the Incubator thought experiment and explains Model 3)."

One suspects that the Nobel Prize committee would be rather reluctant to award the presumptuous philosopher The Big One for this contribution. It is hard to see what the relevant difference is between this case and *Incubator*. If there is no relevant difference, and we are not prepared to accept the argument of the presumptuous philosopher, then we are not justified in using SIA in *Incubator* either.

When discussing the second objection by Korb and Oliver, we remarked that the fact that we don't know our absolute birth ranks if there are extraterrestrial civilizations is not a threat to DA. So why cannot DA be applied in *The Presumptuous Philosopher* to cancel the SIA-induced probability shift in favour of T_2? The answer is that in the absence of knowledge about our absolute birth ranks, DA works by giving us information about what *fraction* of all species are short-lasting. (That we should be at an "early" stage in our species is more likely, according to the DA-reasoning, if a large fraction of all observers find themselves at such an early stage—i.e., if long-lasting species are rare.) This information about what fraction of all species are short-lasting (a larger fraction than we had thought) in turn tells us something about our own fate (that it is more likely that we are a short-lasting species). But it does not tell us anything about how many species, and thus about how many observers there are in total. To get DA to argue in favor of a small number of observers (rather than for a small number of *human* observers), you would need to know your absolute birth rank. Since you don't know that in *The Presumptuous Philosopher* (and, presumably, not in our actual situation either), DA cannot be applied there to cancel the SIA-induced probability shift.

Back in chapter 2, we sketched an explanation of why, owing to observation selection effects, it would be a mistake to view the fine-tuning of our universe as a general ground for favoring hypotheses that imply the existence of a greater number of observer-containing universes. If two competing general hypotheses each implies that there is at least one observer-containing universe, but one of the hypotheses implies the existence of a greater number of observer-containing universes than the other, then fine-tuning is not typically a reason to favor the former. The reasoning in chapter 2 can be adapted to argue that your own existence is not in general a ground for thinking that hypotheses are more likely to be true just by virtue of implying that there is a greater total number of observers. The datum of your existence tends to disconfirm hypotheses on which it would be unlikely that any observers (in your reference class) should exist; but that's as far as it goes. The reason for this is that the sample at hand—you—should not be thought of as randomly selected from the class of all possible observers but only from a class of observers who will actually have existed. It is, so to speak, not a coincidence that the sample you are considering is one that actually exists. Rather, that's a logical consequence of the fact that only actual observers actually view themselves as samples from anything at all.[12]

Harking back to the heavenly-messenger analogy used in chapter 2, we could have considered the following different version, in which reasoning in accordance with SIA would have been justified:

> *Case 5.* The messenger first selected a random observer *from the set of all possible observers.* He then traveled to the realm of physical existence and checked whether this possible observer actually existed somewhere, and brought back news to you about the result.

Yet this variation would make the analogy *less* close to the real case. For while the angel could have learnt from the messenger that the randomly

---

[12] Of course, just as if our universe were found to have "special" properties this could provide justification for using the fact of its existence as part of an argument for there being a great many observer-containing universes, so likewise if you have certain special properties then that could support the hypothesis that there are vast numbers of observers. But it is then the special properties that you are discovered to have, not the mere fact of your existence, that grounds the inference.

selected possible observer didn't actually exit, you could not have learnt that you didn't exist.

Finally, consider the limiting case where we are comparing two hypotheses, one saying that the universe is finite (and contains finitely many observers), the other saying that the universe is infinite (and contains infinitely many observers). SIA would have you assign probability one to the latter hypothesis, assuming both hypotheses had a finite prior probability. But surely, whether the universe is finite or infinite is an open scientific question, not something that you can determine with certainty simply by leaning back in your armchair and registering the fact that you exist!

For these reasons, we should reject SIA.

CHAPTER 8

Observer-Relative Chances in Anthropic Reasoning?[1]

Here we examine an argument by John Leslie (Leslie 1997) purporting to show that anthropic reasoning gives rise to paradoxical "observer-relative chances".[2] We show that the argument trades on the sense/reference ambiguity and is fallacious. We then describe a different case where chances *are* observer-relative in an interesting, but not paradoxical way. The result can be generalized: at least for a very wide range of cases, SSA does not engender paradoxical observer-relative chances.

LESLIE'S ARGUMENT AND WHY IT FAILS

Leslie seeks to establish the following conclusion:

> Estimated probabilities can be observer-relative in a somewhat disconcerting way: a way not depending on the fact that, obviously, various observers often are unaware of truths which other observers know. (p. 435)

Leslie does not regard this as a reductio of anthropic reasoning and recommends that we bite the bullet: "Any air of paradox must not prevent us from accepting these things." (p. 428)

Leslie's argument takes the form of a thought experiment. We start with a batch of one hundred women and divide them randomly into two groups, one with ninety-five and one with five women. By flipping a fair coin, we then assign the name 'the Heads group' randomly to one of these groups and the name 'the Tails group' to the other. According to Leslie, it is now the case that an external observer, i.e. a person not in either of the two groups,

---

[1] This chapter is adapted from a paper previously published in *Erkenntnis* (Bostrom 2000), with permission.

[2] Leslie uses "chances" as synonymous with "epistemic probabilities". I will follow his usage in this chapter and in later passages that refer to the results obtained here. Elsewhere in the book, I reserve the word "chance" for objective probabilities.

ought to derive radically different conclusions than an insider:

> All these persons—the women in the Heads group, those in the Tails group, and the external observer—are fully aware that there are two groups, and that each woman has a ninety-five per cent chance of having entered the larger. Yet the conclusions they ought to derive differ radically. The external observer ought to conclude that the probability is fifty per cent that the Heads group is the larger of the two. Any woman actually in [either the Heads or the Tails group], however, ought to judge the odds ninety-five to five that her group, identified as 'the group I am in', is the larger, regardless of whether she has been informed of its name. (p. 428)

> Even without knowing her group's name, a woman could still appreciate that the external observer estimated its chance of being the larger one as only fifty per cent—this being what his evidence led him to estimate *in the cases of both groups*. The paradox is that she herself would then have to say: 'In view of my evidence of being in one of the groups, ninety-five per cent is what I estimate.' (p. 429)

Somewhere within these two paragraphs a mistake has been made. It is not hard to locate the error if we look at the structure of the reasoning. Let's say there is a woman in the larger group who is called Liz. The "paradox" then takes the following form:

(1) P_{Liz} ("The group that Liz is in is the larger group") = 95%

(2) The group that Liz is in = the Heads group

(3) Therefore: P_{Liz} ("The Heads group is the larger group") = 95%

(4) But $P_{External\ observer}$ ("The Heads group is the larger group") = 50%

(5) Hence chances are observer-relative.

Where it goes wrong is in step (3). The group that Liz is in is indeed identical to the Heads group, but Liz doesn't know that. P_{Liz} ("The Heads group is the larger group") = 50%, not 95% as claimed in step (3). There is nothing mysterious about this, at least not subsequent to Gottlob Freye's classic discussion of Hesperus and Phosphorus. One need not have rational grounds for assigning probability one to the proposition "Hesperus = Phosphorus", even though as a matter of fact Hesperus = Phosphorus. For one might not know that Hesperus = Phosphorus. The expressions "Hesperus" and "Phosphorus" present their denotata under different modes of presentation; they denote the same object while connoting different concepts. While there is still some dispute over how best to characterize this difference and over what general lessons we can pick up from it, the basic observation that you can learn something from being told *"a = b"* (even if a = b) is old hat.

Let's see if Leslie's conclusion can be resuscitated in some way by modifying the thought experiment.

Suppose that we change the example so that Liz knows that the sentence "Liz is in the Heads group" is true. Then step (3) will be correct. But now we run into trouble when we try to take step (5). It is no longer true that Liz and the external observer know about the same facts. Liz now has the information "Liz is in the Heads group"; the external observer doesn't. No interesting observer-relative chances have been produced.

What if we change the example again by assuming that the external observer, too, knows that Liz is in the Heads group? Well, if Liz and the external observer agreed on the chance that the Heads group is the large group before they both learnt that Liz is in the Heads group, they will continue to agree about this chance after they have received that information—*provided* they agree about the conditional probability P(The Heads group is the larger group | Liz is in the Heads group). Do they?

First, look at it from Liz's point of view. Let's go along with Leslie and assume that she should think of herself as a random sample from the batch of one hundred women. Suppose she knows that her name is Liz (and that she is the only woman in the batch with that name). Then, before she learns that she is in the Heads group, she should assign that a probability of 50%. (Recall that what group should be called "the Heads group" was determined by tossing of a fair coin.) She should think that the chance of the sentence "Liz is in the larger group" is 95%, since ninety-five out of the hundred women are in the larger group, and she can regard herself as a random sample from these hundred women. After learning that she is in the Heads group, the chance of her being in the larger group remains 95%. ("The Heads group" and "the Tails group" are just arbitrary labels at this point. Randomly calling one group the Heads group doesn't change the likelihood that it is the big group.) Hence, the probability she should give to "The Heads group is the larger group" is now 95%. Therefore, the conditional probability which we were looking for is P_{Liz} ("The Heads group is the larger group" | "Liz is in the Heads group") = 95%.

Next, consider the situation from the external observer's point of view. What is the probability for the external observer that the Heads group is the larger one, given that Liz is in it? Well, what's the probability that Liz is in the Heads group? In order to answer these questions, we need to know something about (the external observer's beliefs about) how this woman Liz was selected.

Suppose that she was selected as a random sample, with uniform sampling density, from among all the hundred women in the batch. Then the external observer would arrive at the same conclusion as Liz: if the random sample "Liz" is in the Heads group then there is a 95% chance that the Heads group is the bigger group.

If, instead, we suppose that Liz was selected randomly from some subset of the hundred women, then it might happen that the external observer's estimate diverges from Liz's. For example, if the external observer randomly selects one individual x (whose name happens to be "Liz") from the large group, then, when he finds that x is in the Heads group, he should assign a 100% probability to the sentence "The Heads group is the larger group." This is indeed a different conclusion than the one that the insider Liz draws. *She* thought the conditional probability of the Heads group being the larger one given that Liz is in the Heads group was 95%.

In this case, however, we have to question whether Liz and the external observer know about the same evidence. (If they don't, then the disparity in their conclusions doesn't signify that chances are observer-relative in any paradoxical sense.) But it is clear that their information *does* differ in a relevant way. For suppose Liz got to know what the external observer is stipulated to already know: that Liz had been selected by the external observer through some random sampling process from among a certain subset of the hundred women. That implies that Liz is a member of that subset. This information would change her probability assignment so that it once again becomes identical to the external observer's. In the above case, for instance, the external observer selected a woman randomly from the large group. Now, evidently, if Liz gets this extra piece of information, that she has been selected as a random sample from the large group, then she knows with certainty that she is in that group. So her conditional probability that the Heads group is the larger group given that Liz is in the Heads group should then be 100%, the same as what the outside observer should believe.

We see that as soon as we give the two persons access to the same evidence, their disagreement vanishes. No paradoxical observer-relative chances are to be found in this thought experiment.[3]

OBSERVER-RELATIVE CHANCES: ANOTHER GO

In this section we shall give an example where chances could actually be said to be observer-relative in an interesting—though by no means para-

---

[3] The only way, it seems, of maintaining that there are observer-relative chances in a nontrivial sense in Leslie's example is on pain of opening oneself up to systematic exploitation, at least if one is prepared to put one's money where one's mouth is. Suppose there is someone who insists that the odds are different for an insider than they are for an outsider, and not only because the insider and the outsider don't know about the same facts. Let's call this hypothetical person *Mr. L*. (John Leslie, we hope, would not take *this* line of defence.)

At the next major philosophy conference that Mr. L attends we select a group of one hundred philosophers and divide them into two subgroups which we name by means of a coin toss, just as in Leslie's example. We let Mr. L observe this event. Then we ask him what is the probability—for him as an external observer, one not in the selected group—that the large group is the Heads group. Let's say he claims this probability is p. We then repeat the experiment, but this time with Mr. L as one of the hundred philosophers in the batch. Again we ask him what he thinks

doxical—sense. What philosophical lessons we should or shouldn't learn from this phenomenon will be discussed in the next section.

Here is the example:

> Suppose the following takes place in an otherwise empty world. A fair coin is flipped by an automaton and if it falls heads, ten humans are created; if it falls tails, one human is created. In addition to these people, one other human that is created independently of how the coin falls. This latter human we call *the bookie*. The people created as a result of the coin toss we call *the group*. Everybody knows these facts. Furthermore, the bookie knows that she is the bookie, and the people in the group know that they are in the group.

The question is, what would be the fair odds if the people in the group want to bet against the bookie on how the coin fell? One could think that everybody should agree that the chance of it having fallen heads is fifty-fifty, since it was a fair coin. That overlooks the fact that the bookie obtains information from finding that she is the bookie rather than one of the people in the group. This information is relevant to her estimate of how the coin fell. It is more likely that she should find herself being the bookie if one out of two is a bookie than if the ratio is one out of eleven. So finding herself being the bookie, she obtains reason to believe that the coin probably fell tails, leading to the creation of only one other human. In a similar way, the people in the group, by observing that they are in the group, obtain some evidence that the coin fell heads, resulting in a large fraction of all observers observing that they are in the group.

It is a simple exercise to calculate what the posterior probabilities are after this information has been taken into account.

---

the probability is, now from his point of view as an insider, that the large group is the Heads group. (Mr. L doesn't know at this point whether he is in the Heads group or the Tails group. If he did, he would know about a fact that the outsiders do not know about, and hence the chances involved would not be observer-relative in any paradoxical sense.) Say he answers p'.

If either p or p' is anything other than 50% then we can make money out of him by repeating the experiment many times with Mr. L either in the batch or as an external observer, depending on whether it is p or p' that differs from 50%. For example, if p' is greater than 50%, we repeat the experiment with Mr. L in the batch, and we keep offering him the same bet, namely that the Heads group is *not* the larger group, and Mr. L will happily bet against us, e.g. at odds determined by $p^* = (50\% + p') / 2$ (the intermediary odds between what Mr. L thinks are fair odds and what we think are fair odds). If, on the other hand, $p' < 50\%$, we bet (at odds determined by p^*) that the Head's group *is* the larger group. Again Mr. L should willingly bet against us.

In the long run (with probability asymptotically approaching one), the Heads group will be the larger group approximately half the time. So we will win approximately half of the bets. It is easy to verify that the odds to which Mr. L has agreed are such that this will earn us more money than we need pay out. We will be making a net gain, Mr. L a net loss.

Since the coin is fair, we have P(Heads) = P(Tails) = ½.

By SSA, P(I am bookie | Heads) = $\frac{1}{11}$ and P(I am bookie | Tails) = ½. Hence,

P(I am bookie)
= P(I am bookie | Heads) · P(Heads) + P(I am bookie | Tails) · P(Tails)
= $\frac{1}{11} \cdot \frac{1}{2} + \frac{1}{2} \cdot \frac{1}{2} = \frac{13}{44}$.

From Bayes' theorem we then get:

P(Heads | I am bookie)
= P(I am bookie | Heads) · P(Heads) / P(I am bookie)

$= \dfrac{\frac{1}{11} \times \frac{1}{2}}{\frac{13}{44}} = \frac{2}{13}$.

In exactly the same way we get the odds for the people in the group:
P(I am in the group | Heads) = $\frac{10}{11}$
P(I am in the group | Tails) = ½.
P(I am in the group) = $\frac{10}{11} \cdot \frac{1}{2} + \frac{1}{2} \cdot \frac{1}{2} = \frac{31}{44}$.
P(Heads | I am in the group) = P(I am in the group | Heads) · P(Heads) / P(I am in the group)

$= \dfrac{\frac{10}{11} \times \frac{1}{2}}{\frac{31}{44}} = \frac{20}{31}$.

We see that the bookie should think there is a $\frac{2}{13}$ chance that the coin fell heads while the people in the group should think that the chance is $\frac{20}{31}$.

DISCUSSION: INDEXICAL FACTS—NO CONFLICT WITH PHYSICALISM

While it might be slightly noteworthy that the bookie and the people in the group are rationally required to disagree in the above scenario, it isn't the least bit paradoxical, as they have different information. For instance, the bookie knows that "I am the bookie". This piece of information is clearly different from the corresponding one—"I am in the group"—known by the people in the group. So chances have *not* been shown to be observer-relative in the sense that people with the same information can be rationally required to disagree. And if we were to try to modify the example so as to give the participants the same information, we would see that their disagreement evaporates, as it did when we attempted various twists of the Leslie gedanken.

There is a sense, though, in which the chances in the present example can be said to be observer-relative. The sets of evidence that the bookie and the people in the group have, while not identical, are quite similar. They differ only in regard to such indexical facts[4] as "I am the bookie" or "I am in the group". We could say that the example demonstrates, in an interesting way, that chances can be relative to observers in the sense that people whose sets of evidence are the same *up to indexical facts* can be rationally required to disagree about non-indexical facts.

This kind of observer-relativity is not particularly counterintuitive and should not be taken to cast doubt on SSA, from which it was derived. That indexical matters can have implications for what we should believe about nonindexical matters should not surprise us. It can be shown by a trivial example. From "I have blue eyes" it follows that somebody has blue eyes.

The rational odds in the example above being different for the bookie than for the punters in the group, we might begin to wonder whether it is possible to formulate some kind of bet for which all parties would calculate a positive expected payoff? This would not necessarily be an unacceptable consequence since the bettors have different information. Still, it could seem a bit peculiar if we had a situation where purely by applying SSA rational people were led to start placing bets against one another. So it is worth calculating the odds to see if there are cases where they do indeed favour betting. This is done in an appendix to this chapter. The result is negative—no betting. In the quite general class of cases considered, there is no combination of parameter values for which a bet is possible in which both parties would rationally expect a positive non-zero payoff.[5]

---

[4] The metaphysics of indexical facts is not our topic here, but a good starting point for studying that is chapter 10 in (Lewis 1986). David Lewis argues that one can know which possible world is actual and still learn something new when one discovers which person one is in that world. Lewis, borrowing an example from John Perry (Perry 1977) (who in turn is indebted to Henri Castañeda (Castañeda 1966, 1968)) discusses the case of the amnesiacs in the Stanford library. We can imagine (changing the example slightly) that two amnesiacs are lost in the library on the first and second floor respectively. From reading the books they have learned precisely which possible world is actual—in particular they know that two amnesiacs are lost in the Stanford library. Nonetheless, when one of the amnesiacs sees a map of the library saying "You are here" with an arrow pointing to the second floor, he learns something new despite already knowing all non-indexical facts.

[5] One could also worry about another thing: doesn't the doctrine defended here commit one to the view that observation reports couched in the first person should be evaluated by different rules from those pertaining to third-person reports of what is apparently the same evidence? Yes and no. Maybe the best way of putting it is that the evaluation rule is the same in both cases but its application is more complicated in the case of third-person reports (by which we here mean statements about some other person's observations). Third-person reports can become evidence for somebody only by first coming to her knowledge. While you may know your own observations directly, there is an additional step that other people's observations must go through before they become evidence for you: they must somehow be communicated to you. That extra step may involve *additional* selection effects that are not present in the first-person case. This accounts for the apparent evidential difference between first- and third-person reports. For example, what conclusions you can draw from the third-person report "Mr. Ping observes a red room" depends on what your beliefs are about how this report came to be known (as true) to you—why you didn't find out about Mr. Pong instead, who observes a green room. By contrast,

This is an encouraging finding for the anthropic theorizer. Yet we are still left with the fact that there are cases where observers come to disagree with one another other just because of applying SSA. While it is true that these disagreeing observers will have different indexical information, and while there are trivial examples in which a difference in indexical information implies a difference in non-indexical information, it might nonetheless be seen as objectionable that anthropic reasoning should lead to these kinds of disagreements. Doesn't that presuppose that we ascribe some mysterious quality to the things we call "observers", some property of an observer's mind that cannot be reduced to objective observer-independent facts?

The best way to allay this worry is by demonstrating how the above example, in which the "observer-relative" chances appeared, can be recast in purely physicalistic terms:

A coin is tossed and either one or ten human brains are created. These brains make up "the group". Apart from these there is only one other brain, the "bookie". All the brains are informed about the procedure that has taken place. Suppose Alpha is one of the brains that have been created and that Alpha remembers recently having been in the brain states A_1, A_2, ..., A_n. (I.e. Alpha recognizes the descriptions "A_1", "A_2", ..., "A_n" as descriptions of these states, and Alpha knows "this brain was recently in states A_1, A_2, ..., A_n" is true. Cf. Perry (1979).)

At this stage, Alpha should obviously think the probability of Heads is 50%, since it was a fair coin. But now suppose that Alpha is informed that he is the bookie, i.e. that the brain that has recently been in the states A_1, A_2, ..., A_n is the brain that is labeled "the bookie". Then Alpha will reason as follows:

"Let A be the brain that was recently in states A_1, A_2, ..., A_n. The conditional probability of A being labeled 'the bookie' given that A is one of two existing brains is greater than the conditional probability of A being the brain labeled 'the bookie' given that A is one out of eleven brains. Hence, since A does indeed turn out to be the brain labeled 'the bookie', there is a greater than 50% chance that the coin fell tails, creating only one brain."

A parallel line of reasoning can be pursued by a brain labeled "a brain in the group". The argument can be quantified in the same way as in the earlier example and will result in the same "observer-relative" chances. This shows that anthropic reasoning can be understood in a physicalistic framework.

---

there is no analogous underspecification of the first-person report "I observe a red room". There is no relevant story to be told about how it came about that *you* got to know about the observation that *you* are making.

The observer-relative chances in this example too are explained by the fact that the brains have access to different evidence. Alpha, for example, knows that (S_{Alpha}:) *the brain that has recently been in the states* A_1, A_2, ... , A_n *is the brain that is labeled "the bookie"*. A brain, Beta, who comes to disagree with Alpha about the probability of Heads, will have a different information set. Beta might for instance rather know that (S_{Beta}:) *the brain that has recently been in the states* B_1, B_2, ... , B_n *is a brain that is labeled "a member of the group"*. S_{Alpha} is clearly not equivalent to S_{Beta}.

It is instructive to see what happens if we take a step further and eliminate from the example not only all non-physicalistic terms but also its ingredient of indexicality:

> In the previous example we assumed that the proposition (S_{Alpha}) which Alpha knows but Beta does not know was a proposition concerning the brain states A_1, A_2, ... , A_n of Alpha itself. Suppose now instead that Alpha does *not* know what label the brain Alpha has (whether it is "the bookie" or "a brain in the group") but that Alpha has been informed that there are some recent brain states G_1, G_2, ... , G_n of some *other* existing brain, Gamma, and that Gamma is labeled "the bookie".
>
> At this stage, what conclusion Alpha should draw from this piece of information is underdetermined by the given specifications. It depends on what Alpha knows or guesses about how this other brain, Gamma, had been selected to come to Alpha's notice. Suppose we specify the thought experiment further by stipulating that, as far as Alpha's knowledge goes, Gamma can be regarded as a random sample from the set of all existing brains. Alpha may know, say, that one ball for each existing brain was put in an urn and that one of these balls was drawn at random and it turned out to be the one corresponding to Gamma. Reasoning from this information, Alpha will arrive at the same conclusion as if Alpha had learnt that *Alpha* was labeled "the bookie" as in the previous version of the thought experiment. Similarly, Beta may know about another random sample, Epsilon, that is labeled "a brain in the group". This will lead Alpha and Beta to differ in their probability estimates, just as before. In this version of the thought experiment no indexical evidence is involved. Yet Alpha's probabilities differ from Beta's.

What we have here is hardly distinct from any humdrum situation where John and Mary know different things and therefore estimate probabilities differently. The only difference from a standard urn game is that instead of balls or raffle tickets, we're randomizing brains—surely not philosophically relevant.

But what exactly did change when we removed the indexical element? If we compare the two last examples, we see that the essential disparity is in how the random samples were produced.

In the second of the two examples, there was *a physical selection mechanism* that generated the randomness. We said that Alpha knew that there was one ball for each brain in existence, that these balls had been put in an urn, and that one of these balls had then been selected randomly and had turned out to correspond to a brain that was labeled "the bookie".

In the other example, by contrast, there was no such physical mechanism. Instead, there the randomness did somehow *arise from each observer considering herself as a random sample from the set of all observers.* Alpha and Beta observed their own states of mind (i.e. their own brain states). Combining this information with other, non-indexical, information allowed them to draw conclusions about non-indexical states of affairs that they could not draw without the indexical information obtained from observing their own states of mind. But there was no physical randomization mechanism at work analogous to selecting a ball from an urn.

Not that it is unproblematic how such reasoning can be justified or explained—that is after all the subject matter of this book. However, SSA is what is used to get anthropic reasoning off the ground in the first place; so the discovery that SSA leads to "observer-relative" chances, and that these chances arise without an identifiable randomization mechanism, is not something that should add new suspicions. It is merely a restatement of the assumption from which we started.

IN CONCLUSION

Leslie's argument that anthropic reasoning gives rise to paradoxical observer-relative chances does not hold up to scrutiny. We argued that it rests on a sense/reference ambiguity and that when this ambiguity is resolved, the purported observer-relativity disappears. Several ways in which one could try to salvage Leslie's conclusion were explored and it turned out that none of them would work.

We then considered an example where observers applying SSA end up disagreeing about the outcome of a coin toss. The observers' disagreement depends on their having different information and is not paradoxical; there are completely trivial examples of the same kind of phenomenon. We also showed that (at least for a wide range of cases) this disparity in beliefs cannot be marshaled into a betting arrangement where all parties involved would expect to make a gain.

This example was given a physicalistic reformulation, showing that the observers' disagreement does not imply some mysterious irreducible role for the observers' consciousness. What *does* need to be presupposed, however, unless the situation be utterly trivialized, is SSA. This is not a finding that should be taken to cast doubt on anthropic reasoning. Rather, it simply elucidates one aspect of what SSA really means. The absence the sort of paradoxical observer-relative chances that Leslie claimed to have found could even be taken to give some indirect support for SSA.

APPENDIX: THE NO-BETTING RESULTS

This appendix shows, for a quite general set of cases, that adopting and applying SSA does not lead rational agents to bet against one another.

Consider again the case where a fair coin is tossed and a different number of observers are created depending on how the coin falls. The people created as a result of the coin toss make up "the group". In addition to these, there exists a set of people we call the "bookies". Together, the people in the group and the bookies make up the set of people who are said to be "in the experiment". To make the example more general, we also allow there to be (a possibly empty) set of observers who are not in the experiment (i.e. who are not bookies and are not in the group); we call these observers "outsiders".

We introduce the following abbreviations:

Number of people in the group if coin falls heads = h
Number of people in the group if coin falls tails = t
Number of bookies = b
Number of *ou*tsiders = u
For *"The coin fell heads"*, write H
For *"The coin fell tails"*, write $\neg H$
For *"I am in the group"*, write G
For *"I am a bookie"*, write B
For *"I am in the experiment (i.e. I'm either a bookie or in the group)"*, write E

First we want to calculate $P(H|\,G\&E)$ and $P(H|\,B\&E)$, the probabilities that the group members and the bookies, respectively, should assign to the proposition that the coin fell heads. Since G implies E, and B implies E, we have $P(H|\,G\&E) = P(H|\,G)$ and $P(H|\,B\&E) = P(H|\,B)$. We can derive $P(H|\,G)$ from the following equations:

$P(H|\,G) = P(G|\,H)\,P(H)\,/\,P(G)$	(Bayes' theorem)
$P(G|\,H) = h\,/\,(h + b + u)$	(SSA)
$P(G|\,\neg H) = t\,/\,(t + b + u)$	(SSA)
$P(H) = P(\neg H) = \frac{1}{2}$	(Fair coin)
$P(G) = P(G|\,H)\,P(H) + P(G|\,\neg H)\,P(\neg H)$	(Theorem)

This gives us

$$P(H|\,G\&E) = \frac{h \cdot (t + b + u)}{h \cdot (t + b + u) + t \cdot (h + b + u)}.$$

In analogous fashion, using $P(B|H) = b / (h + b + u)$ and $P(B|\neg H) = b / (t + b + u)$, we get

$$P(H|B\&E) = \frac{t+b+u}{(h+b+u)+(t+b+u)}.$$

We see that $P(H|B\&E)$ is not in general equal to $P(H|G\&E)$. The bookies and the people in the group will arrive at different estimates of the probability of Heads. For instance, if we have the parameter values {h = 10, t = 1, b = 1, u = 10} we get $P(H|G\&E) \approx 85\%$ and $P(H|B\&E) \approx 36\%$. In the limiting case when the number of outsiders is zero, {h = 10, t = 1, b = 1, u = 0}, we have $P(H|G\&E) \approx 65\%$ and $P(H|B\&E) \approx 15\%$. In the opposite limiting case, when the number of outsiders is large, {h = 10, t = 1, b = 1, u → ∞}, we get $P(H|G\&E) \approx 91\%$ and $P(H|B\&E) = 50\%$. In general, we should expect the bookies and the group members to disagree about the outcome of the coin toss.

Now that we know the probabilities, we can check whether a bet occurs. There are two types of bet that we will consider. In a type 1 bet, a bookie bets against the group as a whole, and the group members bet against the set of bookies as a whole. In a type 2 bet, an individual bookie bets against an individual group member.

Let's look at the type 1 bet first. The maximum amount $x that a person in the group is willing to pay to each bookie if the coin fell heads in order to get $1 from each bookie if it fell tails is given by

$$P(H|G)(-x)b + P(\neg H|G)b = 0.$$

When calculating the rational odds for a bookie, we have to take into account the fact that depending on the outcome of the coin toss, the bookie will turn out to have betted against a greater or a smaller number of group members. Keeping this in mind, we can write down a condition for the minimum amount $y that a bookie has to receive (from every group member) if the coin fell heads in order to be willing to pay $1 (to every group member) if it fell tails:

$$P(H|B) \, y \cdot b + P(\neg H|B)(-1)t = 0.$$

Solving these two fairness equations, we find that $x = y = \frac{t(h+b+u)}{h(t+b+u)}$, which means that nobody expects to win from a bet of this kind.

Turning now to the type 2 bet, where individual bookies and individuals in the group bet directly against each other, we have to take into account an additional factor. To keep things simple, we assume that it is assured that all of the bookies get to make a type 2 bet and that no person in the group bets against more than one bookie. This implies that the number of bookies isn't

greater than the smallest number of group members that could have resulted from the coin toss; for otherwise there would be no guarantee that all
bookies could bet against a unique group member. But this means that if the
coin toss generated more than the smallest possible number of group members, a selection has to be made as to which of the group members get to
bet against a bookie. Consequently, a group member who finds that she has
been selected obtains reason for thinking that the coin fell in such a way as
to maximize the proportion of group members that get selected to bet
against a bookie. (The bookies' probabilities remain the same as in the previous example.)

Let's say that it is the Tails outcome that produces the smallest group. Let s
denote the number of group members that are selected. We require that $s \leq t$.
We want to calculate the probability for the selected people in the group that
the coin fell heads, i.e. $P(H|G\&E\&S)$. Since S implies both G and E, we have
$P(H|G\&E\&S) = P(H|S)$. From

$$P(H|S) = P(S|H)\,P(H)\,/\,P(S) \qquad \text{(Bayes' theorem)}$$
$$P(S|H) = s\,/\,(h + b + u) \qquad \text{(SSA)}$$
$$P(S|\neg H) = s\,/\,(t + b + u) \qquad \text{(SSA)}$$
$$P(H) = P(\neg H) = \tfrac{1}{2} \qquad \text{(Fair coin)}$$
$$P(S) = P(S|H)P(H) + P(S|\neg H)P(\neg H) \qquad \text{(Theorem)}$$

we then get

$$P(H|G\&E\&S) = \frac{t+b+u}{(t+b+u)+(h+b+u)}.$$

Comparing this to the result in the previous example, we see that
$P(H|G\&E\&S) = P(H|B\&E)$. This means that the bookies and the group
members that are selected now agree about the odds. So there is no possible bet between them for which both parties would calculate a positive non-
zero expected payoff.

We conclude that adopting SSA does not lead observers to place bets
against each other. Whatever the number of outsiders, bookies, group members, and selected group members, there are no bets, either of type 1 or of
type 2, from which all parties should expect to gain.

CHAPTER 9

Paradoxes of the Self-Sampling Assumption[1]

The function of this chapter is that of a wrecking ball. In order to prepare the site for the construction work that we will do in the next two chapters, we must level those current structures that aren't robust enough to build on.

Less metaphorically, we shall present several thought experiments that tease out some counterintuitive consequences of adopting SSA with the universal reference class (the reference class containing all intelligent observers that will have existed). The existence of these consequences is a reason for moving to the more general theory of observation selection effects that we will develop in chapter 10. That theory will permit the reference class to be relativized in a way that makes it possible to avoid the paradoxical consequences we pursue in this chapter.

Among the *prima facie* consequences of applying SSA with the universal reference class is that we have reason to believe in paranormal causation (such as psychokinesis) and that SSA recommends actions that seem radically foolish. A careful analysis, however, reveals that most of these *prima facie* consequences are merely apparent. We show how SSA manages to extricate itself from all of the worst incriminations (we apply a wrecking ball to the wrecking ball).

A subset of counterintuitive consequences remains after the dust has settled. I view them as sufficiently repugnant to motivate going beyond SSA. However, should somebody be willing to accept those implications that remain after we have explained away that which can be explained away, then I don't have any further argument that would compel her to give up SSA. Yet the theory we develop in the next chapter should still be acceptable to her, for she could then hold that all the cases are the "special" kind of cases

---

[1] An early ancestor of this chapter was presented at a conference organized by the *London School of Advanced Study* on the Doomsday argument (London, Nov. 6, 1998). I'm grateful for comments from the participants there, and from referee comments on a more recent ancestor published in *Synthese* (Bostrom 2001), parts of which is used here, with permission.

in which SSA applies, so that the more general theory is sound (albeit super-fluously general and containing an otiose degree of freedom). For the rest of us, who *don't* accept the consequences of SSA that remain at the end of this chapter, the added analytic power of the more general theory is necessary for giving a completely satisfactory account of observation selection effects.

THE *ADAM & EVE* EXPERIMENTS

The three *Adam & Eve* thought experiments that follow are variations on the same theme; they put different problematic aspects of SSA into focus.

First experiment: Serpent's Advice
Eve and Adam, the first two humans, knew that if they gratified their flesh, Eve might bear a child, and if she did, they would be expelled from Eden and would go on to spawn billions of progeny that would cover the Earth with misery.[2] One day a serpent approached the couple and spoke thus: "Pssst! If you embrace each other, then either Eve will have a child or she won't. If she has a child then you will have been among the first two out of billions of people. Your conditional probability of having such early positions in the human species given this hypothesis is extremely small. If, one the other hand, Eve doesn't become pregnant then the conditional probability, given this, of you being among the first two humans is equal to one. By Bayes' theorem, the risk that she will have a child is less than one in a billion. Go forth, indulge, and worry not about the consequences!"

Given SSA and the stated assumptions, it is easy to see that the serpent's argument is sound. We have $P(R \leq 2 | N=2)=1$ and using SSA, $P(R \leq 2 | N > 2 \cdot 10^9) < 10^{-9}$ (where "R" stands for "my birth rank", and "N" for "the total number of observers in my reference class"). We can assume that the prior probability of getting pregnant (based on ordinary empirical considerations) after congress is very roughly one half, $P(N=2) \approx P(N > 2 \cdot 10^9) \approx .5$. Thus we have

$$P(N > 2 \cdot 10^9 \mid R \leq 2)$$

$$= \frac{P(R \leq 2 \mid N > 2 \cdot 10^9)P(N > 2 \cdot 10^9)}{P(R \leq 2 \mid N > 2 \cdot 10^9)P(N > 2 \cdot 10^9) + P(R \leq 2 \mid N = 2)P(N = 2)}$$

$$< 10^{-9}$$

Eve has to conclude that the risk of her getting pregnant is negligible.

[2] We assume that Eve and Adam and whatever descendants they have are the only inhabitants of this world. If we assume, as the Biblical language suggests, that they were placed in this situation and given the knowledge they have by God, we should therefore also assume that God doesn't count as an "observer". Note that for the reasoning to work, Adam and Eve must be extremely confident that if they have a child they will in fact spawn a huge species. One could modify the story so as to weaken this requirement, but empirical plausibility is not an objective in this gedanken.

This result is counterintuitive. Most people's intuition, at least at first glance, is that it would be irrational for Eve to think that the risk is that low. It seems foolish of her to act as if she were extremely unlikely to get pregnant—it seems to conflict with empirical data. And we can assume she is fully aware of these data, at least to the extent to which they are about past events. We can assume that she has access to a huge pool of statistics, maybe based on some population of lobotomized human drones (lobotomized so that they don't belong to the reference class, the class from which Eve should consider herself a random sample). Yet all this knowledge, combined with everything there is to know about the human reproductive system, would not change the fact that it would be irrational for Eve to believe that the risk of her getting pregnant is anything other than effectively nil. This is a strange result, but it follows from SSA.[3]

Second experiment: Lazy Adam
The next example effects another turn of the screw, deriving a consequence that has an even greater degree of initial counterintuitiveness:

> Assume as before that Adam and Eve were once the only people and that they know for certain that if they have a child they will be driven out of Eden and will have billions of descendants. But this time they have a foolproof way of generating a child, perhaps using advanced *in vitro* fertilization. Adam is tired of getting up every morning to go hunting. Together with Eve, he devises the following scheme: *They form the firm intention that unless a wounded deer limps by their cave, they will have a child.* Adam can then put his feet up and rationally expect with near certainty that a wounded deer—an easy target for his spear—will soon stroll by.

One can verify this result the same way as above, choosing appropriate values for the prior probabilities. The prior probability of a wounded deer limping by their cave that morning is one in ten thousand, say.

In the first experiment we had an example of what looked like anomalous precognition. Here we also have (more clearly than in the previous case) the appearance of psychokinesis. If the example works, which it does

---

[3] John Leslie does not accept this result and thinks that Eve should not regard the risk of pregnancy as negligible in these circumstances, on the grounds that the world is indeterministic and the SSA-based reasoning runs smoothly only if the world is deterministic or at least the relevant parts of the future are already "as good as determined" (personal communication; compare also (Leslie 1996), pp. 255–6, where he discusses a somewhat similar example). I disagree with his view that the question about determinism is relevant to the applicability of SSA. But in any case, we can legitimately evaluate the plausibility of SSA by considering what it *would* entail if we knew that the world were deterministic.

if we assume SSA, it almost seems as if Adam is *causing* a wounded deer to walk by. For how else could one explain the coincidence? Adam knows that he can repeat the procedure morning after morning and that he should expect a deer to appear each time. Some mornings he may not form the relevant intention and on those mornings no deer turns up. It seems too good to be mere chance; Adam is tempted to think he has magical powers.

Third experiment: Eve's Card Trick

One morning, Adam shuffles a deck of cards. Later that morning, Eve, having had no contact with the cards, decides to use her willpower to retroactively choose what card lies top. She decides that it shall have been the dame of spades. In order to ordain this outcome, Eve and Adam form the firm intention to have a child unless the dame of spades is top. They can then be virtually certain that when they look at the first card, they will indeed find the dame of spades.

Here it looks as if the couple is in one and the same act performing both psychokinesis and backward causation. No mean feat before breakfast.

These three thought experiments seem to show that SSA has bizarre consequences: strange coincidences, precognition, psychokinesis, and backward causation in situations where we would not expect such phenomena. If these consequences are genuine, they must surely count heavily against the unrestricted version of SSA, with ramifications for DA and other forms of anthropic reasoning that rely on the that principle.

However, we shall now see that such an interpretation misreads the experiments. The truth is more intricate. A careful look at the situation reveals that SSA, in subtle ways, wiggles its way out of the worst of the imputed implications.

ANALYSIS OF *LAZY ADAM*: PREDICTIONS AND COUNTERFACTUALS

This section discusses the second experiment, *Lazy Adam*. The first and the third experiments could be analyzed along similar lines.

Adam can repeat the *Lazy Adam* experiment many mornings. We note that if he intends to repeat the experiment, the number of offspring that he would have to intend to create increases. If the prior probability of a deer appearing is one in ten thousand and the trials are independent, then if he wants to do the experiment twice, he would have to intend to create at least on the order of ten million offspring. If he wants to repeat it ten times, he would have to intend to create 10^{40} offspring to get the odds work out in his favor.

The experiment seems *prima facie* to show that, given SSA, there will be a series of remarkable coincidences between Adam's procreational intentions and appearances of wounded deer. It was suggested that such a series of coincidences could be a ground for attributing paranormal causal powers to Adam.

The inference from a long series of coincidences to an underlying causal link can be disputed. Whether such an inference is legitimate would depend on how long the series of coincidences is, what the circumstances are, and also what theory of causation one should hold. If the series were sufficiently long and the coincidences sufficiently remarkable, intuitive pressure would mount to give the phenomenon a causal interpretation. One can fix the thought experiment so that these conditions are satisfied. For the sake of argument, we may assume the worst case for SSA, namely that if the series of coincidences occurs then Adam has anomalous causal powers. I shall argue that even if we accept SSA, we can still think that neither strange coincidences nor anomalous causal powers would have existed if the experiment had been carried out.

We need to be careful when stating what is implied by the argument given in the thought experiment. All that was shown is that Adam would have reason to believe that his forming the intentions will have the desired outcome. The argument can be extended to show that Adam would have reason to believe that the procedure can be repeated: provided he keeps forming the right intentions, he should think that morning after morning, a wounded deer will turn up. If he doesn't form the intention on some mornings, then on those mornings he should expect deer *not* to turn up. Adam thus has reason to think that deer turn up on those and only those mornings for which he formed the relevant intention. In other words, Adam has reason to believe there will be a coincidence. However, we cannot jump from this to the conclusion that there will actually be a coincidence. Adam could be mistaken. And he could be mistaken even though he is (as the argument in *Lazy Adam* showed, assuming SSA) perfectly rational.

Imagine for a moment that you are looking at the situation from an external point of view. That is, suppose (*per impossible?*) that you are an intelligent observer who is not a member of the reference class. Suppose you know the same non-indexical facts as Adam; that is, you know the same things as he does except such things as that "I am Adam" or "I am among the first two humans", etc. Then the probability you should assign to the proposition that a deer will limp by Adam's cave one specific morning conditional on Adam having formed the relevant intention earlier that morning is the same as what we called Adam's prior probability of deer walking by— one in ten thousand. As an external observer, you would not have reason to believe that there were to be a coincidence.[4]

Adam and the external observer, both being rational but having different information, make different predictions. At least one of them must be mis-

---

[4] The reason why there is a discrepancy between what Adam should believe and what the external observer should believe is of course that they have different information. If they had the same information, they could agree; cf. chapter 8.

taken (although both may be "right" in the sense of doing the best they can with the evidence available to them). In order to determine who was in fact mistaken, we should have to decide whether there would be a coincidence or not. Nothing said so far settles this question. There are possible worlds where a deer does turn up on precisely those mornings when Adam forms the intention, and there are other possible worlds where there is no such coincidence. The description of the thought experiment does not specify which of these two kinds of possible worlds we are referring to.

So far so good, but we want to be able to say something stronger. Let's pretend that there actually once existed these two first people, Eve and Adam, and that they had the reproductive capacities described in the experiment. We would want to say that if the experiment had actually been done (i.e. if Adam had formed the relevant intentions on certain mornings) then almost certainly *he would have found no coincidence.* Almost certainly, no wounded deer would have turned up. That much seems common sense. If SSA forced us to relinquish that conviction, it would count quite strongly as a reason for rejecting SSA.

We therefore have to evaluate a counterfactual: *If Adam had formed the relevant intentions, would there have been a coincidence?* To answer this, we need a theory of conditionals. I will use a simplified version of David Lewis' theory[5] but I think what I will say generalizes to other accounts of conditionals. Let w denote the actual world. (We are pretending that Adam and Eve actually existed and that they had the appropriate reproductive abilities etc.) To determine what would have happened had Adam formed the relevant intentions, we look at the closest[6] possible world w' where he did do the experiment. Let t be the time when Adam would have formed the intentions. When comparing worlds for closeness to w, we are to disregard features of them that exclusively concern what happens after t. Thus we seek a world in which Adam forms the intentions and which is maximally similar to w in two respects: first, in its history up to t; and, second, in its laws. Is the closest such world w', where Adam forms the intentions, one in which deer turn up accordingly, or is it one that lack an Adam-deer correlation?

The answer is quite clearly that there is no Adam-deer correlation in w'. For such a w' can be more similar to w on both accounts than can any world containing the correlation. Regarding the first account, whether there is a coincidence or not in a world presumably makes little difference as to how

---

[5] The parts of Lewis' theory that are relevant to the discussion here can be found in chapters 19 and 21 of (Lewis 1986).

[6] I'm simplifying in some ways, for instance by disregarding certain features of Lewis' analysis designed to deal with cases where there is no closest possible world, but perhaps an infinite sequence of possible worlds, each closer to the actual world than the preceding ones in the sequence. This and other complications are not relevant to the present discussion.

similar it can be to w with respect to its history up to t. But what difference it makes is in favor of no coincidence. This is so because in the absence of a correlation, the positions and states of the deer in the neighborhood at or shortly before t, could be exactly as in w (where none happened to stroll past Adam's cave on the mornings when he did the experiment). The presence of a correlation, on the other hand, would entail a world that is somewhat different from w with regard to the initial states of the deer.

Perhaps more decisively, a world with no Adam-deer correlation would tend to win out on the second account as well. w doesn't (as far as we know) contain any instances of anomalous causation. The laws of w do not support anomalous causation. The laws of any world containing an Adam-deer correlation, at least if the correlation were of the sort that would prompt us to ascribe it to an underlying causal connection, include laws supporting anomalous causation. By contrast, the laws of a world lacking the Adam-deer correlation could easily be exactly like the laws in w. Similarity of laws would therefore also favor a w' that lacks the correlation.

Since there is no correlation in w', the following statement is true: "If Adam had formed the intentions, he would have found no correlation". Although Adam would have had reason to think that there would be a coincidence, he would have found that he was mistaken.

One might wonder: if *we* know all this, why can't Adam reason in the same way? Couldn't he too figure out that there will be no coincidence?

He couldn't, and the reason is that he is lacking some knowledge you and I have. Adam has no knowledge of the future that will show that his innovative hunting technique will fail, whereas we can infer its failure from the fact that many people were born after Adam (ourselves included). If he does his experiment and deer do turn up on precisely those mornings he forms the intention, then it could (especially if the experiment were successfully repeated many times) be the case that the effect should be ascribed to a genuine psychokinetic capacity. If he does the experiment and no deer turns up, then of course he has no such capacity. But he has no means of knowing that no deer turns up. The evidence available to him strongly favors the hypothesis that there *will* be a coincidence. So although Adam may understand the line of reasoning that we have been pursuing here, it will not lead him to the conclusion we arrived at, because he lacks a crucial premiss.

There is a puzzling point here that needs be addressed. Adam knows that if he forms the intentions then he will very likely witness a coincidence. But he also knows that if he doesn't form the intentions then it will be the case that he will live in a world like w, where it is true that had he done the experiment he would most likely *not* have witnessed a coincidence. That looks paradoxical. Adam's forming (or not forming) the conditional procreational intentions gives him relevant information. Yet, the only information he gets is about what choice he made. If that information makes a difference as to whether he should expect to see a coincidence, isn't that just to say that his choice affects whether there will be a coincidence or not? If so, it would seem he has paranormal powers after all.

A more careful analysis reveals that this conclusion doesn't follow. True, the information Adam gets when he forms the intentions is about what choice he made. This information has a bearing on whether to expect a coincidence or not, but that doesn't mean that the choice is a *cause* of the coincidence. It is simply an *indication* of a coincidence. Some things are good indicators of other things without causing them. Take the stock example: the barometer's falling may be a good indicator of impending rain, but it is certainly not a cause of the rain. Similarly, there is no need to think of Adam's decision to procreate if and only if no deer walks by as a *cause* of that event, although it will lead Adam to rationally believe that that event will happen.

One may still perceive a lingering whiff of mystery. Maybe we can put it into words as follows. Let E be the proposition that Adam forms the reproductive intention at time $t = 1$. Let C stand for the proposition that there is a coincidence at time $t = 2$ (i.e. that a deer turns up). It would seem that the above discussion commits one to the view that at $t = 0$ Adam knows (probabilistically) the following:

(1)   If E then C.
(2)   If $\neg E$ then $\neg C$.
(3)   If $\neg E$ then "if E then it would have been the case that $\neg C$".

And there seems to be a conflict between (1) and (3).

I suggest that the appearance of a conflict is due to an equivocation in (3). To bring some light into this, we can paraphrase (1) and (2) as:

(1') $P_{\text{Adam}} (C | E) \approx 1$
(2') $P_{\text{Adam}} (\neg C | \neg E) \approx 1$

But we cannot paraphrase (3) as:

(3') $P_{\text{Adam}} (\neg C | E) \approx 1$

When we said earlier, "If Adam had formed the intentions, he would have found no correlation", we were asserting this on the basis of information that is available to us but not to Adam. Our background knowledge differs from Adam's in respect to both non-indexical facts (we have observed the absence of any subsequent correlation between persons' intentions and the behavior of deer) and indexical facts (we know that we are not among the first two people). Therefore, if (3) is to have any support in the preceding discussion, it must be explicated as:

(3") $P_{\text{We}} (\neg C | E) \approx 1$

This is not in conflict with (1'). We also asserted that Adam could know this. This gives:

(4) P_{Adam} ("P_{We} ($\neg C | E$) ≈ 1") ≈ 1

At first sight, it might seem as if there is a conflict between (4) and (1). However, appearances in this instance are deceptive.

Let's first see why it could *appear* as if there is a conflict. It has to do with the relationship between P_{Adam} and P_{We}. We have assumed that P_{Adam} is a rational probability assignment (in the sense: not just coherent but "reasonable, plausible, intelligent" as well) relative to the background knowledge that Adam has at $t = 0$. And P_{We} is a rational probability assignment relative to the background knowledge that we have, say at $t = 3$. (And of course, we pretend that we know that there actually was this fellow, Adam, at $t = 0$ and that he had the appropriate reproductive abilities etc.) But now, if we know everything Adam knew, and if in addition we have some extra knowledge, *and if Adam knows that*, then it is irrational of him to persist in believing what he believes. Instead he ought to adopt our beliefs, which he knows are based on more information. At least this follows if we assume, as we may in this context, that our a priori probability function is identical to Adam's, and that we haven't made any computational error, and that Adam knows all this. That would then imply (3') after all, which contradicts (1').

The fallacy in this argument is that it assumes that Adam knows that we know everything he knows. Adam doesn't know that, because *he doesn't know that we exist*. He may well know that *if* we exist then we will know everything (at least every objective—non-indexical—piece of information) that he knows and then some. But as far as he is concerned, we are just hypothetical beings.[7] So all that Adam knows is that there is some probability function, the one we designated 'P_{We}', that gives a high conditional probability of $\neg C$ given E. That gets him nowhere. There are infinitely many probability functions. Not knowing that we will actually exist, he has no more reason to tune his own credence to our probability function than to any other.

To summarize, what we have shown so far is the following: Granting SSA, we should think that if Adam and Eve had carried out the experiment, there would almost certainly *not* have been any strange coincidences. There is

---

[7] If he did know that we exist, then it would definitely *not* be the case that he should give a high conditional probability to C given E! Quite the opposite: he would have to set that conditional probability equal to zero. This is easy to see. For by the definition of the thought experiment, we are here only if Adam has a child. Also by stipulation, Adam has a child only if either he doesn't form the intention or he does and no deer turns up. It follows that if he forms the intention and we are here, then no deer turns up. So in this case, his beliefs would coincide with ours; we too know that if he formed the intentions then no deer turned up.

consequently no reason to ascribe anomalous causal powers to Adam. Eve and Adam would rationally think otherwise but they would simply be mistaken. Although they can recognize the line of reasoning we have been pursuing, they won't be moved by its conclusion, because it hinges on a premiss that we, but not they, know is true. Good news for SSA.

One more point needs to be addressed in relation to *Lazy Adam*. We have seen that what the thought experiments demonstrate is not strange coincidences or anomalous causation but simply that Adam and Eve would be misled. Now, there might be a temptation to see this by itself as a ground for rejecting SSA—if a principle misleads people it is unreliable and should not be adopted. This temptation is to be resisted. There is a good answer available to the SSA-proponent, as follows: It is in the nature of probabilistic reasoning that some people using it, if they are in unusual circumstances, will be misled. Eve and Adam were in highly unusual circumstances—they were the first two humans—so we shouldn't be too impressed by the fact that the reasoning based on SSA didn't work for them. For a fair assessment of the reliability of SSA, we have to look at how it performs not only in exceptional cases but in more normal cases as well.

Compare the situation to the *Dungeon* gedanken. There, remember, one hundred people were placed in different cells and were asked to guess the color of the outside of their own cell. Ninety cells were blue and ten red. SSA recommended that a prisoner thinks that with 90% probability he is in a blue cell. If all prisoners bet accordingly, 90% of them will win their bets. The unfortunate 10% who happen to be in red cells lose their bets, but it would be unfair to blame SSA for that. They were simply unlucky. Overall, SSA leads 90% to win, compared to merely 50% if SSA is rejected and people bet at random. This consideration works in favor of SSA.

What about the "overall effect" of everybody adopting SSA in the three experiments pondered above? Here the situation is more complicated because Adam and Eve have much more information than the people in the dungeon cells. Another complication is that these are stories where there are two competing hypotheses about the total number of observers. In both of these respects, the thought experiments are similar to the Doomsday argument and presumably no easier to settle. But here we are trying to find out whether there are some *other* problematic consequences of SSA that are not salient in DA—such as strange coincidences and anomalous causation.

THE UN^{++} GEDANKEN: REASONS AND ABILITIES

We shall now discuss a thought experiment that is similar to Adam & Eve, except that we might one day actually be able to carry it out.

UN^{++}
It is the year 2100 A.D. Technological advances have enabled the formation of an all-powerful and extremely stable world government, UN^{++}.

Any decision about human action taken by the UN^{++} will certainly be implemented. Bad news flash: signs have been detected that a series of n violent gamma ray bursts is about to take place at uncomfortably close quarters, threatening to damage (but not completely destroy) human settlements. For each hypothetical gamma ray burst in this series, astronomical observations give a 90% chance of it coming about. UN^{++} rises to the occasion and passes the following resolution: It will create a list of hypothetical gamma ray bursts, and for each entry on this list it decides that if the burst happens, it will build more space colonies so as to increase the total number of humans that will ever have lived by a factor of m. By arguments analogous to those in the earlier thought experiments, UN^{++} can then be confident that the gamma ray bursts will not happen, provided m is sufficiently great compared to n.

The *UN*$^{++}$ experiment introduces a new difficulty. For although creating UN^{++} and persuading it to adopt the plan would no doubt be a daunting undertaking, it is the sort of project that we could quite conceivably carry out by non-magical means. The *UN*$^{++}$ experiment places *us* in more or less the same situation that Adam and Eve occupied in the other three experiments. This twist compels us to carry the investigation one step further.

Let us suppose that if there is a long series of coincidences ("*C*") between items on the UN^{++} target list and failed gamma ray bursts, then there is anomalous causation ("*AC*"). This supposition is more problematic than was the corresponding assumption in our discussion of *Adam & Eve*. For the point of the *UN*$^{++}$ experiment is that it is claiming some degree of practical possibility, and it is not clear that this supposition could be satisfied in the real world. It depends on the details and on the nature of causation, but it could well be that the list of coincidences would have to be quite long before one would be inclined to regard it as a manifestation of an underlying causal link. And since the number of people that UN^{++} would have to create in case of failure increases rapidly as the list grows longer, it is not clear that such a plan is feasible. But let's shove this scruple to one side in order to give the objector to SSA as good a shot as he can hope to have.

A first point is that even if we accept SSA, it doesn't follow that we have reason to believe that *C* will happen. For we might think that it is unlikely both that UN^{++} will ever be formed and that, if formed, it will adopt and carry out the relevant sort of plan. Without UN^{++} being set up to execute the plan, there is of course no reason to expect *C* (and consequently no reason to believe that there will be *AC*).

But there is a more subtle way of attempting to turn this experiment into an objection against SSA. One could argue that we know that we now have the causal powers to create UN^{++} and make it adopt the plan; and we have good reason (given SSA) to think that if we do this then there will be *C* and hence *AC*. But if we now have the *ability* to bring about *AC* then *we now, ipso facto, have AC*. Since this is absurd, we should reject SSA.

This reasoning is fallacious. Our forming UN^{++} and making it adopt the plan would be an *indication* to us that there is a correlation between the list and gamma ray bursts.[8] But it would not *cause* there to be a correlation unless we do in fact have *AC*. If we don't have *AC*, then forming UN^{++} and making it adopt the plan (call this event "*A*") has no influence whatever on astronomical phenomena, although it misleads us to thinking we have. If we do have *AC* of the relevant sort, then of course the same actions would influence astronomical phenomena and cause a correlation. But the point is this: the fact that we have the ability to do *A* does not determine whether we have *AC*. It doesn't even imply that we have reason to think that we have *AC*.

In order to be perfectly clear about this point, let me explicitly write down the inference I am rejecting. I'm claiming that from the following two premises:

(5) We have strong reasons to think that if we do *A* then we will have brought about *C*.

(6) We have strong reasons to think that we have the power to do *A*.

one cannot legitimately infer:

(7) We have strong reasons to think that we have the power to bring about *C*.

My reason for rejecting this inference is that one can consistently hold the conjunction of (5) and (6) together with the following:

(8) If we don't do *A* then the counterfactual "Had we done *A* then *C* would have occurred" is false.

There might be a temptation to think that the counterfactual in (8) would have been true even if don't do *A*. I suggest that this is due to the fact that (granting SSA) our conditional probability of *C* given that we do *A* is large. Let's abbreviate this conditional probability '$P(C|A)$'. If $P(C|A)$ is large, doesn't that mean that *C* would (probably) have happened if we had done

---

[8] Under the supposition that if there is *AC* then there is *C*, the hypothesis that there will be *C* conflicts, of course, with our best current physical theories, which entail that the population policies of UN^{++} have no significant causal influence on distant gamma ray burst. However, a sufficiently strong probability shift (resulting from applying SSA to the hypothesis that UN^{++} will create a sufficiently enormous number of observers if *C* doesn't happen) would reverse any prior degree of confidence in current physics (so long as we assign it a credence of less than unity).

A? Not so. We must not confuse the conditional probability P(C| A) with the counterfactual "C would have happened if A had happened". For one thing, the reason why your conditional probability P(C| A) is large is that you have included indexical information (about your birth rank) in the background information. Yet one may well choose to exclude indexical information from the set of facts upon which counterfactuals are to supervene. (Especially so if one intends to use counterfactuals to define causality, which should presumably be an objective notion and therefore independent of indexical facts—see the next section for some further thoughts on this.)

So, to reiterate, even though P(C| A) is large (as stated in (5)) and even though we can do *A* (as stated in (6)), we still know that, *given that we don't do A*, *C* almost certainly does not happen and would not have happened even if we had done *A*. As a matter of fact, we have excellent grounds for thinking that we won't do *A*. The UN^{++} experiment, therefore, does not show that we have reason to think that there is *AC*. Good news for SSA, again.

Finally, although it may not be directly relevant to assessing whether SSA is true, it is interesting to ask: *Would it be rational* (given SSA) *for UN^{++} to adopt the plan?*[9]

The UN^{++} should decrease its credence of the proposition that a gamma ray burst will occur if it decides to adopt the plan. Its conditional credence P(Gamma ray burst | A) is smaller than P(Gamma ray burst); that is what the thought experiment showed. Provided a gamma ray burst has a sufficiently great negative utility, non-causal decision theories would recommend that we adopt the plan if we can.

What about causal decision theories? If our theory of causation is one on which no *AC* would be involved even if *C* happens, then obviously causal decision theories would say that the plan is misguided and shouldn't be adopted. The case is more complicated on a theory of causation that says that there is *AC* if *C* happens. UN^{++} should then believe the following: If it adopts the plan, it will have caused the outcome of averting the gamma ray burst; if it doesn't adopt the plan, then it is not the case that had it adopted the plan it would have averted the gamma ray bursts. (This essentially just repeats (5) and (8).) The question is whether causal decision theories would under these circumstances recommend that UN^{++} adopt the plan.

The decision that UN^{++} makes gives it information about whether it has *AC* or not. Yet, when UN^{++} deliberates on the decision, it can only take into account information available to it prior to the decision, and this information

---

[9] The reason this question doesn't seem relevant to the evaluation of SSA is that the answer is likely to be "spoils to the victor": proponents of SSA will say that whatever SSA implies is rational, and its critics may dispute this. Both would be guilty of question-begging if they tried to use it as an argument for or against SSA.

doesn't suffice to determine whether it has AC. UN^{++} therefore has to make its decision under uncertainty. Since on a causal decision theory UN^{++} should do A only if it has AC, UN^{++} would have to act on some preliminary guess about how likely it seems that AC; and since AC is strongly correlated with what decision UN^{++} makes, it would also base its decision, implicitly at least, on a guess about what its decision will be. If it thinks it will eventually choose to do A, it has reason to think it has AC, and thus it should do A. If it thinks it will eventually choose not to do A, it has reason to think that it hasn't got AC, and thus should not do A. UN^{++} therefore is faced with a somewhat degenerate decision problem in which it should choose whatever it initially guesses it will come to choose. More could no doubt be said about the decision theoretical aspects of this scenario, but we will leave it at that. Interested readers may compare the situation to the partly analogous case of the Meta-Newcomb problem presented in an appendix to this chapter.

QUANTUM JOE: SSA AND THE PRINCIPAL PRINCIPLE

Our final thought experiment probes the connection between SSA and objective chance:

> *Quantum Joe*
> Joe, the amateur scientist, has discovered that he is alone in the cosmos so far. He builds a quantum device which according to quantum physics has a one-in-ten chance of outputting any single-digit integer. He also builds a reproduction device which when activated will create ten thousand clones of Joe. He then hooks up the two so that the reproductive device will kick into action unless the quantum device outputs a zero; but if the output is a zero, then the reproductive machine will be destroyed. There are not enough materials left for Joe to reproduce in some other way, so he will then have been the only observer.

We can assume that quantum physics correctly describes the objective chances associated with the quantum device, and that Everett-type interpretations (including the many-worlds and the many-minds interpretations) are false; and that Joe knows this. Using the same kinds of argument as before, we can show that Joe should expect that a zero come up, even though the objective (physical) chance is a mere 10%.

Our reflections on the *Adam & Eve* and *UN⁺⁺* apply to this gedanken also. But here we shall focus on another problem: the apparent conflict between SSA and David Lewis' Principal Principle.

The Principal Principle requires, roughly, that one proportion one's credence in a proposition B in accordance with one's estimate of the objective chance that B will come true (Mellor 1971; Lewis 1980). For example, if you know that the objective chance of B is x%, then your subjective credence of B should be x%, provided you don't have "inadmissible" information. An early formalization of this idea turned out to be inconsistent when applied to so-called "undermining" futures, but this problem has recently been solved through the introduction of the "new Principal Principle", which states that:

$$P(B|HT) = Ch(B|T)$$

H is a proposition giving a complete specification of the history of the world up to time *t*, *T* is the complete theory of chance for the world (giving all the probabilistic laws), P is a rational credence function, and Ch is the chance function specifying the world's objective probabilities at time *t*. (For an explanation of the *modus operandi* of this principle and of how it can constitute the centerpiece of an account of objective chance, see (Hall 1994; Lewis 1994; Thau 1994).)

Now, Quantum Joe knows all the relevant aspects of the history of the world up to the time when he is about to activate the quantum device. He also has complete knowledge of quantum physics, the correct theory of chance for the world in which he is living. If we let *B* be the proposition that the quantum device outputs a zero, the new Principal Principle thus seems to recommend that he should set his credence of *B* equal to $Ch(B|T) \approx \frac{1}{10}$. Yet the SSA-based argument shows that his credence should be ≈ 1. Does SSA therefore require that we give up the Principal Principle?

I think this can be answered in the negative, as follows. True, Joe's credence of getting a zero should diverge from the objective chance of that outcome, even though he knows what that chance is. But that is because he is basing his estimation on inadmissible information. That being so, the new Principal Principle does not apply to Joe's situation. The inadmissible information is indexical information about his Joe's own position in the human species. Normally, indexical information does not affect one's subjective credence in propositions whose objective chances are known. But in certain kinds of cases, such as the one we are dealing with here, indexical information turns out to be relevant and must be factored in.

It not really surprising that the Principal Principle, which expresses the connection between objective chance and rational subjective credence, is trumped by other considerations in cases like these. For objective chances can be seen as concise, informative summaries of patterns of local facts about the world. (That is how they are seen in Lewis' analysis.) But the facts that form the supervenience base for chances are rightly taken not to include indexical facts, for chances are meant to be objective. Since indexical information is not baked into chances, it is only to be expected that your subjective credence may have to diverge from known objective chances if you have additional information of an indexical character that needs be taken into account.

So Quantum Joe can coherently believe that the objective chance (as given by quantum physics) of getting a zero is 10% and yet set his credence in that outcome close to one; he can accept both the Principal Principle and SSA.

UPSHOT

We have considered some challenges to SSA. In *Lazy Adam*, it looked as though on the basis of SSA we should think that Adam had the power to produce anomalous coincidences by will, exerting a psychokinetic influence on the nearby deer population. On closer inspection, it turned out that SSA implies no such thing. It gives us no reason to think that there would have been coincidences or psychic causation if Adam had carried out the experiment. SSA does lead Adam to think otherwise, but he would simply have been mistaken. We argued that the fact that SSA would have misled Adam is no good argument against SSA. For it is in the nature of probabilistic reasoning that exceptional users will be misled, and Adam is such a user. To assess the reliability of SSA-based reasoning one has to look at not only the special cases where it fails but also the normal cases where it succeeds. As we noted that in the *Dungeon* experiment (chapter 4), SSA does well in that regard.

With the UN^{++} gedanken, the scene was changed to one where we ourselves might actually have the ability to step into the role of Adam. We found that SSA does not give us reason to think that there will be strange coincidences or that we (or UN^{++}) have anomalous causal powers. However, there are some hypothetical (empirically implausible) circumstances under which SSA *would* entail that we had reason to believe these things. *If* we knew for certain that UN^{++} existed, had the power to create observers in the requisite numbers, and possessed sufficient stability to certainly follow through on its original plan, and that the other presuppositions behind the thought experiment were also satisfied (particularly, that all observers created would be in our reference class), *then* SSA implies that we should expect to see strange coincidences, namely that the gamma ray bursts on the UN^{++} target list would fizzle. (Intuitively: because this would make it enormously much less remarkable that we should have the birth ranks we have.)

We should think it unlikely, however, that this situation will arise. In fact, if we accept SSA we should think this situation *astronomically* unlikely— about as unlikely as the coincidences would be! We can see this without going into details. If we ever get into the situation where UN^{++} executes the plan, then one out of two things must happen, both of which have extremely low probabilities: a series of strange coincidences, or—which is even more unlikely given SSA—we happen to be among the very first few out of an astronomically large number of humans. If P_1 implies that either P_2 or P_3, and we assign very low probability both to P_2 and to P_3, then we must assign a low probability to P_1 as well.[10]

---

[10] Even if in objective respects we had been in a position to carry out the UN^{++} experiment, there would remain the epistemological problem of how we could ever be sufficiently certain that all preconditions were met. It may seem that only by means of an irrationally exaggerated faith in our capacity to know these things could we ever convince ourselves to the requisite

Finally, in *Quantum Joe* we examined an ostensible conflict between SSA and the Principal Principle. It was argued that this conflict is merely apparent because the SSA-line of reasoning relies on indexical information that should properly be regarded as "inadmissible" and thus outside the scope of the Principal Principle.

These results are at least partially reassuring. All the same, I think it is fair to characterize as deeply counterintuitive the SSA-based advice to Eve, that she need not worry about pregnancy, and its recommendation to Adam, that he should expect a deer to walk by given that the appropriate reproductive intentions are formed, and Quantum Joe's second-guessing of quantum physics. And yet we *seem* to be forced to these conclusions by the arguments given in support of SSA in chapters 4 and 5 (and against SIA in chapter 7).

The next chapter shows a way out of this dilemma. We don't have to accept any of the counterintuitive implications discussed above, and we can still have a workable, unified theory of observation selection effects. The key to this is to take *more* indexical information into account than does SSA.

APPENDIX: THE META-NEWCOMB PROBLEM[11]

The following variant of the Newcomb problem may be compared to the answer to question 4 for the case where C would constitute a causal connection.

Meta-Newcomb. There are two boxes in front of you and you are asked to choose between taking only box B or taking both box A and box B. Box A contains \$1,000. Box B will contain either nothing or \$1,000,000.

---

level of confidence that UN^{++} will forever stick to the plan, that no aliens lurk in some remote corner of the universe, and so on. Likewise in the case of *Adam & Eve*, we may question whether Adam could realistically have known enough about his world for the example to work. Sure, Adam might receive a message from God (or rather the non-observer automaton that has created the world) but can Adam be sufficiently sure that the message is authentic? Or that he is not dreaming it all?

Milan Ćirković (Ćirković 2001) has suggested that "coherence gaps" like these might take some of the sting out of the consequences displayed in this chapter. Maybe so, but my suspicion is that choosing more realistic parameters will not do away with the weirdness so much as make it harder to perceive. The probability shifts would be smaller but they would still be there. One can also consider various ways of fleshing out the stories so that fairly large probability shifts could be attained, e.g. by postulating that the people involved have spent a great deal of time and effort verifying that all the preconditions are met, that they have multiple independent strands of evidence showing that to be the case, and so on.

The bottom line, however, is that if somebody can live comfortably with the SSA-implications discussed in this chapter, there is nothing to prevent them from continuing to use SSA with the universal reference class. The theory we'll present in the next chapter subsumes this possibility as a special case while also allowing other solutions that avoid these implications.

[11] This appendix was first published in *Analysis* (Bostrom 2001) and is reprinted here with permission.

What *B* will contain is (or will be) determined by Predictor, who has an excellent track record of predicting your choices. There are two possibilities. Either Predictor has already made his move by predicting your choice and putting a million dollars in *B* iff he predicted that you will take only *B* (as in the standard Newcomb problem); or else Predictor has not yet made his move but will wait and observe what box you choose and then put a million dollars in *B* iff you take only *B*. In cases like this, Predictor makes his move before the subject roughly half of the time. However, there is a Metapredictor, who has an excellent track record of predicting Predictor's choices as well as your own. You know all this. Metapredictor informs you of the following truth functional: Either you choose *A* and *B*, and Predictor will make his move after you make your choice; or else you choose only *B*, and Predictor has already made his choice. Now, what do you choose?

"Piece of cake!" says the naïve non-causal decision theorist. She takes just box *B* and walks off, her pockets bulging with a million dollars.

But if you are a causal decision theorist you seem to be in for a hard time. The additional difficulty you face compared to the standard Newcomb problem is that you don't know whether your choice will have a causal influence on what box *B* contains. In a sense, the decision problem presented here is the opposite of the one faced by UN^{++}. There, a preliminary belief about what you will choose would be transformed into a reason for making that choice. Here, a preliminary decision would seem to undermine itself (given a causal decision theory). If Predictor made his move before you make your choice, then (let us assume) your choice doesn't affect what's in the box. But if he makes his move after yours, by observing what choice you made, then you certainly do causally determine what *B* contains. A preliminary decision about what to choose seems to undermine itself. If you think you will choose two boxes then you have reason to think that your choice will causally influence what's in the boxes, and hence that you ought to take only one box. But if you think you will take only one box then you should think that your choice will *not* affect the contents, and thus you would be led back to the decision to take both boxes; and so on *ad infinitum*.

CHAPTER 10

Observation Selection Theory
A Methodology for Anthropic Reasoning

This chapter brings all the lessons from the foregoing chapters together and presents a theory of observation selection effects. It provides a method for taming anthropic biases and a general framework for connecting theory and observation.

BUILDING BLOCKS, THEORY CONSTRAINTS AND DESIDERATA

Let's start by reviewing some of the materials and tools that we have on our workbench:

Chapter 2 established several preliminary conclusions concerning the use of anthropic arguments in cosmology. We shall want to revisit these when we have formulated the observation selection theory and see if it replicates the earlier findings or if some revisions are required.

Chapter 3 homed in on what seemed to lie at the core of anthropic reasoning and expressed it in a tentative principle, SSA, which described a way of taking into account indexical information about which observer one has turned out to be.

Chapter 4 developed several thought experiments in support of SSA. The *Incubator* gedanken is especially important because it provided the link to the Doomsday argument and the various paradoxical results we examined in chapter 9.

Chapter 5 showed how something like SSA is needed to make sense of certain types of scientific theorizing such as in linking Big-World cosmological models to empirical data.

Chapter 6 analyzed the Doomsday argument. We found shortcomings in the versions that have been presented in the literature, we argued that John Leslie's proposal for solving the reference class problem is unworkable, and we showed that DA has alternative interpretations and is inconclusive. However, it has not been refuted by any of the easy objections that we examined in chapter 7. In particular, we rejected the claim that SIA is the way to neutralize the counterintuitive effects that SSA can have in certain applications.

Chapter 8 proved a kind of "coherence" for SSA-based reasoning: it was shown not to lead to alleged paradoxical "observer-relative" chances or implausible betting-frenzy between rational agents (in the wide range of cases considered).

In chapter 9, the *Adam & Eve*, UN^{++}, and *Quantum Joe* thought experiments demonstrated counterintuitive consequences of SSA, although we also saw that these consequences do not include the *prima facie* one that SSA gives us reason to believe in paranormal causation. The genuine implications of SSA are not impossible to accept; John Leslie, for one, is quite willing to bite the bullets. Yet many of us, endowed with less hardy epistemic teeth and stomachs, may find a meal of such ammunition a rather unpalatable experience and would prefer an alternative theory that does not have these implications, supposing one can be found that is satisfactory on other accounts.

Let's list what some of these criteria are that an observation selection theory should satisfy:

• The observation selection effects described by the Carter-Leslie versions of WAP and SAP must be heeded; these should come out as special case injunctions of a more general principle.

• The theory *must* be able to handle the problem of freak observers in Big-World cosmological models.

• More generally, observation selection effects in cosmology, including ones of a probabilistic nature, must be taken into account. The theory should connect in constructive ways with current research in physical cosmology that is addressing these issues.

• The theory should also make it possible to model observation selection effects in other sciences, including the applications in evolutionary biology, thermodynamics, traffic analysis, and quantum physics that we reviewed in chapter 5.

• The arguments set forth in the thought experiments in chapter 4 must be respected to the extent that they are sound.

• The theory should not explicitly or implicitly rely on SIA or on any supposition that amounts to the same thing. (Or if it does, a very strong defense against the objections raised against SIA in chapter 7, including *The Presumptuous Philosopher* gedanken, would have to be provided.) Also, the theory must obviously not employ any of the defective ideas and misunderstandings we exposed when scrutinizing the various objection against DA in chapter 6.

• Not strictly a criterion, but certainly a desideratum, is that the counterintuitive implications of SSA discussed in chapter 9 be avoided.

• Something needs to be said about the reference class problem: Where is the boundary of how the reference class can be defined? What are the considerations that determine this boundary?

• In most general terms, the theory should provide a sound methodology for linking up theory with observational data, including ones that have indexical components.

When these specific criteria and desiderata are combined with the usual generic theoretical goals—simplicity, coherence, non-arbitrariness, exactness, intuitive plausibility, etc.—we have enough constraints that we will be happy if we can find even one theory that fits the bill.

THE OUTLINE OF A SOLUTION

In order to reach the observation selection theory we are searching for, we shall have to traverse the following sequence of ideas.

Step one: We recognize that there is additional indexical information—apart from the information you might have about which observer you are—that needs to be taken into account. In particular, you may also have relevant information about which temporal part of a given observer that you currently are. We must strengthen SSA in a way that lets us model the evidential import of such information.

Step two: We zoom in on the *Incubator* gedanken as the simplest situation where SSA leads to the kind of reasoning that we saw in the previous chapter gives counterintuitive results if it is applied to *Adam & Eve* etc. We need to think carefully about what is going on in this example and study what happens when we apply the strengthened version of SSA to it.

Step three: We note that the answer given by applying SSA to *Incubator* in accordance with Model 2 (described in chapter 4) can be avoided if we relativize the reference class in a certain way.

Step four: We realize that the arguments given for Model 2 are defeated by the strengthened version of SSA. Since this version takes more indexical information into account, it trumps SSA in cases of disagreement. This gives us the authority to reject the claim that Model 2 has to be used in all cases where the number of observers is a variable. Instead, a new model using relativized reference classes is formulated which is more generally valid and which enables us to resolve the paradoxes of chapter 9.

Step five: We abstract from the particulars and find a general probabilistic formula that specifies the relation between evidence, hypotheses, and reference classes.

Step six: We show how this formula embodies a methodology that meets the criteria and desiderata listed in the previous section.

SSSA: Taking account of indexical information of observer-moments

Just as one can be ignorant about which observer one is, and one can get new information by finding out, and this information can be relevant evidence for various non-indexical hypotheses—so likewise can one be ignorant about which temporal part of an observer one currently is, and such indexical information can bear on non-indexical hypotheses. Observation selection effects can be implicated in both cases. Not surprisingly, there are extensive similarities in how we should model reasoning using these two types of indexical information.

We shall use the term "*observer-moment*" to refer to a brief time-segment of an observer. We can now consider the obvious analogue to SSA that applies to observer-moments instead of observers. Call this the *Strong Self-Sampling Assumption*:

> *(SSSA)* One should reason as if one's present observer-moment were a random sample from the set of all observer-moments in its reference class.

Consider the simple case of Mr. Amnesiac (depicted in figure 3):

> *Mr. Amnesiac*
> Mr. Amnesiac, the only observer ever to exist, is created in Room 1, where he stays for two hours. He is then transported in into Room 2, where spends one hour, whereupon he is terminated. His severe amnesia renders him incapable of retaining memories for any significant period of time. The details about the experimental situation he is in, however, are explained on posters in both rooms; so he is always aware of the relevant non-indexical features of his world.

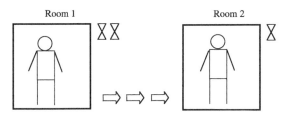

Figure 3: Mr. Amnesiac spending different amounts of time in two rooms

It is plausible to require that Mr. Amnesiac's credence at each point that he is currently in Room 1 be twice as large as his credence that he is in Room 2. In other words, all observer-moments in this gedanken should set P("This observer-moment is in Room 1 | Information about the setup) = ⅔. Arguments to back up this claim can be obtained easily by adapting the reasoning we used to support the view that in the *Dungeon* gedanken (chapter 4), one's credence of being in a blue cell should equal 90% (the fraction of cells that are blue). This in agreement with SSSA. By varying the proportions of Mr. Amnesiac's lifespan that he spends in various rooms, we can generalize the finding to a larger set of cases.

In the same manner, we can handle the case where instead of one observer being moved between the rooms, we have two different observers who exist, one in each room, for two hours and one hour, respectively (figure 4). We assume that the lights are out so that the observers cannot see what color beard they have, and that they have amnesia so that they can't remember how long they have been in a room.

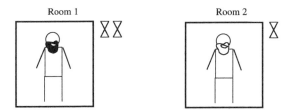

Figure 4: Two amnesiacs spending different amounts of time in two rooms

By SSSA, both observers should at each point in time set:

P(I am currently in Room 1 | Information about the setup) = ⅔
P(I am currently in Room 2 | Information about the setup) = ⅓.

This result can be backed up by betting arguments similar to those used to justify our analysis of *Dungeon* in chapter 4. We may suppose, for example, that every five minutes the observers are called upon to bet on which room they are in, and we can then calculate the fair odds at which their combined expected gain is zero.

Before we proceed, we should note that the definition did not specify the exact duration of an observer-moment. Doesn't this omission generate a serious degree of vagueness in the formulation of SSSA? Not so. So long as we are consistent and partition observers into time-segments of equal duration, it doesn't matter how long a unit of subjective time is (provided it is sufficiently fine-grained for the problem at hand). For example, in *Mr. Amnesiac* it does not matter whether an observer-moment lasts for five seconds or five minutes or one hour. In either case, there are twice as many observer-moments (of the same reference class) being spent in Room 1, and that is enough for SSSA to recommend a credence of ⅔ of being in Room 1 for all observer-moments.

For the purposes of SSSA, it may be appropriate to partition observers into segments of equal *subjective* time. If one observer has twice the amount of experience in a given time interval as another observer, it seems quite plausible to associate twice as many observer-moments to the former observer during the interval. Thus, for instance, if two similar observers could be similarly implemented on two distinct pieces of silicon hardware (Drexler 1985; Moravec 1989), and we run one of the computers at a faster clock rate, then on this line of reasoning that would result in more observer-moments being produced per second in the faster computer.[1] Subjective

---

[1] One science-fiction method of uploading a human mind to a computer is as follows: (1) Through continued progress in computational neuroscience, create a catalogue of the functional properties of the various types of neurons and other computational elements in the human brain. (2) Use e.g. advanced nanotechnology to disassemble a particular human brain and create a three-dimensional map of its neuronal network at a sufficient level of detail (presumably at least on the neuronal level but if necessary down to the molecular level). (3) Use a powerful computer to run an emulation of this neuronal network. This means that the computations that took place in the original biological brain are now performed by the computer. (4) Connect the emulated intellect to suitable input/output organs if you want it to be able to interact with the external world. Assuming computationalism is true, this will result in the uploaded mind continuing to exist (with the same memories, desires, etc.) on its new computational substrate. (The intuitive philosophical plausibility of the scenario may be increased if you imagine a more gradual transformation, with one neuron at a time being replaced by a silicon microprocessor that performs the same computation. At no point would there be a discontinuity in behavior, and the subject would not be able to tell a difference; and at the end of the transformation we have a silicon implementation of the mind. For a more detailed analysis, see e.g. (Merkle 1994).

time, thus, is not about how long an observer *thinks* an interval is—one can easily be mistaken about that—but it is, rather, a measure of the actual amount of cognition and experience that have taken place. However, nothing in the following discussion hinges on this idea.[2]

SSSA is a strengthening of SSA in the sense that it takes more indexical information into account: not only information about which observer you are but also information about which temporal part of that observer you currently are. SSSA is *not* necessarily a strengthening of SSA in the sense that it has all the same implications that SSA has and then some. Au contraire, we shall argue that the extra informational component that SSSA includes in its jurisdiction introduces new degrees of freedoms for rational belief compared to SSA—basically because this added information can be legitimately evaluated in divergent ways. Consequently, there is a potential for rational disagreements (on the basis of this larger set of indexical information now underlying our judgments) that didn't exist before (in relation to the more limited set of information that SSA deals with). This means that some limitations on rational belief that would obtain if SSA were all we had are no longer applicable once we realize that SSA left out important considerations. So in one sense, SSSA is sometimes weaker than SSA, namely, because in some cases it imposes fewer restrictions on rational credence assignments.

REASSESSING INCUBATOR

Next we zero in on a key lesson that emerges from the preceding investigations: that the critical point, the fountainhead, of all the paradoxical results seems to be the contexts where the hypotheses under consideration have different implications about the total number of observers in existence. Such is the way with DA, the various *Adam & Eve* experiments, *Quantum Joe*, and UN^{++}. By contrast, things seem to be humming along perfectly nicely so long as the total number of observers is held constant.

---

[2] If subjective time is a better measure of the duration of observer-moments than chronological time, this might suggest that an even more fundamental entity for self-sampling to be applied to would be (some types of) thoughts, or occurrent ideas. SSSA can lead to longer-lived observers getting a higher sampling density by virtue of their containing more observer-moments. One can ponder whether one should not also assign a higher sampling density to certain types of observer-moments, for example those that have a greater degree of clarity, intensity, or focus. Should we say that if there were (counterfactually!) equally many deep and perspicacious anthropic thinkers as there are superficial and muddled ones then one should, other things equal, expect to find one's current observer-moment to be one of the more lucid observer-moments? And should one think that one were more likely to find oneself as an observer who spends an above-average amount of time thinking about observation selection effects? This would follow if only observer-moments spent pondering problems of observation selection effects are included in one's current reference class, or if such observer-moments are assigned a very high sampling density. And if one does in fact find oneself as such an observer, who is rather frequently engaged in anthropic reasoning, could one take that as private evidence in favor of the just-mentioned approach?

Here is another clue: Recall that we remarked in chapter 4 that the cases in which the definition of the reference class is relevant for our probability assignments seem to be precisely those in which the total number of observers depends on which hypothesis is true. This suggests that the solution we are trying to find has something to with how the reference class is defined.

So that we may focus our beam of attention as sharply as possible on the critical point, let us contemplate the simplest case where the number of observers is a variable and that we can use to model the reasoning in DA and the problematic thought experiments: *Incubator.* Now that we have SSSA, it is useful to add some details to the original version:

> *Incubator*, version III
> The incubator tosses a fair coin in an otherwise empty world. If the coin falls heads, the incubator creates one room with a black-bearded observer and one room with one white-bearded observer; if it falls tails, the incubator creates only a room with a black-bearded observer. Observers first spend one hour in darkness (being ignorant about their beard color), and then one hour with the lights on (so they can see their beard in a mirror). Everyone knows the setup. After two hours, the experiment ends and everybody is killed.

The situation is depicted in figure 5. For simplicity, we can assume that there is one observer-moment per hour and observer.

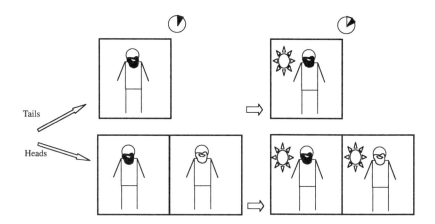

Figure 5: *Incubator*, version III

We discussed three models for how to reason about *Incubator* in chapter 4. We rejected Model 1 and Model 3 and were thus left with Model 2—the model embodying the kind of reasoning that got us into trouble in Chapter 9. Is it perhaps possible that there is fourth model, a better way of reasoning that can be accessed by means of the more powerful analytical resources provided by SSSA? Let's consider again what the observer-moments in *Incubator* should believe.

To start with, suppose that all observer-moments are in the same reference class. Then it follows directly from SSSA that[3]

P("This is an observer-moment that knows it has a black beard" | Tails) = ½

P("This is an observer-moment that knows it has a black beard" | Heads) = ¼

Together with the fact that the coin toss is known to have been fair, this implies that after the light comes on, the observer-moment that knows it has a black beard should assign a credence of ⅓ to Heads. This is the conclusion that, when transposed to DA and the *Adam & Eve* thought experiments, leads to the problematic probability shift in favor of hypotheses that imply fewer additional observers.[4]

This suggests that if we are unwilling to accept these consequences, we should not place all observer-moments in the same reference class. Suppose that we instead put the early observer-moments in one reference class and the late observer-moments in separate reference classes. We'll see how this move might be justified in the next section, but we can already note that

---

[3] From now on, we suppress information about the experimental setup, which is assumed to be shared by all observer-moments and is thus implicitly conditionalized on in all credence assignments.

[4] It would be an error to regard these probability shifts as representing some sort of "inverse SIA". SIA would have you assign a higher a priori (i.e. conditional only on the fact that you exist) probability to worlds that contain greater numbers of observers. But the DA-like probability shift in favor of hypotheses entailing fewer observers does not represent a general a priori bias in favor of worlds with fewer observers. What it does, rather, is reduce the probability of those hypotheses on which there would be many additional observers beyond yourself compared to hypotheses on which it also *was guaranteed* that an observer like you would exist although not accompanied by as many other observers. Thus is is because there would still be "early" observers whether or not the human species lasts for long that finding yourself one of these early observers gives you reason, according to DA, to think that there will not be hugely many observers after you. This probability shift is a posteriori and applies only to those observers who know that they are in the special position of being early (or who have some other such property that is privileged in the sense that the number of people likely to have it is independent of which of the hypotheses in question happens to be true).

making the choice of reference class context-dependent in this way is not entirely arbitrary. The early observer-moments, which are in very similar states, are in the same reference class. The observer-moment that has discovered that it has a black beard is in an importantly different state (no longer wondering about its beard color) and is thus placed in a different reference class. The observer-moment that has discovered it has a white beard is again different from all the other observer-moments (it is, for instance, in a state of no uncertainty as to its beard color and can deduce logically that the coin fell heads), and so it also has its own reference class. The differences between the observer-moments are significant at least in the respect that they concern what information the observer-moments have that is relevant to the problem at hand, viz. to guess how the coin fell.

If we use this reference class partitioning, then SSSA no longer entails that the observer-moment who has discovered that it has a black beard should favor the Tails hypothesis. Instead, that observer-moment will now assign equal credence to either outcome of the coin toss. This is because on either Tails or Heads, *all* observer-moments in its reference class (which is now the singleton consisting only of that observer-moment itself) observe what it is observing; so SSSA gives:

P("This is an observer-moment that knows it has a black beard" | Tails) = 1

P("This is an observer-moment that knows it has a black beard" | Heads) = 1

The problematic probability shift is thus avoided.

It remains the case that the early observer-moments, who are ignorant about their beard-color, assign an even credence to Heads and Tails; so we have not imported the illicit SIA criticized in chapter 7.

As for the observer-moment that discovers that it has a white beard, SSSA gives the following conditional probabilities:

P("This is an observer-moment that knows it has a black beard" | Tails) = 0

P("This is an observer-moment that knows it has a black beard" | Heads) = 1

So that observer-moment is advised to assign zero credence to the Tails hypothesis (which would have made its existence impossible).

HOW THE REFERENCE CLASS MAY BE OBSERVER-MOMENT RELATIVE

Can it be permissible for different observer-moments to use different reference classes? We can turn this question around by asking: Why should different observer-moments not use different reference classes? What argument is there to show that such a way of assigning credence would necessarily be irrational?

In chapter 4, we gave an argument for accepting Model 2, the model asserting that the observer who knows he has a black beard should assign a greater than even credence to Tails. The argument had the following form: First consider what you should believe if you don't know your beard color; second, in this state of ignorance, assign conditional probabilities to you having a given beard color given Heads or given Tails; third, upon learning your beard color, use Bayesian kinematics to update the credence function obtained through the first two steps. The upshot of this process is that after finding that you have a black beard, your credence of Tails should be ⅔.

Let's try to recapture this chain of reasoning in our present framework using observer-moments. The early observer-moments don't know whether they have black or white beard, but they can consider the conditional probabilities of that given a particular outcome of the coin toss. They know that on Heads, one out of two of the observer-moments in their epistemic situation has a black beard; and on Tails, one out of one has a black beard:

P("This observer-moment has a black beard" | Tails & Early) = 1

P("This observer-moment has a black beard" | Heads & Early) = ½

("Early" stands for "This observer-moment exists during the first hour".) One can easily see that this credence assignment is independent of whether one uses the universal reference class is used or the partition of reference classes described above. Moreover, since the observer-moments know that the coin toss is fair, they also assign an even credence to Heads and Tails.[5] This gives (via Bayes' theorem):

P(Tails | "This observer-moment has a black beard" & Early) = ⅔
(C1)

P(Heads | "This observer-moment has a black beard" & Early) = ⅓
(C2)

When the lights come on, one observer discovers he has a black beard. The old argument that is now being questioned would now have him update his credence by applying Bayesian conditionalization to the condi-

---

[5] Note that in this case there is no DA-like probability-shift from finding that you are an "early" observer-moment, because the proportion of observer-moments that are early is the same on the Heads and the Tails hypotheses. Even if the universal reference classed were used, the DA-shift would come only from discovering that you have black beard.

tional credence assignments (C1 & C2) that he made when he was ignorant about his beard color. And this where the argument fails. For the later
observer-moment's evidence is not equivalent to the earlier observer-
moment's evidence conjoined with the proposition that it has a black
beard. The later observer-moment has also *lost* knowledge of the indexical proposition "Early", and moreover, the indexical proposition expressed
by "This observer-moment has a black beard" is a different one when the
thought is entertained by the later observer-moment, since "this" then
refers to a different observer-moment.

Therefore, we see that the argument that would force the acceptance of
Model 2 relies on the implicit premiss that the only relevant epistemological difference between the observer before and after he discovers his
beard color is that he gains the information that is taken into account by
the Bayesian conditionalization referred to in step three. If there are other
relevant informational changes between the "early" and the "late" states of
the observer, then there is no general reason to think that his credence
assignments in the latter state should be obtained by simply conditionalizing on the finding that he is an observer with black beard. In chapter 4,
were we had by stipulation limited our consideration to only such indexical information as concerned which observer one is, this hidden premiss
was satisfied; for the latter state of the observer then differed from the
early one in precisely one regard, namely, by having acquired the indexical information that he is the observer with the black beard—the information that was conditionalized on in step three. *Now*, however, this tacit
assumption is no longer supported. For we now have also to consider
changes in other kinds of indexical information that might have occurred
between the early and the late stages. This includes the change in the
indexical information about which temporal part of the observer (i.e.
which observer-moment) one currently constitutes. Before the observer
finds that he has a black beard, he knows the piece of indexical information that "this current observer-moment is one that is ignorant about its
beard color". After finding out that he has a black beard, he has *lost* that
piece of indexical information (the indexical fact no longer obtains about
him); and the information he has gained includes the indexical fact that
"this current observer-moment is one that knows that it has a black beard".
These differences in information (which the argument for Model 2 fails to
take into account) could potentially be relevant to what credence the
observer should assign to the Tails and Heads hypotheses after he has
found out that he has a black beard.

Consider now the claim that the reference class is observer-moment relative, more specifically, that the early and the late observer-moments should
use different reference classes, as described above. Then, since the reference class is what determines the conditional probabilities that are used in

the calculation of the posterior probabilities of Heads or Tails, we have to acknowledge that the difference in indexical information just referred to *is* directly relevant and must therefore be taken into account. The indexical information that the early observer-moments use to derive the conditional probabilities C1 and C2 (namely, the indexical information that they are early observer-moments, which is what determines that their reference class is, which in turn determines these conditional probabilities) is lost and replaced by different indexical information when we turn to the later observer-moments. The later observer-moments, having different indexical information, belong, ex hypothesi, in a different reference classes mandating a different set of conditional probabilities. If a late observer-moment's reference class does not include early observer-moments, then its conditional probability (given either Heads or Tails) of being an early observer-moment is zero. Conditionalizing on being a late observer-moment would therefore have no influence on the credence that the late observer-moment assigns to the possible outcomes of the coin toss. (The late observer-moment that has discovered it has a white beard has of course got *another* piece of relevant information, which implies Tails, so that's what it should believe, with probability unity.)

The argument I've just given does not show that the difference in indexical information about which observer-moment one currently is *requires* that different reference classes be used. All it does is to show that this is now an open possibility, and that the argument to the contrary that was earlier used to support model 2 can no longer be applied once the purview is expanded to SSSA which takes into account a more complete set of indexical information. What this means is that the arguments relying on Model 2 can now be seen to be *inconclusive*; they don't prove what they set out to prove. We are therefore free to reject DA and the assertion that Adam and Eve, Quantum Joe and UN^{++} should believe the counterintuitive propositions which, if the sole basis of evaluation were the indexical information taken into account by SSA, they might have been rationally required to accept.

Indeed, the fact that the choice of a universal reference class leads to the implausible conclusions of chapter 9 is a reason for rejecting the universal reference class as the exclusively rational alternative. It suggests that, instead, choosing reference in a more context-dependent manner is a preferable method. I am not claiming that this reason is conclusive. One *could* choose to accept the consequences discussed in *Adam & Eve*, *Quantum Joe* and *UN^{++}*. If one is willing to do that then nothing that has been said here stops one from using a universal reference class. But if one is unwilling to embrace those results, then the way in which one can coherently avoid doing so is by insisting that one's choice of reference class is to some degree dependent on context (specifically, on indexical information concerning which observer-moment one currently is).

The task now awaiting us is to explain how an observation selection theory can be developed that meets all the criteria and desiderata listed above and that can operate with a relativized reference class. The framework we shall propose is neutral in regard to the reference class definition. It can therefore be used either with a universal reference class or with a relativized reference class. The theory specifies how credence assignments are to be made *given* a choice of reference class. This is a virtue because in the absence of solid grounds for claiming that only one particular reference class definition can be rationally permissible, it would be wrong to rule out other definitions by fiat. This is not to espouse a policy of complete laissez-faire as regards the choice of reference class. We shall see that there are interesting limits on the range of permissible choices.

FORMALIZING THE THEORY: THE OBSERVATION EQUATION

A centerpiece of our observation selection theory is the probabilistic connection between theory and observation that enables one to derive observational consequences from theories about the distribution of observer-moments in the world. Here we shall first propose an equation that gives a specification of this fundamental methodological link. Then we shall illustrate how it works by applying it to *Incubator*.

Let α be an observer-moment whose subjective probability function is P_α. Let Ω_α be the class of all possible observer-moments that belong to the same reference class as α (according to α's reference class definition $\Re_\alpha$).[6] Let w_α be the possible world in which α is located. Let e be some evidence and h some hypothesis, and let Ω_e and Ω_h be the classes of possible observer-moments "about whom" e and h are true, respectively. (If h ascribes a property to observer-moments—e.g. h:= "This is an observer-moment that has a black beard"—then we say that h is *true about* those and only those possible observer-moments that have the property in question; if h is non-indexical, not referring to any particular observer-moment, then h is *true about* all and only those possible observer-moments that live in possible worlds where h holds true. And similarly for e.) Finally, let $\Omega(w)$ be the class of observer-moments in the possible world w. We then have:

---

[6] Earlier we included only actually existing observer-moments in the reference class. It is expedient for present purposes, however, to have a concise notation for this broader class which includes possible observer-moments, so from now on we use the term "reference class" for this more inclusive notion. This is merely a terminological convenience and does not by itself reflect a substantive deviation from our previous approach.

$$P_\alpha(h|e) = \frac{1}{\gamma} \sum_{\sigma \in \Omega_h \cap \Omega_e} \frac{P_\alpha(w_\sigma)}{|\Omega_\sigma \cap \Omega(w_\sigma)|} \qquad \text{(OE)}$$

where γ is a normalization constant

$$\gamma = \sum_{\sigma \in \Omega_e} \frac{P_\alpha(w_\sigma)}{|\Omega_\sigma \cap \Omega(w_\sigma)|}.$$

Let us apply OE to *Incubator* to calculate what credence an observer should assign to Heads upon finding that he has a black beard. In order to do that we must first specify what reference class definition is used by the corresponding possible observer-moments (i.e. those that are in a state of knowing that they have black beards). Let's call these possible observer-moments β_2 and β_4 (see figure 6). We need two such possible observer-moments in our model of the problem since there are two relevant possible worlds, one (w_1) where Heads is true and one (w_2) where Tails is true, and there is one possible observer-moment knowing it has a black beard in each of these possible worlds. For the sake of illustration, let's assume that the reference class definition $\mathfrak{R}_{\beta_{2,4}}$ used by β_2 and β_4 is the one discussed above that places these two possible observer-moments in a separate reference from the possible observer-moments that don't know their beard color and places the possible observer-moment that knows it has a white beard in a third reference class on its own. (In the interest of brevity, we shall from now on frequently refer to possible observer-moments simply as "observer-moments", when context makes it clear what is meant.)

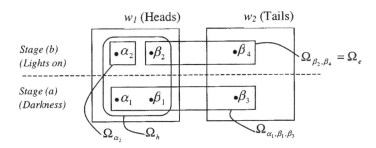

Figure 6: *Incubator* III, observer-moment representation

We can assume that the observer-moments share the prior $P(w_1) = P(w_2) = $ ½. Let *h* be the hypothesis that the coin fell heads, and *e* the total information available to an observer-moment that knows it has a black beard. As shown in the diagram (where the α-observer-moments are those belonging to the possible white-bearded observer) we have:

$$\Omega_e = \Omega_{\beta_2} = \Omega_{\beta_4} = \{\beta_2, \beta_4\}$$

$$\Omega_e \cap \Omega_b = \{\beta_2\}$$

$$w_{\beta_2} = w_1$$

$$w_{\beta_4} = w_2$$

$$\Omega_{\beta_2} \cap \Omega(w_{\beta_2}) = \{\beta_2\}$$

From this it follows that $P_{\beta_{2,4}}(h\,|\,e) = \frac{1}{2}$ (and $\gamma = 1$). The observer, upon finding he has a black beard, should consequently profess prefect ignorance about the outcome of the coin toss.

A QUANTUM GENERALIZATION OF OE

If one adopts a many-worlds interpretation of quantum physics of the type that postulates a primitive connection between the quantum measure of an observer-moment and the probability of finding oneself currently as that observer-moment, then one needs to augment OE by assigning a weight $\mu(\sigma)$ to each observer-moment that is being summed over, representing that observer-moment's quantum measure. This gives us

$$P_\alpha(h\,|\,e) = \frac{1}{\gamma} \sum_{\sigma \in \Omega_h \cap \Omega_e} \frac{P_\alpha(w_\sigma)\mu(\sigma)}{\sum_{\tau \in \Omega_\sigma \cap \Omega(w_\sigma)} \mu(\tau)} \qquad \text{(QOE)}$$

where γ is a normalization constant:

$$\gamma = \sum_{\sigma \in \Omega_e} \frac{P_\alpha(w_\sigma)}{\sum_{\tau \in \Omega_e \cap \Omega(w_\sigma)} \mu(\tau)}$$

(No assertion is made here about the virtues of the many-worlds version; we just point out how it can be modeled within the current framework.) This formula can also be used in a non-quantum context if one wishes to assign different kinds of observer-moments different weights, for example a larger weight to observer-moments that are clearer or more intense or contain more information.

One might have a similar expression with an integral instead of a sum if one is dealing with a continuum of observer-moments, but we shall not explore that suggestion here.[7]

NON-TRIVIALITY OF THE REFERENCE CLASS: WHY $\mathfrak{R}^0$ MUST BE REJECTED

We thus see how making use of the more fine-grained indexical information represented by observer-moments (rather than observers as wholes) makes it possible to move to a relativized definition of the reference class, and how this enables us to avoid the counterintuitive consequences that flow from applying SSA with a universal reference class in DA, *Adam-and-Eve*, *Quantum Joe*, and UN^{++}.

It was noted that the *Incubator* observer-moments that were on this approach placed in different reference classes were different in ways that are not small or arbitrary but importantly relevant to the problem at hand. Is it possible to say something more definite about the criteria for membership in an observer-moment's reference class? This section establishes one important constraint on how the reference class can rationally be defined.

What we shall call $\mathfrak{R}^0$, the minimal reference class definition, is the beguilingly simple idea that the reference class for a given observer-moment consists of those and only those observer-moments from which it is subjectively indistinguishable:

$$(\forall\alpha)\Omega_\alpha = \{\alpha_j : \alpha_j \text{ is subjectively indistinguishable from } \alpha\} \qquad (\mathfrak{R}^0)$$

Two observer-moments are subjectively indistinguishable iff they can't tell which of them they are. (Being able to say "I am *this* observer-moment, not *that* one" does not count as being able to tell which observer-moment you are.) For example, if one observer-moment has a pain in his toe and another has a pain in his finger then they are *not* subjectively indistinguishable; for they can identify themselves as "this is the observer-moment with the pain in his toe" and "this is the observer-moment with the pain in his finger", respectively. By contrast, if two brains are in the precisely the same state, then (assuming epistemic states supervene on brain states) the two corresponding observer-moments are subjectively indistinguishable. The same holds if the brains are in slightly different states but the differences are imperceptible to the subjects.

There are some cases where using the extreme minimalism of $\mathfrak{R}^0$ doesn't prevent one from constructing acceptable models. For instance, if the possible states that the observer in *Incubator* may end up in upon discovering that he has a black beard (i.e. β_2 or β_4) are subjectively indistinguishable, then $\mathfrak{R}^0$ replicates the reference class partition that we used above and will thus yield the same credence assignment.

---

[7] For some relevant ideas on handling infinite cases that arise in inflationary cosmological models, see (Vilenkin 1995).

One can model *Incubator* using $\mathfrak{R}^0$ even if we assume that there are two subjectively distinguishable states that the blackbearded observer might be in after learning about his beard color. In order to do that, one has to expand our representation of the problem by considering a more fine-grained partition of the possibilities involved. To be concrete, let us suppose that the blackbearded observer might or might not experience a pain in his little toe during the stage where he knows he has a black beard. If he knew that this pain would occur only if the coin fell Tails (say) then the problem would be trivial; so let's suppose that he doesn't have know of any correlation between having the pain and the outcome of the coin toss. We then have four possible worlds to consider (figure 7):

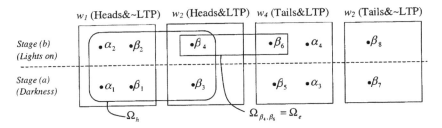

Figure 7: *Incubator* III with potential toe-pain

The possible worlds w_1-w_4 represent the following possibilities:

w_1: Heads and the late blackbeard has no little-toe pain.

w_2: Heads and the late blackbeard has a little-toe pain.

w_3: Tails and the late blackbeard has a little-toe pain.

w_4: Tails and the late blackbeard has no little-toe pain.

We can assume that the observer-moments share the prior $P(w_i) = \frac{1}{4}$ (for $i = 1,2,3,4$). Let h be the hypothesis that the coin fell heads, and e the information available to an observer-moment that knows it has a black beard and pain in the little toe. By $\mathfrak{R}^0$, the reference class for such an observer-moment is

$$\Omega_e = \Omega_{\beta_4, \beta_6} = \{\beta_4, \beta_6\}$$

As can be seen in the diagram, we have

$$\Omega_e \cap \Omega_h = \{\beta_4\}$$

OE then implies that $P_{\beta_{4,6}}(h|e) = \frac{1}{2}$ (with $\gamma = \frac{1}{2}$). That is, we get the same result here with the minimal reference class definition that we got on the revised approach of the previous section.

So $\mathfrak{R}^0$ can be made to work in *Incubator* even if the participants are never in subjectively indistinguishable states. $\mathfrak{R}^0$ is neat, clear-cut, non-arbitrary, and it expunges the counterintuitive implications stemming from using the universal reference class definition, $\mathfrak{R}^u$. Yet the temptation to accept $\mathfrak{R}^0$ has to be resisted.

Recall the "freak-observer problem" plaguing Big World theories that we discussed in chapters 3 and 5. This is one application where $\mathfrak{R}^0$ falls short.

Suppose T_1 and T_2 are two Big World theories. According to T_1, the vast majority of observers observe values of physical constants in agreement with what we observe and only a small minority of freak observers are deluded and observe the physical constants having different values. According to T_2, it is the other way around: the normal observers observe physical constants having other values than what we observe, and a minority of freak observers make observations that agree with ours. We want to say that our observations favor T_1 over T_2. Yet this is not possible on $\mathfrak{R}^0$. For according to $\mathfrak{R}^0$, the reference class to which we belong consists of all and only those observers-moments who make the same observations as we do, since other observer-moments are subjectively distinguishable from ours. If T_1 and T_2 both imply that the universe is big enough for it to be certain (or very probable) that it contains at least some observer making the observations that we are actually making, then on $\mathfrak{R}^0$ our evidence would not favor T_1 over T_2. Here is the proof:

> Consider an observer-moment α, who, in light of evidence e, considers what probability to assign to the mutually exclusive hypotheses h_j ($1 \leq j \leq n$). By $\mathfrak{R}^0$ we have $\Omega_\alpha = \Omega_e$.[8] OE then gives

---

[8] According to $\mathfrak{R}^0$, $\sigma \in \Omega_\alpha$ iff σ has the same total evidence as α. (For an observer-moment σ that has different total evidence from α would thereby be subjectively distinguishable from α; and an observer-moment that is subjectively indistinguishable from α must per definition share all of α's evidence and can have no evidence that α does not have, and it would thus have the same total evidence as α.) What we need to show, thus, is that σ has the same total evidence as α iff $\sigma \in \Omega_e$. Note first that Ω_e, the class of all possible observer-moments about whom e is true, is one in which α is a member (for since α knows e, e is true about α; this is so because any non-indexical part p of e is true of those and only those observer-moments that are in possible worlds where p holds true, and any indexical part p' of e of the form "this observer-moment has property P" is true about those and only those possible observer-moments who have property P). Moreover, Ω_e is the narrowest class that α knows it is a member of, because if α knew it was a member of some proper subset Ω_{e*} of Ω_e, then e wouldn't be the total evidence of α since α would then know e^*, which is stronger than e. We can now show that σ has the same total evidence as $\alpha \Leftrightarrow \sigma \in \Omega_e$:

(⇒) Suppose first that σ has the same total evidence as α. Then α is subjectively indistinguishable from σ. Therefore, if $\sigma \notin \Omega_e$, then α wouldn't know it was in Ω_e, since α cannot distinguish itself from σ. $\perp$. Hence $\sigma \in \Omega_e$.

$$P_\alpha(h_j|e) = \frac{1}{\gamma} \sum_{\sigma \in \Omega_{h_j} \cap \Omega_e} \frac{P_\alpha(w_\sigma)}{\left|\Omega_e \cap \Omega(w_\sigma)\right|} .$$

Let $M(h_j)$ be the class of worlds w_i where h_j is true and for which $\Omega(w_i) \cap \Omega_e$ is non-empty. We can thus write:

$$P_\alpha(h_j \mid e) = \frac{1}{\gamma} \sum_{w_i \in M(h_j)} \sum_{\sigma \in \Omega_{h_j} \cap \Omega_e \cap \Omega(w_i)} \frac{P_\alpha(w_\sigma)}{\left|\Omega_e \cap \Omega(w_\sigma)\right|} .$$

Since h_j is true in w_i if $w_i \in M(h_j)$, we have $\Omega(w_i) \subseteq \Omega_{h_j}$, giving:

$$P_\alpha(h_j \mid e) = \frac{1}{\gamma} \sum_{w_i \in M(h_j)} \frac{P_\alpha(w_i)}{\left|\Omega_e \cap \Omega(w_i)\right|} \cdot \left|\Omega_e \cap \Omega(w_i)\right|$$

$$= \frac{1}{\gamma} \sum_{w_i \in M(h_j)} P_\alpha(w_i) .$$

For each h_j that implies the existence of at least one observer-moment compatible with e[9], $\Omega(w_i) \cap \Omega_e$ is non-empty for each w_i in which h_j is true. For such an h_j we therefore have

$$\frac{1}{\gamma} \sum_{w_i \in M(h_j)} P_\alpha(w_i) = \frac{1}{\gamma} P_\alpha(h_j) .$$

Forming the ratio between two such hypotheses, h_j and h_k, we thus find that this is unchanged under conditionalization on e,

$$\frac{P_\alpha(h_j|e)}{P_\alpha(h_k|e)} = \frac{P_\alpha(h_j)}{P_\alpha(h_k)} .$$

This means that e does not selectively favour any of the hypotheses h_j that implies that some observer-moment is compatible with e.

Since this consequence is unacceptable, we must reject $\mathfrak{R}^0$. Any workable reference class definition must permit reference classes to contain observer-moments that are subjectively distinguishable. The reference class definition is in this sense non-trivial.

Observer-moments that are incompatible with e can thus play a role in determining the credence of observer-moments whose total evidence is e. This point is important. To emphasize it, we will give another example (see figure 8):

($\Leftarrow$) Take a σ such that $\sigma \in \Omega_e$. Suppose σ doesn't have the same total evidence as α. Then α can subjectively distinguish itself from σ. Hence there is a narrower class than Ω_e (namely Ω_e-σ) that α knows it is a member of.⊥. Hence σ has the same total evidence as α.

This completes the proof that $\Omega_\alpha = \Omega_e$.

[9] We say that an observer-moment α is incompatible with e iff $\alpha \notin \Omega_e$.

Blackbeards & Whitebeards

Two theories, T_1 and T_2, each say that there are three rooms, and the two theories are assigned equal prior probabilities. On T_1, two of the rooms contain observers with black beards and the third room contains an observer with a white beard. On T_2, one room contains a black-bearded observer and the other two contain white-bearded observers. All observers know what color their own beard is (but they cannot see into the other rooms). You find yourself in one of the rooms as a blackbeard. What credence should you give to T_1?

We can see, by analogy to the Big World cosmology case, that the answer should be that observing that you are a blackbeard gives you reason to favor T_1 over T_2. But if we use $\mathfrak{R}^0$, we do not get that result.

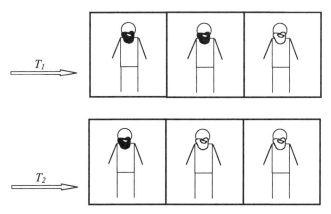

Figure 8: The *Blackbeards & Whitebeards* thought experiment

In the observer-moment graph of this gedanken (figure 9), α_1, β_1, and α_2 are the blackbeard observer-moments, and e is the information possessed by such an observer-moment ("this observer-moment is a blackbeard"). h is the hypothesis that T_1 is true. Given OE&$\mathfrak{R}^0$ the observer-moments are partitioned into two reference classes: the blackbeards and the whitebeards (assuming that they are not subjectively distinguishable in any other way than via their beard color). Thus, for example, α_1 belongs to the reference class $\Omega_{\alpha_1} = \{\alpha_1, \beta_1, \alpha_2\}$.

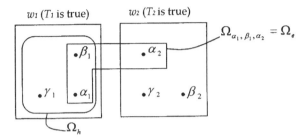

Figure 9: Applying OE to *Blackbeards & Whitebeards* using $\mathfrak{R}^0$ (an incorrect reference class definition)

This gives $P_{\alpha_1}(b \mid e)=\frac{1}{2}$ (with $\gamma =1$). Hence, according to $\mathfrak{R}^0$, the blackbeards' credence of T_1 should be the same as their credence of T_2, which is wrong.

A broader definition of the reference class will give the correct result. Suppose all observer-moments in *Blackbeards and Whitebeards* are included in the same reference class (figure 10):

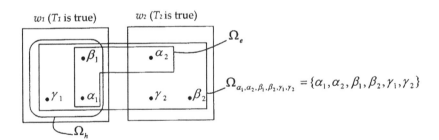

Figure 10: Applying OE to *Blackbeards & Whitebeards* using a wider reference class definition.

This gives $P_{\alpha_1}(b) = \frac{2}{3}$. That is, observer-moments that find that they have black beards obtain some reason to think that T_1 is true.

This establishes boundaries for how the reference class can be defined. The reference class to which an observer-moment α belongs consists of those and only those observer-moments that are relevantly similar to α. We have just demonstrated that observer-moments can be relevantly similar even if they are subjectively distinguishable. And we saw earlier that if we reject the paradoxical recommendations in *Adam & Eve, Quantum Joe,* and

UN^{++} that follow from using the universal reference class definition $\mathfrak{R}^{U}$ then we also must maintain that not all observer-moments are relevantly similar. We thus have ways of testing a proposed reference class definition. On the one hand, we may not want it to be so permissive as to give counterintuitive results in *Adam & Eve,* et al. (Scylla). On the other hand, it must not be so stringent as to make cosmological theorizing impossible because of the freak-observer problem (Charybdis). A maximally attractive reference class definition would seem to be one that steers clear of both these extremes.

A SUBJECTIVE FACTOR IN THE CHOICE OF REFERENCE CLASS?

A reference class definition is a partition of possible observer-moments; each equivalence class in the partition is the reference class for all the observer-moments included in it. If $\mathfrak{R}$ is any permissible reference class definition then we have in general $\mathfrak{R}^{0} \subseteq \mathfrak{R} \subseteq \mathfrak{R}^{U}$, where "$\subseteq$" denotes the relation "less (or equally) coarse-grained than". We have argued above that there are cases showing that ("$\subset$" meaning "strictly less coarse-grained than"):

$\mathfrak{R}^{0} \subset \mathfrak{R}$ ("$\mathfrak{R}^{0}$-bound")

And *if* we reject the counterintuitive advice to *Adam & Eve,* et al. then there also are cases committing us to:

$\mathfrak{R} \subset \mathfrak{R}^{U}$ ("$\mathfrak{R}^{U}$-bound")

One may also want to impose a condition of "non-arbitrariness" to the effect that completely arbitrary or irrelevant differences between two observer-moments are not a ground for placing them in separate reference classes. Of course, we haven't defined what counts as a "non-arbitrary" or "relevant" difference—indeed, it might be one of those notions that do not permit of an exact definition; but it may still be useful to have a label for this generic theoretical desideratum that significant distinctions be based on relevant differences.

Within these constraints, there is room for diverging reference class definitions. In the next chapter, we shall establish a further constraint as well as identify several considerations that are pertinent in electing a reference class. One cannot rule out that there are new arguments waiting to be discovered that will impose additional limitations on legitimate reference class definitions, conceivably even narrowing the field to one uniquely correct choice.

One idea that might be worth exploring is that in anthropic reasoning one should reason in such a way that one is following a rule that one thinks will maximize the expected fraction of all observer-moments applying it that will be right.[10]

---

[10] A refinement would be to recognize that being right or wrong is not a binary matter, so one may instead say we should try to minimize the expected value of an error-term that takes into account how much an observer-moment's degree of belief in a proposition Ψ deviates from the truth value of Ψ.

If many of the different observer-moments in the Big-World cosmology case (including both many of those observing CMB = 2.7 K and those observing CMB = 3.1 K) are said to be applying the same rule (and likewise the black-beard and the whitebeard observer-moments in *Blackbeards & Whitebeards*), and yet the later observer-moments in e.g. the Adam & Eve gedanken are taken to be applying a different rule than the early observer-moments (since the later ones are, after all, in no uncertainty at all about the outcome of the carnal embrace and may thus not be applying any non-trivial rule of anthropic reasoning to the problem at hand), then this meta-principle may be able to give the results we want. In order to move forward with this idea, however, we would need to have good criteria for determining which observer-moments should be said to be applying the same rule, and rule-following is notoriously a tricky concept to explicate. Another problem is that when calculating the expected fraction of rule-applying observer-moments that will be right, one needs credences as input in order to perform the calculation, and what these credences should be is itself dependent on which rule is adopted—so that maybe the best one could hope for from this approach would be to eliminate those rules that by their own standards are inferior to some other rule.

My suspicion is that at the end of the day there will remain a subjective factor in the choice of reference class. Yet, I think there is a subjective element too in the choice of an ordinary Bayesian prior credence function over the set of non-centered possible worlds. I don't believe that *every* such possible non-indexical function is rationally defensible; but I think that after everything has been said and done, there is a class of non-indexical credence functions that would all be defensible in the sense that intelligent, rational, and reasonable thinkers could have any of these credence functions even in an idealized state of reflective equilibrium. (This could perhaps be said to be something of a "received view" among Bayesian epistemologists.) What we are suggesting here is that a similar subjective element exists in credence assignments to *indexical* propositions, and that this is reflected in the fact that there are many permissible choices of reference class. And isn't this just what one should have expected? Why think there is no room for rational disagreement regarding the indexical part of belief-formation while there is very considerable room for disagreement between rational thinkers in regard the non-indexical part of belief-formation? Our theory puts the two domains, the indexical and the non-indexical, on an equal footing. In both, there are constraints on what can be reasonably believed, but these constraints may not single out a uniquely correct credence function.

We are free to seek arguments for additional constraints (we shall find some in the next chapter) and it is an open question how far one can shrink the class of defensible reference class definitions. New constraints can simply be added to the theory since OE itself (along with its quantum sibling) is neutral with respect to choice of reference class.

It may be worth noting that the question of whether there is a subjective factor in the choice of reference class is logically independent from the question of whether the reference class is relative to observer-moments. For conceivably, it could be the case that for any observer-moment there is a unique objectively correct choice of reference class, but it is a different one for different observer-moments. Then we would have relativity together with complete objectivity. Moreover, one could alternatively have the view that if everybody is perfectly rational then every observer-moment must use the same reference class, while admitting that there is no objective ground determining exactly what this common reference class should be. Then we would have a degree of subjectivity together with complete absence of relativity. An example of this latter kind of view would be to think that there is compelling argument for adopting a universal reference class definition ($\mathfrak{R}^u$) while admitting that there is no compelling reason for picking any particular delineation of what counts as an observer-moment.

We shall continue our discussion of the reference class problem at the end of the next chapter.

CHAPTER 11

Observation Selection Theory Applied

The proof of the pudding being in its eating, we shall in this final chapter apply the observation selection theory to the fine-tuning and freak-observer problems in cosmology, to the Sleeping Beauty problem in game theoretic modeling of imperfect recall, and to the other scientific issues that we have studied (in evolution theory, thermodynamics, traffic analysis, and quantum physics). Then, towards the end, we shall argue that one can say something about how scientifically rigorous a given application is by looking at what sort of demand it places on how the reference class be defined. In general, weaker demands correspond to greater scientific rigor. Paradoxical applications are distinguished from the more scientific ones by the fact that the former work only for a rather special set of reference classes (which one may well reject) whereas the latter hold for a much wider range of reference classes (which arguably any reasonable person is required not to transgress). We will also tie this in with the foregoing discussion of the element of subjectivity that may exist in the choice of reference class.

COSMOLOGICAL THEORIZING: FINE-TUNING AND FREAK OBSERVERS

In chapter 2, we argued, *inter alia*, for three preliminary conclusions regarding fine-tuning as evidence for multiverse hypotheses:

> (1) Fine-tuning favors (other things equal) hypotheses h_+ on which it is likely that one or more observer-containing universes exist over hypotheses h_- on which this is unlikely.

> (2) If two competing general hypotheses each imply that there is at least some observer-containing universe, but one of them implies a

greater number of observer-containing universes, then fine-tuning is not a reason to favor the latter (other things equal).

(3) Although $P(e|h_M)$ may be much closer to zero than to one (h_M being the multiverse hypothesis, and e the evidence we actually have), it could nonetheless easily be large enough to make the multiverse hypothesis supported by e.

We can now reexamine these theses in the new light of our theory. To begin with (1), let's determine under what circumstances we will have $P_\alpha(h_+|e) > P_\alpha(h_-|e)$.

Suppose that

P_α(there is at least one actual observer-moment compatible with $e|h_+) \approx 1$.

Since $P(A|B) = P(A\&B) / P(B)$, this can be expressed as

$$\frac{\sum_{w_i \in M(h_+)} P_\alpha(w_i)}{P_\alpha(h_+)} \approx 1.$$

($M(h)$, remember, is the class of worlds w_i where h is true and for which $\Omega(w_i) \cap \Omega_e$ is non-empty.) Similarly, if we suppose that

P_α(there is at least one actual observer-moment compatible with $e|h_-) \approx 0$, we get

$$\frac{\sum_{w_i \in M(h_-)} P_\alpha(w_i)}{P_\alpha(h_-)} \approx 0.$$

If the hypotheses in question have about equal prior probability, $P_\alpha(h_+) \approx P_\alpha(h_-)$, this implies that

$$\sum_{w_i \in M(h_+)} P_\alpha(w_i) \gg \sum_{w_i \in M(h_-)} P_\alpha(w_i) \qquad (\$)$$

which is equivalent[1] to

---

[1] To see this, consider the worlds over which the sums range in ($\$$): these worlds all have at least one observer-moment in Ω_e and are such that h_+ (or h_-) is true in them; and $P_\alpha(w_i)$ appears in the sum once for every such world. In the second inequality ($\$\$$), the sum again includes only terms corresponding to worlds that have at least one observer-moment in Ω_e and are such that h_+ (or h_-) is true in them. The difference is that terms relating to such worlds occur multiple times in ($\$\$$): a term $P_\alpha(w_\sigma)$ occurs once for every such observer-moment σ in each such world. Thus after dividing each term $P_\alpha(w_\sigma)$ with the number of such observer-moments ($|\Omega_e \cap \Omega(w_\sigma)|$), the sum is the same as in ($\$$).

$$\sum_{\sigma \in \Omega_{h_+} \cap \Omega_e} \frac{P_\alpha(w_\sigma)}{\left|\Omega_e \cap \Omega(w_\sigma)\right|} >> \sum_{\sigma \in \Omega_{h_-} \cap \Omega_e} \frac{P_\alpha(w_\sigma)}{\left|\Omega_e \cap \Omega(w_\sigma)\right|} \qquad (\$\$)$$

Now, according to OE, $P_\alpha(h_+ \mid e) > P_\alpha(h_- \mid e)$ is equivalent to

$$\sum_{\sigma \in \Omega_{h_+} \cap \Omega_e} \frac{P_\alpha(w_\sigma)}{\left|\Omega_\sigma \cap \Omega(w_\sigma)\right|} > \sum_{\sigma \in \Omega_{h_-} \cap \Omega_e} \frac{P_\alpha(w_\sigma)}{\left|\Omega_\sigma \cap \Omega(w_\sigma)\right|} \qquad (\pounds)$$

We may thus tell under what circumstances e will preferentially support h_+ over h_- by considering what is required for ($\$\$$) to yield ($\pounds$). And from this we can learn three lessons:

• If $\Omega_e = \Omega_\sigma$ for each $\sigma \in \Omega_e \cap (\Omega_{h+} \cup \Omega_{h-})$ then ($\pounds$) follows from ($\$\$$). This means that if all the observer-moments that the hypotheses say may exist and which are compatible with our evidence e are in the same reference class (Ω_e) then a hypothesis h_+ on which it is likely that one or more observer-moments compatible with e exist is supported vis-à-vis a hypothesis h_- on which that is unlikely.

• In principle, it is possible for a hypothesis h_- that makes it less likely that there should be some observer-moment compatible with e to get preferential support from e vis-à-vis a hypothesis h_+ which makes that more likely. For example, if h_+ makes it likely that there should be one observer-moment compatible with e but at the same time makes it very likely that there are very many other observer-moments in our reference class that are not compatible with e, then h_+ may be disfavored by e compared to a hypothesis h_- on which it is quite unlikely that there should be any observer-moment compatible with e but on which also it is highly unlikely that there should be a substantial number of observer-moments in our reference class that are not compatible with e.

• In practice (i.e. regarding (3)), if we think of h_+ as a multiverse theory and h_- as a single-universe theory, it seems that the concrete details will sometimes be such that ($\pounds$) follows from ($\$\$$) together with the facts about these details. This is the case when h_+ entails a higher probability than does h_- to there being some actual observer-moment that is compatible with e, while at the same time the expected ratio between the number of actual observer-moments that are compatible with e that are in our reference class and the number of actual observer-moments that are in our reference class that are incompatible with e is about the same on h_+ as on h_- (or greater on h_+ than on h_-). Crudely put: it is alright to infer a bigger cosmos in order to make it probable that at least some observer-moment compatible with e exists, but only if this can be done without sacrificing too much of the desideratum of making it probable that a large fraction of the actual observer-moments that are in our reference class are compatible with e.

We'll continue the discussion of (3) in a moment, but first let's direct the spotlight on the second preliminary thesis. The analysis of (2) follows a path parallel to that of (1).

Suppose that

P_α(there are many actual observer-moments compatible with $e \mid h_{++}) \approx 1$

P_α(there is at least one actual observer-moment compatible with $e \mid h_+) \approx 1$

$P_\alpha(h_{++}) \approx P_\alpha(h_+)$

Since the first expression implies that

P_α(there is at least one actual observer-moment compatible with $e \mid h_{++}) \approx 1$

we get, in a similar way to above,

$$\sum_{\sigma \in \Omega_{h_{++}} \cap \Omega_e} \frac{P_\alpha(w_\sigma)}{\left|\Omega_e \cap \Omega(w_\sigma)\right|} \approx \sum_{\sigma \in \Omega_{h_+} \cap \Omega_e} \frac{P_\alpha(w_\sigma)}{\left|\Omega_e \cap \Omega(w_\sigma)\right|} \qquad (\$\$*)$$

Meanwhile, by OE, is equivalent to

$$\sum_{\sigma \in \Omega_{h_{++}} \cap \Omega_e} \frac{P_\alpha(w_\sigma)}{\left|\Omega_\sigma \cap \Omega(w_\sigma)\right|} \approx \sum_{\sigma \in \Omega_{h_+} \cap \Omega_e} \frac{P_\alpha(w_\sigma)}{\left|\Omega_\sigma \cap \Omega(w_\sigma)\right|} \qquad (\pounds*)$$

Again we can compare ($\$\$*$) to ($\pounds*$) to see under what circumstances the former implies the latter. We find that

- As before, if $\Omega_e = \Omega_\sigma$ for each $\sigma \in \Omega_e \cap (\Omega_{h+} \cup \Omega_{h-})$ then ($\pounds*$) follows from ($\$\$*$). This means that if the observer-moments that are compatible with e and with at least one of the hypotheses h_{++} and h_+ are all in the same reference class (Ω_e) then a hypothesis h_{++} on which it is likely that there are a great many observer-moments compatible with e is *not* preferentially supported vis-à-vis a hypothesis h_+ on which it is likely that there are relatively few observer-moments compatible with e.

• Generally speaking, *e* will fail to distinguish between h_{++} and h_+ if, for those observer-moments that are in our reference class, both hypotheses imply a similar expected ratio between the number of ones compatible with *e* and the number of ones incompatible with *e*. This means that ceteris paribus there is no reason to prefer a hypothesis that implies a greater number of observer-moments, beyond what is required to make it likely that there should be at least one actual observer-moment that is compatible with *e*.

Armed with these results, we can address (3). Let's suppose for the moment that there are no freak observers.

First, consider a single-universe theory h_U on which our universe is fine-tuned, so that conditional on h_U there was only a very small probability that an observer-containing universe should exist. If we compare h_U with a multiverse theory h_M, on which it was quite likely that an observer-containing universe should exist, we find that if h_U and h_M had similar prior probabilities, then there are prima facie grounds for thinking h_M to be more probable than h_U given the evidence we have. Whether these *prima facie* grounds hold up on closer scrutiny depends on the distributions of observer-moments that h_U and h_M make probable. Supposing that the nature of the observer-moments that would tend to exist on h_U (if there were any observer-moments at all, which would improbable on h_U) are similar to the observer-moments that (most likely) exist on h_M, then we do in fact have such grounds.

The precise sense of the proviso that our evidence *e* may favor h_M over h_U only if the observer-moments most likely to exist on either hypothesis are of a similar nature is specified by OE and the lessons we derived from it above. But we can say at least something in intuitive terms about what sorts of single-universe and multiverse theories for which this will be the case. For example, we can consider the case where there is a single relevant physical parameter, λ. Suppose the prior probability distribution over possible values of λ that a universe could have is smeared out over a broad interval (representing a priori ignorance about λ and absence of any general grounds, such as considerations of simplicity or theoretical elegance, for expecting that λ should have taken on a value within a more narrow range). In the archetypal case of fine-tuning, there is only a very small range of λ-values that give rise to a universe that contains observers. Then the conditional probability of *e* given h_U is very small. By contrast, the conditional probability of *e* given h_M can be quite large, since there will most likely be observers given h_M and these observer-moments will all be living in universes where λ has a value within the small region of fine-tuned (observer-generating) values. In this situation, h_M would be preferentially supported by *e*.

Now consider a different case that doesn't involve fine-tuning but merely "ad hoc" setting of a free parameter. This is the case when observers can exist over the whole range of possible values of λ (or a fairly large part thereof). The conditional probability of *e* given h_U is the same as before (i.e. very small), but in this case the conditional probability of *e* given h_M is about equally small. For although h_M makes it likely that there should be some observers, and even that there should be some observers compatible with *e*, h_M also makes it highly likely that there should be very many other observers who are *not* compatible with *e*. These are the observers who live in other universes in the multiverse, universes where λ takes a different value than the one we have observed (and hence incompatible with *e*). If these other observers are in the same reference class as us (and there is no clear reason why they shouldn't be, at least if the sort of observers living in universes with different λ are not too dissimilar to ourselves), then this means that the conditional probability of *e* given h_M is very small. If enough other-λ universes contain substantial quantities of observers who are in the same reference class as us, then h_M will not get significant preferential support from *e* compared to h_U.

We see here the sense in which fine-tuning suggests a multiverse in a way that mere free parameters do not. In the former case, h_M tends to be strongly supported by the evidence we have (given comparable priors); in the latter case, not.

On this story, how does one fit in the scenario where we discover a simple single-universe theory h_U^* that accounts well for the evidence? Well, if h_U^* is elegant and simple, then we would assign it a relatively high prior probability. Since h_U^* by assumption implies or at least gives a rather high probability to *e*, the conditional probability of h_U^* given *e* would thus be high. This would be support for the single-universe hypothesis and against the multiverse hypothesis.

One kind of candidate for such a single-universe theory are theories involving a creator who chose to create only one universe. *If* one assigned one such theory h_C^* a reasonably high prior probability, and *if* it could be shown to give a high probability to there being one universe precisely like the one we observe and no other universes, then one would have support for h_C^*. Creator-hypotheses on which the creator creates a whole ensemble of observer-containing universes would be less supported than h_C^*. However, if our universe is not of the sort that one might have suspected a creator to create if he created only one universe (if our universe is not the "nicest" possible one in any sense, for example), then the conditional probability of *e* on any creator-hypothesis involving the creation of only one universe might well be so slim that even if one assigned such a creator-hypothesis a high prior probability it would still not be tenable in light of *e* if there were some plausible alternative theory giving a high conditional probability to *e* (e.g. a multiverse theory successfully riding on fine-tuning and its concomitant selection effects, or a still-to-be-discovered simple and elegant single-universe theory that fits the facts). If there were no such plausible alternative theory, then one may believe either a fine-tuned single-universe theory, a multiverse-theory not benefiting from observation selection effects, or a creator hypothesis (either of the single-universe or the multiverse kind)—these would be roughly on a par regarding how well they'd fit with the evidence (quite poorly for all of them) and the choice between them would be determined mainly by one's prior probability function.

In chapter 2 we also touched on the case where our universe is discovered to have some "special feature" F. One example of this is if we were to find inscriptions saying "God created this universe and it's the only one he created" in places where it seems only a divine being would have made them (and we thought that there was a significant chance that the creator was being honest). Another example is if we find specific evidence that favors on ordinary (non-anthropic) grounds some physical theory that either implies a single-universe world or a multiverse. Such new evidence e' would be conjoined with the evidence e we already have. What we should believe in the light of this depends on what conditional probability various hypotheses give to $e\&e'$ and on the prior probabilities we give to these hypotheses. With e' involving special features, $e\&e'$ might well be such as to preferentially favor hypotheses that specifically accounts for the special features, and this favoring may be strong enough to dominate any of the considerations mentioned above. For example, if we find all those inscriptions, that would make the creator-hypothesis seem very attractive even if one assigned it a low prior probability and even if the conditional probability of there being a single universe with F given the creator-hypotheses would be small; for other plausible hypotheses would presumably give very much smaller conditional probabilities to our finding that our universe has F. (On h_U, it would be extremely unlikely that there would be any universe with F. On h_M, it might be likely that there should be some universe with F, but it would nonetheless be extremely unlikely that we should be in that universe, since on any plausible multiverse theory not involving a creator it would seem that if it were likely that there should be one universe with F then it would also be most likely that there are a great many other universes not having F and in which the observers, although many of them would be in the same reference class as us, would thus not be compatible with the evidence we have.) Similar considerations hold if F is not divine-looking inscriptions but something more of the nature of ordinary physical evidence for some particular physical theory.

Finally, we have to tackle the question of how the existence of freak observers affects the story. The answer is: hardly at all. Although once we take account of freak observers there will presumably be a broad class of single-universe theories that make probable that some observers compatible with e should exist, this doesn't help the case for such theories. For freak observers are random. Whether they are generated by Hawking radiation or by thermal fluctuations or by some other phenomena of a similar kind, these freak observers would not be preferentially generated to be compatible with *e*. Only an extremely minute fraction of all freak observers would be compatible with *e*. The case would therefore be essentially the same as if we have a multiverse where many universes contain observers (that are in our reference class) but only a tiny fraction of them contain observers who are compatible with *e*. Just as *e* didn't especially favor such multiverse-theories over ad hoc single-universe theories, so likewise *e* is not given a sufficiently high probability by the there-is-a-single-universe-sufficiently-big-to-contain-all-kinds-of-freak observers theory (h_F) to make such a theory supported by our evidence. In fact, the case for h_F is much worse than the case for such a multiverse theory. For the multiverse theory, even if not getting any assistance from fine-tuning, would at least have a bias towards observers who have evolved (i.e. most observers would be of that kind). Evolved observers would tend to be in epistemic states that to some degree reflect the nature of the universe they are living in. Thus if not every logically possible universe is instantiated (with equal frequency) in the multiverse but instead the universes it contains tend to share at least some basic features with our actual universe, then a much greater fraction of the observers existing in the multiverse would be compatible with *e* than of the observers existing given h_F. On h_F the observers would be distributed roughly evenly over all logically possible epistemic states (of a given complexity)[2] whereas on the multiverse theory they'd be distributed over the smaller space of epistemic states that are likely to be instantiated in observers evolving in universes that share at least some basic features (maybe physical laws, or some physical laws, depending on the particular multiverse theory) with our universe. So h_F is strongly disfavored by *e*.

Freak observers, therefore, cannot rescue an otherwise flawed theory. At the same time, the existence of freak observers would not prevent a theory that is otherwise supported by our evidence from still being supported once the freak observers are taken into account—provided that the freak observers make up a small fraction of all the observers that the theory says exist. In the universe we are actually living in, for example, it seems that there may well be vast numbers of freak observers (if only it is sufficiently big). Yet these freak observers would be in an astronomically small minority[3] compared to the regular observers who trace their origin to life that evolved by normal pathways on some planet. For every observer that pops out of a black hole, there are countless civilizations of regular observers. Freak observers can thus, in the light of our observation selection theory, be ignored for all practical purposes.

---

[2] If you were to generate lumps of matter at random and wait until a brain in a conscious state emerged, you'd most likely find that the first conscious brain-state was some totally weird psychedelic one, but at any rate not one consistent with the highly specific and orderly set of knowledge represented by *e*.

[3] Again, we are disregarding the infinite case. It seems that in order to handle the infinite case one would have to strengthen OE with something that is formulated in terms of spatial densities of observer-moments rather than classes of observer-moments. But that is beyond the scope of this investigation.

THE FREAK-OBSERVER PROBLEM PLACES ONLY LAX DEMANDS ON THE REFERENCE CLASS

We saw in chapter 10 that in order to solve the freak-observer problem, we must use a reference class definition that puts some subjectively distinguishable observer-moments in the same reference class. It is worth pointing out, however, that for the purpose of dealing with freak observers, it suffices to select a reference class definition $\mathfrak{R}^{\varepsilon}$ that is only *marginally* more inclusive than $\mathfrak{R}^{0}$. The reason for this is illustrated in figure 11.

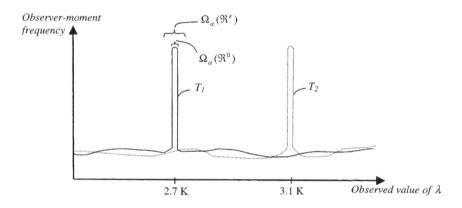

Figure 11: How a marginally more inclusive reference class ($\mathfrak{R}^{0}$) solves the freak-observer problem.

The fraction of the observer-moments in $\Omega_{\alpha}(\mathfrak{R}^{0})$ (i.e. our reference class as specified by $\mathfrak{R}^{0}$) that have the same total evidence e as we have (which includes observing a value of about 2.7 K for the cosmic microwave background radiation) is the same on T_2 as it is on T_1 (namely, 100% in either case). Therefore, on $\Omega_{\alpha}(\mathfrak{R}^{0})$, e could not distinguish between T_1 and T_2. Yet, if we move to the reference class $\Omega_{\alpha}(\mathfrak{R}^{\varepsilon})$ specified by the only slightly more inclusive $\mathfrak{R}^{\varepsilon}$ (which places in our reference class also observer-moments that are just a tiny bit subjectively different from our own), then our evidence e will distinguish strongly between T_1 and T_2 (and strongly favor the former). This is so because the frequency distribution of observer-moments is strongly peaked around observer-moments that observe the true current value of CMB rather than one of the alternative values that are observed only by observer-moments suffering from illusions. In the figure, if we look at the interval marked "$\Omega_{\alpha}(\mathfrak{R}^{\varepsilon})$", we see that the proportion of area under the T_1-curve in this interval that is inside the area under the smaller interval representing $\Omega_e = \Omega_\alpha$ is much larger than the corresponding proportion for the T_2-curve. The effect is actually more extreme than is apparent from the graph, both because the graph is not drawn to scale and because there are other dimensions, apart from the observed value of CMB, on which the randomly generated observer-moments will have a relatively broad and flat distribution compared to those observer-moments that have evolved in regular ways. The regular observer-moments will tend to be clustered in the region that a theory claims to represent the properties of the actual world.

We can thus lay down another constraint that any legitimate reference class definition must satisfy: it must be no less inclusive than $\mathfrak{R}^\varepsilon$ ("$\mathfrak{R}^\varepsilon$-bound").

THE SLEEPING BEAUTY PROBLEM: MODELING IMPERFECT RECALL

We'll continue our exploration of how the observation selection theory applies to scientific problems a few sections hence, but we pause to interject a discussion of the Sleeping Beauty problem, a thought experiment involving imperfect recall. *Sleeping Beauty* is closely related to two other problems that have been discussed in recent game theory literature: *Absent-Minded Driver* and the *Absent-Minded Passenger*. One's views on one of these problems is likely to determine how one thinks about the others. Therefore, we can regard *Sleeping Beauty* as a template for a broader class of imperfect recall problems. (The purpose of investigating these problems here is partly to see if our theory may shed light on them and partly to give a further illustration of how the theory works. Towards the end of this chapter, when tying various loose ends together in an attempt to capture some general lesson, we shall also find it useful to have a broad range of sample cases to draw from.)

> *Sleeping Beauty*
> On Sunday afternoon Beauty is given the following information. She will be put to sleep on Sunday evening and will wake up on Monday morning. Initially she will not know what day it is, but on Monday afternoon she'll be told it is Monday. On Monday evening she will be put to sleep again. Then a fair coin will be tossed and if and only if it falls tails will she be awakened again on Tuesday. However, before she is woken she will have her memory erased so that upon awakening on Tuesday morning she has no memory of having been awakened on Monday. When she wakes up on Monday, what probability should she assign to the hypothesis that the coin landed heads?

Views diverge as to whether the correct answer is P(Heads) = ⅓ or P(Heads) = ½. In support of the former alternative is the consideration that if there were a long series of Sleeping Beauty experiments then on average one third of the awakenings would be Heads-awakenings. One might therefore think that on any particular awakening, Beauty should believe with a credence of ⅓ that the coin landed heads in that trial. In support of the view that P(Heads) = ½ there is the consideration that the coin is known to be fair and it appears as if awakening does not give relevant new information to somebody who knew all along that she would at some point be awakened. The former view is advocated in e.g. (Elga 2000) and the latter in e.g. (Lewis 2001); but see also (Aumann, Hart, et al. 1997; Battigalli 1997; Gilboa 1997; Grove 1997; Halpern 1997; Lipman 1997; Piccione and Rubinstein 1997a, 1997b; Wedd 2000) for earlier treatments of the same or similar problems.

My position is that the issue is more complicated than existing analyses admit and that the solution is underdetermined by the problem as formulated above. It contains ambiguities that must be recognized and disentangled. Depending on how we do that, we get different answers. In particular, we need to decide whether there are any outsiders (i.e. observer-moments other than those belonging to Beauty while she is in the experiment), and what Beauty's reference class is. Once these parameters have been fixed, it is straightforward to calculate the answer using OE.

THE CASE OF NO OUTSIDERS

Consider first the case of no outsiders. Suppose that Beauty is the only observer in the world and that she is created specifically for the experiment and that she is killed as soon as it is over. We can simplify by representing each possible period of being awake as a single possible observer-moment. (As shown earlier, it makes no difference how many observer-moments we associate with a unit of subjective time, provided we use a sufficiently fine-grained metric to accurately represent the proportions of subjective time spent in the various states.) We can then represent *Sleeping Beauty* graphically as follows (figure 12):

The diagram shows the possible observer-moments, and groups those

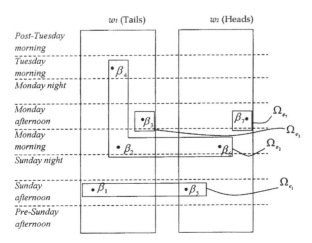

Figure 12: The *Sleeping Beauty* problem (with no outsiders).

that have the same total information together in equivalence classes. Thus, for instance, let β_2, β_4, and β_6 denote the "Monday-morning-in-the-Tails-world" observer-moment, the "Tuesday-morning-in-the-Tails-world" observer-moment, and the "Monday-morning-in-the-Heads-world" observer-moment, respectively. Since they have the same evidence (not shared by any other observer-moment), they constitute an equivalence class. This equivalence class, which we have denoted by "Ω_{e_2}", represents the evidence that each of these observer-moments has.

To find the solution, we must also know Beauty's reference class. Consider first the case where Beauty puts only subjectively indistinguishable observer-moments in her reference class,

$$R_{\beta_{2,4,6}} = \{\beta_2, \beta_4, \beta_6\}$$

It is then easy to verify that OE entails

$$R_{\beta_{2,4,6}}(Heads \mid e_2) = \tfrac{1}{2}$$

So when Beauty wakes up on Monday morning (and of course likewise if and when she wakes up on Tuesday) she should think that the probability of Heads is ½. Intuitively, this is because all the possible observer-moments that are in the just awakened Beauty's reference class (i.e. β_2, β_4 and β_6— or "$\beta_{2,4,6}$" for short) share the same evidence e_2 ("I know the set-up and I've just woken up but haven't yet been told what day it is") and this reference class was guaranteed to be non-empty independently of how the coin fell.

In the case where Beauty includes all observer-moments in her reference class,

$$R_{\beta_2} = R_{\beta_2} = R_{\beta_2} = \{\beta_1, \beta_2, \beta_3, \beta_4, \beta_5, \beta_6, \beta_7\}$$

OE entails

$$P_{\beta_{2,4,6}}(Heads \mid e_2) = \tfrac{2}{5}$$

In this case, when Beauty wakes up she should think that the probability of Heads is ⅖. The reason why the probability is less than ½ is that a smaller fraction of all observer-moments in her reference class would have her evidence if Heads (namely, one out of three observer-moments) than if Tails (two out of four). The exact figure of ⅖, however, depends on the detailed stipulations about the version of *Sleeping Beauty* we are considering and is not generic to the scenario.

THE CASE WITH OUTSIDERS

Turning to the case where there are outsiders (figure 13), we note first that their existence makes no difference unless they are included in the awakened Beauty's reference class. If they are not included—if, for instance, Beauty's reference class (at that time) is $R_{\beta_{2,4,6}} = \{\beta_2, \beta_4, \beta_6\}$—then her credence in Heads when wakening on Monday morning is ½. "Outsiders", however numerous, do not affect Beauty's probabilities given this choice of reference class.

We can also note in passing that the assumption that the outsiders are not in $R_{\beta_{2,4,6}}$ (the reference class of $\beta_{2,4,6}$) implies that $\beta_{2,4,6}$ all know that they are in the experiment and consequently that they are not among the outsiders. For as we have argued earlier, every observer-moment's reference class must include all other observer-moment that are subjectively indistinguishable from itself, i.e. all observer-moments that share the same total evidence that it has. So if the outsiders are not in $R_{\beta_{2,4,6}}$ then $\beta_{2,4,6}$ can infer that the outsiders have different evidence from their own, and thus that $\beta_{2,4,6}$ are not outsiders.

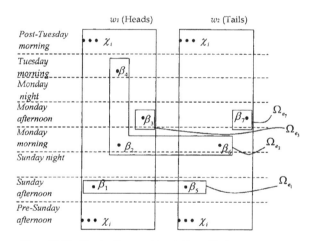

Figure 13: The *Sleeping Beauty* problem (with outsiders).

We get a different answer than ½, however, if there are possible outside observer-moments that *are* included in $R_{\beta_{2,4,6}}$. Let's assume that the number and nature of the outsiders are independent of the outcome of the coin toss. Then an observer-moment observing that it is in the experiment (e.g. β_2) thereby gets reason to increase its credence in the hypothesis (Tails) that entails that a greater fraction of all observer-moments in its reference class are in the experiment than does the rival hypothesis (Heads). In the limiting case where the number of outsiders (that are included in $R_{\beta_{2,4,6}}$) gets very large, OE yields $P_{\beta_{2,4,6}}(Heads\,|\,e_2) \rightarrow \frac{1}{3}$.

SYNTHESIS OF THE ½- AND THE ⅓-VIEWS

The account presented here shows how we can accommodate both of the rivaling intuitions about what Beauty's credence should be when she wakes up.

On the one hand, the intuition that her credence of Heads should be ⅓ because that would match the long-run frequency of heads among her awakenings is vindicated if we assume that there is an actual series of experiments resulting in an actual long-run frequency. For there are then many observer-moments that are outside the particular run of the experiment that β_2 is in whilst nonetheless being in β_2's reference class. This leads, as we saw, to $P_{\beta_{2,4,6}}(Heads \mid e_2) \approx \frac{1}{3}$.

On the other hand, the intuition that Beauty's credence of Heads should be ½ is justified in cases where there is only one run of the experiment and there are no other observer-moments in the awakened Beauty's reference class than her other possible awakenings in that experiment. For in that case, the awakened Beauty does not get any relevant information from finding that she has been awakened, and she therefore retains the prior credence of ½.

Those who feel strongly inclined to answer P(Heads) = ½ on Beauty's behalf even in cases were various outsiders are known to be present are free to take that intuition as a reason for choosing a reference class that places outsiders (as well as Beauty's own pre- and post-experiment observer-moments) outside the reference class they would use as awakened observer-moments in the experiment. It is, hopefully, superfluous to here re-emphasize that such a restriction of one's reference class also needs to be considered in the broader context of other inferences that one wishes to make from indexical statements or observations about one's position in the world. For instance, jumping to the extreme view that only subjectively indistinguishable observer-moments get admitted into one's reference class would be unwise, because it would bar one from deriving observational consequences from Big-World cosmologies.

OBSERVATION SELECTION THEORY APPLIED TO OTHER SCIENTIFIC PROBLEMS

Having now shown in detail how the observation selection theory replicates and extends earlier chapters' informal findings about fine-tuning arguments and the freak-observer problem in cosmology, we can proceed more quickly in describing how it applies to the other scientific problems we have discussed. We will focus on what these applications presuppose about the reference class.

Consider first the criticism of Boltzmann's attempt to explain time's arrow. The criticism was that if Boltzmann's picture were right, we should have expected to live in a much smaller low-entropy bubble than we in fact do. What definitions of the reference class are compatible with this conclusion? The answer is that any of a very broad range of reference class definitions would work. Let's consider some examples.

The universal reference class definition $\mathfrak{R}^u$ would work, of course—it was the one implicitly used in our original discussion of this topic in chapter 5. But a narrower reference class definition would also work fine. The argument goes through so long as our reference class includes those possible observer-moments that are exactly like ours except that they observe themselves living in a somewhat smaller low-entropy region than we do. For if Boltzmann were right, the vast majority of observer-moments in such a reference class would find themselves in smaller low-entropy regions than we do. This would entail, via OE, that the conditional probability of our data on the Boltzmann theory would be extremely small, and hence (making only very weak assumptions about the prior probability of Boltzmann's theory and its rivals) that our data disconfirms the Boltzmann theory. This claim does not depend on any assumption about the world being very big so that all relevant types of observations were likely to be made whether Boltzmann is right or wrong. Supposing the reference class definition has at least the diminutive degree of inclusiveness just described, our observations would have a much higher probability conditional on the theory that the universe as a whole is in a low-entropy state than on the theory that our region is a thermal fluctuation in a high-entropy bath. In fact, we can lower the requirements even further by considering that if we were the result of a thermal fluctuation then we would most likely have been the result of the smallest possible thermal fluctuation that would have produced observer-moments in our reference class, and the size of such a fluctuation would at any rate not be larger than the size of a human brain (which we know can produce such observer-moments). This means that we could fall back on the argument given for why we should not believe that we are freak observers; and for *that* we saw that the highly restrictive reference class definition $\mathfrak{R}^\varepsilon$ would suffice.

Ponder, next, the point we made about it being a mistake to conclude from the fact that intelligent life evolved on Earth that the evolution of intelligent life on a given Earth-like planet is not highly improbable (assuming there are sufficiently many Earth-like planets to make it probable that intelligent life would evolve somewhere). Does this point depend very sensitively on a particular choice of reference class? Again, the answer is no. Here, however, there is a slight qualification. The point about an observation selection effect vitiating the attempt to learn about how hard it is for intelligent life to evolve depends on the assumption that the universe contains sufficiently many Earth-like planets (so that the selection effect has a sufficient pool from which to select). More specifically, the argument depends on the probability of at least some civilization "like ours" coming to exist being almost independent on which of the hypotheses under consideration (about the improbability of our evolution) being correct. In more technical terms, what this means is that the argument presupposes that it was approximately equally likely that some observer-moment in your reference class should come to exist whichever of the rival hypotheses is true. But how many Earth-like planets there have to be in total in order for that premiss this to hold true depends on how wide your reference class is. The broader your reference class, the fewer Earth-like planets are required to make the probability approach unity that some possible observer-moment in the reference class should be actualized. So it is not exactly true to say that how we define the reference class has no relevance for this application. Nonetheless, in practice this qualification may make little difference. For instance, if we suppose that the world contains an *infinite* number of Earth-like planets (as seems to be the case) then every legitimate reference class definition (which is no less inclusive than $\Re^0$) gives the same result in this application.

What of Carter's ideas about how we might be able to estimate the number of critical steps in human evolution? Here, what the argument presupposes as far as the reference class is concerned is, roughly speaking, that the observers that would have existed if intelligent life on Earth had arisen earlier or later than it actually did would be in the same reference class as us. More accurately, we need not assume that all these different possible observers would be in our reference class (we don't even have to suppose that another run of evolution on an Earth-like planet would be likely to produce observers in our reference class even if their evolution took the same time as ours did). Rather, what we need to suppose in order for the argument to work without complications is that the probability that an evolutionary process that leads to intelligent observers should produce observer-moments that are in our reference class is roughly independent of how long the process takes (within a largish interval). The easiest way to grasp the gist of this qualification is to consider a hypothetical case where it is contravened. Suppose that only observer-moments that were thinking "this planet that I am living on has existed for about 4.5 billion years" were included in our reference class (call this reference class "$\Re^{4.5Gyrs}$"). Since such observer-moments would not exist (or would be vastly less frequent) among intelligent species that took, say, eight billion years to evolve, we should by $\Re^{4.5Gyrs}$ find no significant information in the fact that our evolution took 4.5 billion years. In particular, we could not reason that if there were very many critical steps in human evolution then we would most likely have come into existence closer to the cut-off date (i.e. when Earth becomes inimical to the emergence of intelligent life, which occurs no later than when our sun becomes a red giant) and that therefore, since we arose so early, there most likely weren't very many critical steps. For given $\Re^{4.5Gyrs}$, the relevant observer-moments *had* to arise after 4.5 billion years (i.e. long before the cut-off) or not arise at all. Even if the evolution of intelligent life took much more than 4.5 billion years on the vast majority of the planets where it occurred, the type of observer-moments that are in $\Re^{4.5Gyrs}$ would still overwhelmingly be found on planets where evolution progressed exceptionally rapidly. So

Carter's argument would not work with $\mathfrak{R}^{4.5Gyrs}$.

In the actual case, however, there do not seem to be strong reasons for thinking that civilizations that take somewhat longer or shorter to evolve than ours did would be significantly less likely to contain observer-moments that are in our reference class than are civilizations that take the same time as ours. The main *systematic* differences in observer-moments between various such civilizations would seem to be in regard to what the observer-moments believe about how long it took for their civilization to develop. (Of course, different civilizations may contain very different kinds of observer-moments, but there seems currently no good argument for thinking that most of these differences would be strongly correlated with how long a civilization takes to arise.) So it seems that Carter's ideas for estimating the number of critical steps relies only on fairly weak assumptions about the reference class. What's required is that we don't adopt a reference class like $\mathfrak{R}^{4.5Gyrs}$, which excludes observer-moments primarily on the basis of what they believe about how long their species took to evolve. Yet, this is a defeasible claim. Further research *might* reveal that there is the kind of systematic correlation between how late a civilization arises and fundamental aspects of the subjective qualities of the observer-moments it is likely to contain that would weaken or destroy Carter's argument even with a rather more inclusive choice of reference class than $\mathfrak{R}^{4.5Gyrs}$.

Traffic analysis.—If the explanandum is why it appears that one tends to end up in a slow lane, what the explanation we suggested in chapter 5 presupposes in terms of the reference class is that observer-moments of the kind that are in one's reference class are likely to exist in larger numbers in slow lanes than in fast ones. This holds, for example, if the proportion of a lane's observer-moments that are in one's reference class is the same for fast and slow lanes (since there are more observer-moments in slow lanes). It would *not* hold if fast-lane observer-moments were much more likely to be in your reference class than slow-lane observer-moments (extreme example: if it were the case that people in slow lanes usually got so bored that their brains stopped working!) But realistically, it seems that when you are in a slow lane and puzzling about why that is so, then you have no reason to think that a fast lane observer-moment would be more likely to be sufficiently similar to your current observer-moment to be in its reference class than a slow lane observer-moment. (If anything, one would expect the opposite: that observer-moments that are in the same situation as you would be more likely to be in states that are similar to yours.)

We also noted in chapter 5 that observation selection effects may provide us with a method for observationally distinguishing between different interpretations, or versions, of quantum mechanics. This point holds under a wide range of choices of reference class definitions. Consider one of the toy models that we discussed:

World A: 10^{10} observers; measure or probability 1–10^{-30}

World B: 10^{50} observers; measure or probability 10^{-30}

A single-history version of quantum mechanics predicts that we should observe World A whereas a many-worlds version predicts that we should observe World B. This tenet presupposes that observer-moments in one of the worlds are not vastly more likely to be in our reference class than observer-moments in the other world. Again, it seems rather plausible, in the absence of arguments to the contrary, that this presupposition would hold in any real attempt to create an empirical test to distinguish between the two sorts of versions of quantum theory; but of course one cannot firmly proclaim on that issue until a concrete scenario has been specified. (Because of the difficulty of deriving the quantum measure for a suitable pair of possibilities to apply the test to, the task of describing a feasible empirical way of discriminating between the rival versions in this way is a non-trivial challenge for quantum cosmologists.) For the sake of illustration, we can imagine a hypothetical case where the presupposition *fails*: Suppose that all the "observers" in World B are kangaroos, and that you don't take observer-moments of kangaroos to be in your present observer-moment's reference class. Then even if you find yourself in World A, this would not be evidence against the many-worlds version.

ROBUSTNESS OF REFERENCE CLASS AND SCIENTIFIC SOLIDITY

Thus what we find is that the scientific arguments appealing to observation selection effects that we described in chapter 5 make various assumptions about the reference class, *but that these assumptions are quite weak*. That is to say, in these applications, *any* non-arbitrary reference class definition satisfying some relatively mild constraints gives basically the same result.

I wish to suggest that insensitivity (within limits) to the choice of reference class is exactly what makes the applications just surveyed scientifically respectable. Such *robustness* is one hallmark of scientific objectivity.

Again, it is useful to draw attention to the parallel to non-indexical scientific arguments. Such arguments also depend for their persuasiveness on assumptions about the shape of our prior credence function, as Hume taught us. That the moon is smaller than the Earth is as well established as any scientific truth. Yet this truth does not, of course, follow *logically* from any sensory data we have. Rather, it is a hypothesis that gets an extremely high credence after one conditionalizes on the available body of evidence—*provided* one has a suitable prior credence function. There exist, trivially, credence functions that give a puny probability to the moon being smaller than the Earth when conditionalized on current data; but this is irrelevant, for only a highly unreasonable person would have such a credence function. To say that there is strong scientific evidence for a hypothesis might just mean (roughly) that the evidence is such that any reasonable person considering the data carefully would accept the hypothesis.[4] I submit that the same holds with regard to reasoning that involves indexical propositions and observation selection effects. The indexical and the non-indexical are on *a par*, and the scientifically rigorous anthropic arguments are those that work under any choice of reference class that a reasonable person could have (the choice of reference class being a reflection of the indexical part of one's prior credence function).

Scientific rigor is a matter of degree. We might even informally rank the scientific applications we examined in order of their rigor and objectivity. At one extreme, we have the solution to the problem of freak observers. Any non-arbitrary reference class that is at least as inclusive as $\mathfrak{R}^\varepsilon$ delivers the same verdict (namely, that we are extremely unlikely to be freak-observers), so this result is very solid. Likewise for the criticism against Boltzmann's account of time's arrow. The results regarding traffic analysis are also very firm. The arguments in evolutionary biology make slightly stronger assumptions about the choice of reference class and are therefore somewhat less rigorous (and of course some of these arguments—especially Carter's argument that there were only few critical steps in human evolution—are also shaky because of the empirical modeling assumptions that they include, quite apart from what they suppose about observation selection effects). Regarding the quantum physics idea, we cannot really tell until we are presented with a concrete plan; but it at least conceivable that it could turn out to yield something that is solid as far as its invocation of observation selection effects is concerned (although it could well be that we'll never find a rigorous way of establishing the prior quantum measure for a suitable set of possibilities, so that this application could fail to ever become firmly established for that reason).

It pays to contrast this list of scientific applications with the various *paradoxical* applications that we discussed in earlier chapters. Take the Doomsday argument. In order for it to work, one has to assume that the beings who will exist in the distant future if humankind avoids going extinct soon will contain lots of observer-moments that are in the same reference class as one's current observer-moment. If one thinks that far-future humans or human descendants will have quite different beliefs than we have, that they will be concerned with very different questions, and that their minds might even be implemented on some rather different (perhaps technologically enhanced) neural or computational structures, then requiring that the observer-moments existing under such widely differing conditions are all in the same reference class is to make a very strong assumption. The same can

---

[4] This is actually saying very little, since we don't have much of an independent grasp of what it means to be reasonable other than that one accepts those results that are strongly supported by the evidence one has; but it seems about right as far as it goes. Compare also these suggestions about robustness to Brian Skyrms' ideas about resilience (Skyrms 1980).

be said about the cases of *Adam & Eve*, *UN*$^{++}$, and *Quantum Joe*. These arguments will fail to persuade anybody who doesn't use the particular kind of very inclusive reference class they rely on—indeed, reflecting on these arguments may well lead a reasonable person to adopt a more narrow reference class. Because they presuppose a very special shape of the indexical parts of one's prior credence function, they are not scientifically rigorous. At best, they work as ad hominem arguments for those people who happen to accept the appropriate sort of reference class—but we are under no rational obligation to do so.[5]

WRAP-UP

An elusive, controversial, and multifariously paradoxical set of problems, branded "anthropic", formed the subject matter of our investigation. We have tried to show that something of importance can be found behind the smoke and confusion: the appreciation of *observation selection effects* and of their relevance for scientific and philosophical inferences. We have tried to describe what these things are, how they operate, and how they apply to concrete cases.

Part of our method was to take philosophical paradoxes seriously. We argued, for instance, that the Doomsday argument does not fail for any *trivial* reason. There are some gaps in its presentation, but we saw that many of these can be filled in. In parallel to this obsession with philosophical paradox, we pursued a detailed investigation of the role of observation selection effects in various concrete scientific contexts.

The theory we have developed in this book, and formalized in chapter 10, provides an exact and systematic framework for taking observation selection effects into account. From the Observation Equation, it is possible to derive as special cases many of the results established by other authors or in earlier chapters of this work. The Carter and Leslie versions of the weak and the strong anthropic principles, for example, are vindicated and extended. The theory solves the freak-observer problem. It explains how to evaluate fine-tuning arguments in cosmology. And it clarifies some murky issues in several other scientific disciplines.

We have seen that it is not necessary to adopt the Self-Indication Assumption (and thus to agree with the Presumptuous Philosopher) in order to avoid the counterintuitive conclusions of the Doomsday argument, *Adam*

---

[5] As regards DA, we can distinguish versions of it that have a greater degree of persuasiveness than others. For example, DA provides stronger grounds for rejecting the hypothesis that humans will exist in very great numbers in the future in states that are very similar to our current ones (since for this, only relatively weak assumptions are needed: that the reference class definition be at least somewhat inclusive) than for rejecting the hypothesis that humans will continue to exist in *any* form in large numbers (which would require that a highly diverse set of possible observer-moments be included in our current reference class).

& *Eve*, *UN*$^{++}$, and *Quantum Joe*. For the principle that led to those conclusions, the Self-Sampling Assumption, while being a helpful first step, left out a certain kind of relevant indexical information, namely information about which temporal segment of an observer one currently is. Including this extra information undercuts the inferences that led to strange results by sanctioning the use of a reference class that is relative to observer-moments. The Self-Sampling Assumption can thus be seen as a ladder that can be kicked away now that we have climbed it (or better yet, as something to be retained as a simplified special-case version of the Observation Equation).

The Observation Equation itself is neutral with regard to the definition of the reference class. We did, however, establish some constraints on permissible definitions ($\mathfrak{R}^0$-bound, non-arbitrariness, $\mathfrak{R}^\varepsilon$-bound, and the less firm $\mathfrak{R}^u$-bound). We also pointed out some considerations that are relevant for choosing a reference class within these constraints. It was speculated that although further arguments may impose additional restrictions, it is likely that there will remain some latitude for subjective epistemic factors to influence the choice of reference class. If so, then our theory reflects a symmetry between the indexical and the non-indexical components of our prior credence function. In both components, there are limitations on what can reasonably be held, but these limitations do not pick out a uniquely correct credence assignment: rational thinkers could disagree to some extent even given the same evidence. This view has the virtue of enabling us to explain the differing degrees of scientific rigor and objectivity that pertain to different applications, ranging from solving the freak-observer problem (extremely rigorous) to the Doomsday argument (much shakier and hence non-compelling, especially in its more ambitious versions). Generally speaking, the weaker the assumptions that an application needs to make about the reference class, the more scientifically solid it is.

There we have, thus, a framework for connecting up indexical beliefs with non-indexical ones; a delineation of the element of subjectivity in both kinds of inferences; and a method for applying the theory to help solve concrete philosophical and scientific problems, ranging from the question of God's existence to analyzing claims about perceptual illusions among motorists.

Yet some issues remain mysterious. In particular, I feel that the problem of the reference class, the problem of generalizing to infinite cases, and the problem of attaining a more intuitively transparent understanding of the relation between the indexical and the non-indexical may each enclose deep enigmas. These mysteries may even somehow be connected. I hope that others will see more clearly than I have and will be able to advance further into this fascinating land of thought.

Bibliography

Achinstein, P. (1993). "Explanation and "Old Evidence." *Philosophia* 51(1): 125–137.

Aguirre, A. (2001). "The Cold Big-Bang Cosmology as a Counter-example to Several Anthropic Arguments." *Physics preprint archive astro-ph/0106143.*

Albert, D. D. (1989). "On the possibility that the present quantum state of the universe is the vacuum." *Proceedings of the 1988 biennial meeting of the philosophy of science association.* A. Fine and J. Lepli. Michigan, East Lansing. 2: 127–133.

Angrilli, A., P. Cherubini, et al. (1997). "The Influence of Affective Factors on Time Perception." *Perception Psychophysics* 59: 972–982.

Aumann, R. J., S. Hart, et al. (1997). "The Forgetful Passenger." *Games and Economic Behaviour* 20: 117–120.

Bacon, F. (1620). *Novum Organum.* London, Routledge.

Barrow, J. D. (1983). "Anthropic definitions." *Quarterly Journal of the Royal Astronomical Society.* 24: 146–153.

———— and F. J. Tipler (1986). *The anthropic cosmological principle.* Oxford, Oxford University Press.

Bartha, P. and C. Hitchcock (1999). "No One Knows the Date of the Hour: An Unorthodox Application of Rev. Bayes's Theorem." *Philosophy of Science (Proceedings)* 66: S329–S353.

———— and C. Hitchcock (2000). "The Shooting-Room Paradox and Conditionalizing on Measurably Challenged Sets." *Synthese* 108(3): 403–437.

Bartholomew, D. J. (1984). *The God of Chance.* London, SCM Press Ltd.

Battigalli, P. (1997). "Dynamic Consistency and Imperfect Recall." *Games and Economic Behaviour* 20: 31–50.

Belot, G., J. Earman, et al. (1999). "The Hawking Information Loss Paradox: The Anatomy of a Controversy." *British Journal for the Philosophy of Science* 50(2): 189–229.

Bigelow, J., J. Collins, et al. (1993). "The big bad bug: what are the Humean's chances." *British Journal for the Philosophy of Science* 44: 443–63.

Black, R. (1998). "Chance, Credence, and the Principal Principle." *British Journal for the Philosophy of Science* 49: 371–85.

Bostrom, N. (1997). "Investigations into the Doomsday argument." *Preprint* http://www.anthropic-principles.com/preprints/inv/investigations.html.

⸻ (1998). "How Long Before Superintelligence?" *International Journal of Futures Studies* 2.

⸻ (1999). "The Doomsday Argument is Alive and Kicking." *Mind* 108(431): 539–50.

⸻ (1999). "A Subjectivist Theory of Objective Chance." *British Society for the Philosophy of Science Conference*, July 8–9, Nottingham, U.K.

⸻ (2000). "Observer-relative chances in anthropic reasoning?" *Erkenntnis* 52: 93–108.

⸻ (2001). "The Doomsday argument, Adam & Eve, UN++, and Quantum Joe." *Synthese* 127(3): 359–387.

⸻ (2001). "The Meta-Newcomb Problem." *Analysis* 61(4): 309–310.

⸻ (2002). "Existential Risks: Analyzing Human Extinction Scenarios and Related Hazards." *Journal of Evolution and Technology*, Vol. 9

Brin, G. D. (1983). "The 'Great Silence': The Controversy Concerning Extraterrestrial Intelligent Life." *Quarterly Journal of the Royal Astronomical Society* 24: 283–309.

Brown, S. J. (1995). "Survival." *The Journal of Finance* 50(3): 853–873.

Buch, P. (1994). "Future prospects discussed." *Nature* 368(10 March): 108.

Carlson, E. and E. J. Olsson (1998). "Is our existence in need of further explanation?" *Inquiry* 41: 255–75.

Carter, B. (1974). "Large number coincidences and the anthropic principle in cosmology." *Confrontation of Cosmological Theories with Data*. M. S. Longair. Dordrecht, Reidel: 291–8.

⸻ (1983). "The anthropic principle and its implications for biological evolution." *Philosophical Transactions of the Royal Society* A 310(347–363).

⸻ (1989). "The anthropic selection principle and the ultra-Darwinian synthesis." In *The Anthropic Principle*. F. Bertola and U. Curi. Cambridge, Cambridge University Press: 33–63.

⸻ (1990). "Large Number Coincidences and the Anthropic Principle in Cosmology." In *Physical Cosmology and Philosophy*. J. Leslie, Macmillan Publishing Company.

Castañeda, H.-N. (1968). "On the Logic of Attributions of Self-Knowledge to Others." *Journal of Philosophy* 65: 439–56.

———— (1966). "'He': A Study in the Logic of Self-Consciousness." *Ratio* 8: 130–57.

Castell, P. (1998). "A Consistent Restriction of the Principle of Indifference." *British Journal for the Philosophy of Science* 49: 387–395.

Caves, C. M. (2000). "Predicting future duration from present age: A critical assessment." *Physics preprint archive astro-ph/0001414*(24 Jan 2000).

Ćirković, M. (2001). "On Agencies and Capacities in the Anthropic Self-Selection: A Comment on Bostrom." Unpublished manuscript.

———— and N. Bostrom (2000). "Cosmological Constant and the Final Anthropic Hypothesis." *Astrophysics and Space Science* 274(4): 675–687.

Coles, P. and Ellis, G. (1994). "The Case for an Open Universe." *Nature* 370(6491): 609–615.

Craig, W. L. (1988). "Barrow and Tipler on the anthropic principle vs. Divine design." *British Journal for the Philosophy of Science* 38: 389–395.

———— (1997). "Hartle-Hawking cosmology and atheism." *Analysis* 57(4): 291–295.

Delahaye, J.-P. (1996). "Recherche de modèles pour l'argument de l'Apocalypse de Carter-Leslie". Unpublished manuscript.

DeWitt, B. S. (1970). "Quantum mechanics and reality." *Physics Today* 23: 30.

Dicke, R. H. (1961). "Dirac's Cosmology and Mach's principle." *Nature* 192: 440–441.

Dieks, D. (1992). "Doomsday—Or: the Dangers of Statistics." *Philosophical Quarterly* 42(166): 78–84.

———— (1999). The Doomsday Argument. Unpublished manuscript.

Dowe, P. (1998). "Multiple universes, fine-tuning and the inverse gambler's fallacy." Unpublished manuscript.

Drexler, E. (1985). *Engines of Creation: The Coming Era of Nanotechnology.* London, Fourth Estate.

———— (1992). *Nanosystems.* New York, John Wiley & Sons, Inc.

Earman, J. (1987). "The SAP also rises: a critical examination of the anthropic principle." *Philosophical Quarterly* 24(4): 307–17.

———— (1992). *Bayes or Bust? A Critical Examination of Bayesian Confirmation Theory.* Cambridge, MIT Pres.

Eckhardt, W. (1992). "A Shooting-Room view of Doomsday." *Journal of Philosophy* 94(5): 244–259.

———— (1993). "Probability Theory and the Doomsday Argument." *Mind* 102(407): 483–88.

Eddington, A. (1939). *The Philosophy of Physical Science.* Cambridge, Cambridge University Press.

Eells, E. (1990). "Bayesian Problems of Old Evidence." *Scientific Theories.* Minneapolis, University of Minnesota Press.

Efstathiou, G. et al. (1995). "A model for the Infrared Continuum Spectrum of NGC-1068." *Monthly Notices of the Royal Astronomical Society* 277(3): 1134–44.

Elga, A. (2000). "Self-locating Belief and the Sleeping Beauty problem." *Analysis* 60(2): 143–147.

Feinberg, G. and R. Shapiro (1980). *Life beyond Earth: The Intelligent Earthling's Guide to Life in the Universe.* New York, Morrow.

Feller, W. (1966). *An Introduction to Probability Theory and its Applications.* New York, Wiley.

Franceschi, P. (1998). "Une Solution pour l'Argument de l'Apocalypse." *Canadian Journal of Philosophy* 28(2): 227–246.

———— (1999). "Comment l'Urne de Carter et Leslie se Déverse dans celle de Hemple." *Canadian Journal of Philosophy* 29(1): 139–56.

Freedman, W. L. (2000). "The Hubble constant and the expansion age of the Universe." *Physics Letters* 333(1–6): 13–31.

Freitas Jr., R. A. (1999). *Nanomedicine.* Austin, Landes Bioscience.

Gale, G. (1981). "The Anthropic Principle." *Scientific American* 245 (June): 154–171.

———— (1996). "Anthropic-principle cosmology: physics or metaphysics?" *Final Causality in Nature and Human Affairs.* R. Hassing. Washington, D. C., Catholic University Press.

Gardner, M. (1986). "WAP, SAP, FAP & PAP." *New York Review of Books* 33(May 8): 22–25.

Garriga, J., V. F. Mukhanov, et al. (2000). "Eternal inflation, black holes, and the future of civilizations." *International Journal of Theoretical Physics* 39(7): 1887–1900.

———— and A. Vilenkin (2001). "Many worlds in one." *Physical Review* D 64(043511).

Gilboa, I. (1997). "A Comment on the Absent-Minded Driver Paradox." *Games and Economic Behaviour* 20: 25–30.

Gilovich, T., B. Vallone, et al. (1985). *Cognitive Psychology* 17: 295–314.

Goodman, S., N. (1994). "Future prospects discussed." *Nature* 368(10 March): 108.

Gott, J. R. (1996). *Clusters, Lensing, and the Future of the Universe. Astronomical Society of the Pacific Conference Series.* V. Trimble and A. Reisenegger. San Francisco. 88.

———— (1993). "Implications of the Copernican principle for our future prospects." *Nature* 363(27 May): 315–319.

———— (1994). "Future prospects discussed." *Nature* 368(10 March): 108.

———— (1997). "A Grim Reckoning." *New Scientist.* 2108: 36–39.

————. (2000). "Random Observations and the Copernican principle." *Physics Web,* February.

———— (2001). *Time Travel in Einstein's Universe: The Physical Possibilities of Travel Through Time.* New York: Houghton Mifflin.

Gould, S. J. (1985). *The Flamingo's Smile, Reflections in Natural History.* London, Penguin Books.

——— (1990). "Mind and Supermind." *Physical Cosmology and Philosophy.* New York, Collier Macmillan.

Greenberg, M. (1999). "Apocalypse Not Just Now." *London Review of Books* 1 July 1999: 19–22.

Grove, A. J. (1997). "On the Expected Value of Games with Absentmindedness." *Games and Economic Behaviour* 20: 51–65.

Hacking, I. (1987). "The inverse gambler's fallacy: the argument from design. The anthropic principle applied to wheeler universes." *Mind* 76: 331–40.

Hall, N. (1994). "Correcting the guide to objective chance." *Mind* 103(412): 505–17.

Halpern, J. Y. (1997). "On Ambiguities in the Interpretation of Game Trees." *Games and Economic Behaviour* 20: 66–96.

Halpin, J. L. (1994). "Legitimizing Chance: The Best-System Approach to Probabilistic Laws in Physical Theory." *Australasian Journal of Philosophy* 72(3): 317–338.

Hanson, R. (1998). "Must early life be easy? The rhythm of major evolutionary transitions." Unpublished manuscript.

Hart, M. H. (1982). "Atmospheric Evolution, the Drake Equation, and DNA: Sparse life in an Infinite Universe." In *Extraterrestrials: Where are they?* M. H. Hart and B. Zuckerman. New York, Pergamon Press.

Hawking, S. (1974). "The Anisotropy of the Universe at Large Times." In *Confrontation of Cosmological Theories with Observational Data.* M. S. Longair. Dordrecht, Reidel.

Hawking, S. W. and W. Israel, Eds. (1979). *General Relativity: An Einstein Centenary Survey.* Cambridge, Cambridge University Press.

Hoefer, C. (1997). "On Lewis' objective chance: 'Humean supervenience debugged'." *Mind* 106(422): 321–34.

——— (1999). "A Skeptic's Guide to Objective Chance". Unpublished manuscript.

Horwich, P. (1982). *Probability and evidence.* Cambridge, Cambridge University Press.

Howson, C. (1991). "The 'Old Evidence' Problem." *British Journal for the Philosophy of Science* 42(4): 547–555.

Jorion, P. and W. N. Goetzmann (2000). "A Century of Global Stock Markets." *National Bureau of Economic Research*, working paper 7565.

Kane, G. L. (2000). "The Beginning of the End of the Anthropic Principle." *Physics preprint archive astro-ph/0001197.*

Kanitscheider, B. (1993). "Anthropic arguments—are they really explanations?" *The Anthropic Principle: Proceedings of the Venice Conference on Cosmology and Philosophy.* F. Bertola and U. Curi. Cambridge, Cambridge University Press.

Klapdor, H. V. and K. Grotz (1986). "Evidence for a nonvanishing energy density of the vacuum (or cosmological constant)." *Astrophysical Journal* 301(L39–L43).

Kopf, T., P. Krtous, et al. (1994). "Too soon for doom gloom." *Physics preprint archive gr-gc/9407002* (v3, 4 Jul.).

Korb, K. and J. Oliver (1999a). "A Refutation of the Doomsday Argument." *Mind* 107: 403–10.

———— and J. J. Oliver (1999b). "Comment on Nick Bostrom's "The Doomsday Argument is Alive and Kicking." *Mind* 108(431): 551–3.

Kurzweil, R. (1999). The *Age of Spiritual Machines: When computers exceed human intelligence.* New York, Viking.

Kyburg Jr., H. (1981). "Principle Investigation." *Journal of Philosophy* 78: 772–777.

Lachièze-Rey, M. and J.-P. Luminet (1995). "Cosmic Topology." *Physics Reports* 254(3): 135–214.

Larson, R. C. (1987). "Perspectives on Queues—Social-Justice and the Psychology of Queuing." *Operations Research.* 35(6): 895–904.

Ledford, A., P. Marriott, et al. (2001). "Lifetime prediction from only present age: fact or fiction?" *Physics Letters* A 280: 309–311.

Leslie, J. (1972). "Ethically required existence." *American Philosophical Quarterly* July: 215–24.

———— (1979). *Value and Existence.* Oxford, Blackwell.

———— (1985). "Modern Cosmology and the Creation of Life." In *Evolution and Creation.* Notre Dame, University of Notre Dame Press.

———— (1985). "The Scientific Weight of Anthropic and Teleological Principles." *Conference on Teleology in Natural Science, Center for Philosophy of Science*, Pittsburgh.

———— (1988). "No inverse gambler's fallacy in cosmology." *Mind* 97(386): 269–272.

———— (1989). "Risking the world's end." *Bulletin of the Canadian Nuclear Society* May, 10–15.

———— (1989). *Universes.* London, Routledge.

———— (1990). "Is the end of the world nigh?" *Philosophical Quarterly* 40(158): 65–72.

———— (1992). "Doomsday Revisited." *Philosophical Quarterly* 42(166): 85–87.

———— (1992). "Time and the Anthropic Principle." *Mind* 101(403): 521–540.

———— (1993). "Doom and Probabilities." *Mind* 102(407): 489–91.

———— (1996). "The Anthropic Principle Today." In *Final Causality in Nature and Human Affairs.* R. Hassing. Washington, D. C., Catholic University Press.

———— (1996). "A difficulty for Everett's many-worlds theory." *Inernational Studies in the Philosophy of Science* 10(3): 239–246.

———— (1996). *The End of the World: the Science and Ethics of Human Extinction.* London, Routledge.

————— (1997). "Observer-relative Chances and the Doomsday argument." *Inquiry* 40: 427–36.

Lewis, D. (1980). "A Subjectivist Guide to Objective Chance." In Richard C. Jeffrey, ed., *Studies in Inductive Logic and Probability*, vol. II. Berkeley: University of California Press. Reprinted with postscripts in Lewis 1986, pp. 83–132.

Lewis, D. (1986). *Philosophical Papers*. New York, Oxford University Press.

————— (1994). "Humean Supervenience Debugged." *Mind* 103(412): 473–90.

————— (2001). "Sleeping Beauty: reply to Elga." *Analysis* 61(271): 171–176.

Linde, A. (1990). *Inflation and Quantum Cosmology*. San Diego, Academic Press.

————— and A. Mezhlumian (1996). "On Regularization Scheme Dependence of Predictions in Inflationary Cosmology." *Physics Review* D 53: 4267–4274.

Lipman, B. L. (1997). "More Absentmindedness." *Games and Economic Behaviour* 20: 97–101.

Mackay, A. L. (1994). "Future prospects discussed." *Nature* 368(10 March): 108.

Manson, N. A. (1989). *Why Cosmic Fine-tuning Needs to be Explained. Doctoral Dissertation*, Department of Philosophy, Syracuse University.

Martel, H., P. R. Shapiro, et al. (1998). "Likely values of the cosmological constant." *Astrophysical Journal* 492(1): 29–40.

Martin, J. L. (1995). *General Relativity*. 3rd edition. London, Prentice Hall.

Mayr, E. (1985). "The probability of extraterrestrial intelligent life." In Ext*raterrestrials, Science and Alien Intelligence*. J. Edward Regis. New York, Cambridge University Press: 23–30.

McGrath, P. J. (1988). "The inverse gambler's fallacy." *Mind* 97(386): 265–268.

McMullin, E. (1993). "Indifference Principle and Anthropic Principle in Cosmology." *Studies in the History of the Philosophy of Science* 24(3): 359–389.

Mellor, H. (1971). *The matter of chance*. Cambridge, Cambridge University Press.

Merkle, R. (1994). "The Molecular Repair of the Brain." *Cryonics* 15(1 and 2).

Minsky, M. (1994). "Will Robots Inherit the Earth?" *Scientific American*. October.

Moravec, H. (1989). *Mind Children*. Cambridge, Harvard University Press.

————— (1998). "When will computer hardware match the human brain?" *Journal of Evolution and Technology* 1.

————— (1999). *Robot: mere machine to transcendent mind*. New York, Oxford University Press.

Morris, M. S., K. S. Thorne, et al. (1988). "Wormholes, Time Machines, and the Weak Energy Condition." *Physical Review Letters* 61(13): 1446–1449.

Nielsen, H. B. (1981). "Did God have to fine tune the laws of nature to create light?" In *Particle Physics*. L. Amdric, L. Dadic and N. Zovoko, North-Holland Publishing Company: 125–142.

————— (1989). "Random dynamics and relations between the number of fermion generations and the fine structure constants." *Acta Physica Polonica* B20: 427–468.

Oliver, J. and K. Korb (1997). "A Bayesian analysis of the Doomsday Argument," *Technical report* 97/323, Department of Computer Science, Monash University.

Olum, K. (2002). "The Doomsday Argument and the Number of Possible Observers." *Philosophical Quarterly* April. *Preprint at Physics preprint archive gr-qc/0009081.*

Page, D. (1996). "Sensible Quantum Mechanics: Are Probabilities Only in the Mind?" *International Journal of Physics* 5(6):583–596.

———. (1997). "Sensible Quantum Mechanics: Are Only Perceptions Probabilistic?" Unpublished manuscript.

———. (1999). "Can Quantum Cosmology Give Observational Consequences of Many-Worlds Quantum Theory?" In *General Relativity and Relativistic Astrophysics*, C. P. Burgess and R.C. Myers, Eighth Canadian Conference, Montreal, Quebec. Melville, N.Y.: American Institute of Physics, 225–232.

Papagiannis, M. D. (1978). "Could we be the only advanced technological civilization in our galaxy?" *Origin of Life.* H. Noda. Tokyo, Center Acad. Publishing.

Papineau, D. (1995). "Probabilities and the many minds interpretation of quantum mechanics." Analysis 55(4): 239–246.

——— (1997). "Uncertain decisions and the many-worlds interpretation of quantum mechanics." *The Monist* 80(1): 97–117.

Parfit, D. (1998). "Why anything? Why this?" *London Review of Books* Jan 22: 24–27.

Perlmutter, S., G. Aldering, et al. (1998). *Nature* 391(51).

——— et al. (1999). "Measurements of Omega and Lambda from 42 high-redshift supernovae." *Astrophysical Journal* 517: 565–586.

Perry, J. (1977). "Frege on Demonstratives." *Philosophical Review* 86: 474–97.

——— (1979). "The Problem of the Essential indexical." *Noûs* 13: 3–21.

Piccione, M. and A. Rubinstein (1997a). "The Absent-Minded Driver's Paradox: Synthesis and Responses." *Games and Economic Behaviour* 20: 121–130.

——— and A. Rubinstein (1997b). "On the Interpretation of Decision Problems with Imperfect Recall." *Games and Economic Behaviour* 20: 3–24.

Polkinghorne, J. C. (1986). *One World: The Interaction of Science and Theology.* London.

Ramsey, F. P. (1990). "Chance." In *Philosophical Papers.* D. H. Mellor. New York, Cambridge University Press.

Raup, D. M. (1985). "ETI without intelligence." In *Extraterrestrials, Science and Alien Intelligence.* J. Edward Regis. New York, Cambridge University Press: 31–42.

Redelmeier, D. A. and R. J. Tibshirani (1999). "Why cars in the other lane seem to go faster." *Nature* 401: 35.

———. and R. J. Tibshirani (2000). "Are Those Other Drivers Really Going Faster?" *Chance* 13(3): 8–14.

Reiss, D. et al. (1998). "Constraints on cosmological models from Hubble Space Telescope observations of high-z supernovae." *Astrophysical Journal* 493(2).

Reiss, A. (2000). "The Case for an Accelerating Universe from Supernovae." *Publications of the Astronomical Society of the Pacific* 122: 1284–1299.

Sagan, C. (1995). "The abundance of life-bearing planets." *Bioastronomy News* 7(4): 1–4.

Schlesinger, G. (1991). *The Sweep of Probability.* Notre Dame, University of Notre Dame Press.

Schmidhuber, J. (1997). "A Computer Scientist's View of Life, the Universe, and Everything." In *Foundations of Computer Science: Potential-Theory-Cognition.* C. Freska and M. Jantzen. Berlin, Springer. 1337: 201–208.

Schopf, W. J. (ed.), (1992). *Major Events in the History of Life.* Boston, Jones and Barlett.

Simpson, G. G. (1964). "The nonprevalence of humanoids." *Science* 143(769).

Singh, A. (1995). "Small nonvanishing cosmological constant from vacuum energy: Physically and observationally." *Physical Review* D 52(12): 6700–7.

Sklar, L. (1989). "Ultimate explanations: comments on Tipler." In *Proceedings of the 1988 Biennial Meeting of the Philosophy of Science Association.* A. Fine and J. Lepli. Michigan, East Lansing. 2: 49–55.

——— (1993). *Physics and Chance: Philosophical issues in the foundations of statistical mechanics.* Cambridge, Cambridge University Press.

Skyrms, B. (1980). *Causal necessity.* London, Yale University Press.

Smith, Q. (1985). "The Anthropic Principle and Many-Worlds Cosmologies." *Australasian Journal of Philosophy* 63: 336–48.

——— (1998). "Critical Notice: John Leslie, The end of the world." *Canadian Journal of Philosophy* 28(3): 413–434.

Smolin, L. (1997). *The life of the cosmos.* New York, Oxford University Press.

Snowden, R. J., N. Stimpson, et al. (1998). *Nature* 392: 450.

Strevens, M. (1995). "A closer look at the 'new' principle." *British Journal for the Philosophy of Science.* 46: 545–61.

——— (1998). "Inferring Probabilities from Symmetries." *Noûs* 32(2): 231–246.

Sturgeon, S. (1998). "Humean Chance: Five Questions for David Lewis." *Erkenntnis* 49: 321–335.

Swinburne, R. (1990). "Argument from the fine-tuning of the universe." In *Physical cosmology and philosophy.* J. Leslie. New York, Collier Macmillan: 154–73.

——— (1991). *The Existence of God.* Oxford, Oxford University Press.

Tännsjö, T. (1997). "Doom Soon?" *Inquiry* 40: 243–52.

Tegmark, M. (1996). "Does the universe in fact contain almost no information?" *Foundations of Physics Letters* 9(1): 25–42.

———— (1997). "Is "the theory of everything" merely the ultimate ensemble theory?" *Physics preprints archive gr-gc/9704009*(3 Apr).

Tegmark, M. (1997). "On the dimensionality of spacetime." *Classical and Quantum Gravity* 14: L69–L75.

Thau, M. (1994). "Undermining and admissibility." *Mind* 103(412): 491–503.

Tipler, F. J. (1982). "Anthropic-principle arguments against steady-state cosmological theories." *Observatory* 102: 36–39.

———— (1994). *The Physics of Immortality: Modern Cosmology, God, and the Resurrection of the Dead.* New York, Doubleday.

Tversky, A. and D. Kahneman (1981). "The Framing of Decisions and the Psychology of Choice." *Science* 211(4481): 453–8.

———— and D. Kahneman (1991). "Loss aversion in riskless choice—a reference-dependent model." *Quarterly Journal of Economics* 106(4): 1039–1061.

van Inwagen, P. (1993). *Metaphysics.* Oxford, Oxford University Press.

Vilenkin, A. (1995). "Predictions From Quantum Cosmology." *Physical Review Letters* 74(6): 846–849.

———— (1998). "Unambiguous probabilities in an eternally inflating universe." *Physical Review Letters.* 81: 5501–5504.

Vranas, P. (1998). "Who's Afraid of Undermining? Why the Principal Principle Need Not Contradict Humean Supervenience." In *Sixteenth Biennial Meeting of the Philosophy of Science Association,* Kansas City, Missouri.

Walton, D. and J. Bathurst (1998). "An exploration of the perceptions of the average driver's speed compared to perceived driver safety and driving skill." *Accident Analysis and Prevention* 30(6): 821–830.

Wedd, N. E. (2000). "Some 'Sleeping Beauty' postings." *Web-based document* http://www.maproom.demon.co.uk/sb.html#motorist.

Weinberg, S. (1987). "Anthropic bound on the Cosmological Constant." *Physical Review Letters* 59(22): 2607–2610.

Wheeler, J. A. (1957). "Assessment of Everett's 'Relative State' Formulation of Quantum Theory." *Review of Modern Physics* 29: 463–465.

———— (1975). *The nature of scientific discovery.* O. Gingerich. Washington, Smithsonian Press: 261–96 and 575–87.Wheeler, J. A. (1977). *Foundational Problems in the Special Sciences.* R. E. Butts and J. Hintikka. Dordrecht, Reidel: 3.

Whitaker, M. A. B. (1988). "On Hacking's criticism of the Wheeler anthropic principle." *Mind* 97(386): 259–264.

White, R. (2000). "Fine-Tuning and Multiple Universes." *Noûs* 34(2) 260–276.

Wilson, P. A. (1991). "What is the explanandum of the anthropic principle?" *American Philosophical Quarterly* 28(2): 167–73.

———— (1994). "Carter on Anthropic Principle Predictions." *British Journal for the Philosophy of Science* 45: 241–253.

Worrall, J. (1996). "Is the idea of a scientific explanation unduly anthropocentric? The lessons of the anthropic principle." *Technical report*. London, LSE: Centre for the philosophy of the natural and social sciences.

Zehavi, I. and Dekel, A. (1999). "Evidence for a positive cosmological constant from flows of galaxies and distant supernovae." *Nature* 401(6750): 252–254.

Zuboff, A. (1991). "One Self: The Logic of Experience." *Inquiry* 33: 39–68.

Index

CPSIA information can be obtained at www.ICGtesting.com
Printed in the USA
LVOW01s2140070814

398123LV00011B/364/P

9 780415 883948